CONSILIENCE, BRAINS
AND
MARKETS

CONSILIENCE, BRAINS AND MARKETS

Saving the Free Enterprise Market for a Global Society

Gerald A. Cory, Jr.

Academic Vice President and Professor
International Technological University
Sunnyvale, California
Senior Fellow, Graduate Studies and Research
San Jose State University
San Jose, California

with Foreword by
Osvald M. Bjelland

ITUgreen
PRESS
SUNNYVALE · CALIFORNIA

ITU*green* Press for International Technological University
www.itugup.com

ISBN: 978-0-9841864-4-0

ISBN: 978-0-9841864-2-6

10 9 8 7 6 5 4 3 2 1

A C. I. P. record for this book is available from the Library of Congress

Printed in the United States of America

*to my grandchildren
and great-grandchildren*

CONTENTS

PART ONE

LEGACY AND FOUNDATIONS

PART TWO

APPLICATIONS TO THE
MARKET AND ECONOMICS

PART THREE

APPLICATIONS TO
SOCIETY AND POLITICS

CONCLUSION AND EPILOGUE

FOREWORD

In 2004, I invited Jerry Cory to give the keynote speech at The Performance Theater. That year we staged the event in Budapest, using the occasion to celebrate Hungary's entry into the European Union and the World Trade Organization. Jerry's presentation, on the human brain and human motivation, resonated.

The Performance Theater, organized annually by The Performance Theater Foundation for a small group of top-rung executives, aims to inspire better, bolder business leadership—leadership that is capable of looking beyond quarterly results—to deliver value to both shareholders and society as a whole. Jerry's work in Dual Motive Theory tells us that attempting this "double-act" is not callow or quixotic, but is rather the logical fulfillment of our natural impulses that drive us to pursue not only our own interests but also those of our fellow humans.

In short, we are not neurologically predestined to be callously self-interested. Nor is the free market, by definition, a zero-sum game. We can make the market work, for not just a few, but for many. We can make economic growth work with—rather than against—the environment on which our collective long-term progress ultimately depends.

Jerry is the leading architect of the dual motive approach to *consilience*, which champions the unity of the natural and social sciences. Consilience is an ancient approach to learning that recognizes the "oneness" of knowledge—a vision at odds with the twentieth century trend towards greater and greater fragmentation into a plethora of disciplines and specializations. In 1998, consilience was resurrected by E.O. Wilson in *Consilience: The Unity of Knowledge*. Jerry has helped feed this revival.

Dual Motive Theory evolved from Jerry's doctoral work and dissertation at Stanford University in 1974, and was first introduced to the scientific academic community in his impressive monograph, *The Reciprocal Modular Brain in Economics and Politics: Shaping the Rational and Moral Basis of Organization, Exchange, and Choice* (Plenum, 1999). In it he demonstrated the differences between the brain elements we inherit from early vertebrates such as fish, amphibians, and early reptiles and those elements we inherit from early caregiving mammals.

Dual Motive Theory has thus helped open up a new way of thinking about human motivation. In so doing, it has expanded the horizons of economic theory.

In this present book, *Consilience, Brains and Markets*, Jerry draws upon evolutionary neuroscience and physiology to establish that our social exchange brain architecture is made up of a set of physiological processes resulting from the dynamic interplay of neural circuits derived from our ancestral vertebrate and mammalian heritages. This dynamic interplay, augmented by our higher brain structures, produces the dual motives of self-interest and other-interest as the foundations of all social exchange activity.

Drawing on alternative perspectives from anthropology, economics, sociology, political science, and ethics, Jerry argues persuasively that we have wrongly defined free enterprise as a soulless, materialistic system based exclusively on a single primary motive — self-interest. We are, in reality, driven by two core motives: self-interest *and* other-interest. The free market can, therefore, deliver both human value and business value.

By enlightening us to this possibility, Jerry makes a contribution toward answering what is perhaps the biggest question of our day: How can we radically expand the benefits of the free market system without destroying the planet?

Osvald M. Bjelland, PhD
Founder of The Performance Theater and Chairman of Xyntéo, an advisory firm specializing in low-carbon growth solutions

ACKNOWLEDGMENTS

The ideas presented in this book evolved over a period of a half-century during which I accumulated many intellectual debts. My early interest in the brain goes back to my employment at Tidewater Hospital, a private psychiatric institution (1950–1951) in Beaufort County, South Carolina. Under the supervision of psychiatrist, A. K. Fidler, I participated extensively in patient care and studied the greats of psychiatry and brain science. I have pursued my study of neuroscience unflaggingly since that time. I also wish to acknowledge Robert H. Wienefeld, former chair of history at the University of South Carolina, who during my undergraduate years in the early 1950s, helped me to think historically and economically.

I wish, especially, to thank Kurt Steiner of Stanford University for his guidance and encouragement. His support of the ideas and concepts that lead to this work have been of great value to me since we first met at Stanford in 1970. I also want to thank Robert North, Nobutaka Ike, Hans Weiler, Peter Corning, Donald Kennedy, Charles Drekmeier, Tilo Schabert, Alexander George, Richard Fagen, Daryl Bem, and Robert Packenham, all of Stanford University, who gave their advice and support in the development of these ideas many years ago.

I owe special and more recent thanks to the late Paul MacLean, of the National Institutes of Mental Health, for his review, helpful comments, and longtime encouragement; also to Elliott White, *emeritus* of Temple University, for helpful review and comments on earlier work. I also wish to thank Edward O. Wilson of Harvard University for his acknowledgment of my work and his encouragement.

For their review and endorsement of earlier related works, I wish to thank Russell Gardner, Jr., formerly professor of psychiatry at the University of Texas, Daniel Levine, professor of psychology, University of Texas Arlington; Kent Bailey, emeritus professor of psychology, Virginia Commonwealth University;

and Daniel R. Wilson, chair, department of psychiatry, Creighton University with whom I co-authored a recent work on the evolutionary epidemiology of mania and depression.

For their friendship and support I owe special thanks to Shu-Park Chan, founder of International Technological University (ITU), Yau-Gene Chan, my business partner at ITU, as well as to Mikel Duffy, Manisha Pai, Betty Hayes, Lisa Jiang, Betty Ban, and all the ITU faculty and staff. Sophie Yin deserves special thanks for her work in translating this book into Chinese.

My team at ITUgreen, Marie Kivley, Shawn Lovering, and Anastasia Savvina, not only reviewed and critiqued my work but kept me focused and motivated throughout this project.

Also, thank you to Chris Buehler and Lorraine Okun Nogee of Formative, Inc. and to the people of Sheridan Books for their wonderful customer service and expertise in modern publishing.

1

INTRODUCTION:
THE EMERGENCE
OF DUAL MOTIVE THEORY

These are stressful times. Globally we face many challenges, such as climate change, energy depletion, regional wars, hunger and deprivation. Confronting these effectively and successfully requires a sound economic and market system. One that works worldwide. One that is not ethnocentric but universally applicable across the developed and developing regions of the globe.

As I began this book in Fall 2008, the United States economy was again in crisis. This time it was the subprime mortgage debacle requiring an unprecedented taxpayer bailout estimated to move into the trillions. Less than 20 years ago it was the junk bond binge leading to the savings and loan bailout. Between the two, we had the over-speculation of the dotcom bust.

Although many factors may contribute to these recurring crises, by general agreement flagrant greed stands out among them.

Additionally and globally, we've seen the rise of radical terrorist movements that view our economic system as a soulless materialistic system.

So what's wrong with our vaunted free enterprise system? Why does it fail so regularly and flagrantly? Why does it get a bad press from radicals, and some not so radical, in the developing world?

One important cause is the very definition we give the free enterprise system. Classical economics and derived business theory have for the past two centuries, been defined in the halls of academia and science as based upon a sole primary motive of self-interest.

In our best business colleges and universities, mostly in the Western world, we teach this definition to the future leaders of the business world. And we teach that it is science—a fundamental fact of human nature and human exchange.

The logic follows: when all is fundamentally self-interest, it is only a short and slippery slide into greed itself. Ultimately, a sole primary motive of self-interest is a not so subtle justification for greed. Viewed from a multidisciplinary perspective of psychiatry and psychology, anyone who acts only on self-interest is a sociopath. Even if we are not attracting only sociopaths to the pursuit of economics and business—which I believe we certainly are not—we are encouraging sociopathic behavior.

But is self-interest really science? And, moreover, is it a proper definition of our free enterprise system?

In this book, as in earlier ones, I offer a new interpretation based on multidisciplinary scientific findings, some old, some new. I offer an evidenced argument from hard science—specifically, physiology, medicine, and evolutionary neuroscience that we got the definition only half right.

The answer is: our free enterprise system—the market—is based not on a sole primary motive of self-interest but, more accurately, on the interplay of two motives, self- and other-interest or Ego and Empathy, as expressions of archetypal neural circuitries from different periods of our evolution.

And the effect of being half right over so many decades was to skew market and business behavior toward excessive self-interest or greed.

A redefinition on the basis of dual primary motives, a Dual Motive Theory, will not cure all of our systemic ills, but getting the definition right is a beginning. It allows a proper vision and appreciation of the market, perhaps even an ideal in which to anchor our free enterprise market behavior and justify its global acceptance and application.

To achieve this definition and the vision that follows from it, we must begin with the necessary science.

This book, therefore, follows in a series of books and other publications I have written aimed at consilience, the bridging of the natural with the social sciences. It responds to the call for consilience (1998), a concerted effort toward unifying the natural and social sciences, by Harvard sociobiologist E. O. Wilson.

From the perspective of evolutionary neurophysiology, the human brain is in essence a *social* brain. As such, it *creates* the social sciences. The human brain, then, is the necessary unifying or bridging mechanism through which we must go to achieve the consilient unification of the natural and the social sciences. Only humans with their highly developed social brain create markets and social sciences.

The study of the brain is advancing rapidly. This book, and its predecessors, draw not only upon this new research and findings but also upon an extensive body of research in medicine, physiology, and evolutionary neuroscience that has been accumulating over the past several decades going back so far as the early 20th and even late 19th centuries.

Brain study got a great boost when the U. S. government declared the 1990s to be the decade of the brain. More federal funding became available for brain research. And neuroscience, the scientific study of the brain, became increasingly important on our university and college campuses. That situation continues to the present day.

But the new emphasis on neuroscience spurred by new imaging technologies and Federal grants, to fulfill its potential, must build on a body of research and experimentation that had been building up for decades before.

Important to the study of the consilient or unifying social brain is the work of the late Paul D. MacLean and other scholars who shared his perspective and research interests. MacLean was the longtime chief of the Laboratory of Brain Evolution and Behavior of the National Institutes of Health.

Unlike mainstream behavioral and cognitive neuro-scientists, MacLean studied the brain from the standpoint of evolution. This is the only way to truly understand it—to trace it through a long, long period of history and development going back into deep time—to the beginning of life itself.

This book, while drawing on all areas of neurophysiology, builds on the evolutionary perspective pioneered by MacLean and others like him. It also draws upon medical research, specifically the findings from the well-intentioned but misguided and regrettable practice of psychosurgery (luekotomies, lobotomies, etc.) during the 1930s through the 1950s.

The book is divided into three parts. The first part, made up of six chapters, is foundational. Like MacLean, I place the brain in evolutionary context.

MacLean (1990) refers to the primary function of the human brain as the preservation of the individual self and the human species. Although this may be said of the nervous system of any organism which must survive to reproduce, MacLean leads us to consider not just automatisms or automatic, tightly wired instinctual mechanisms, but the evolved social architecture of the human brain upon which choices are made.

From the evolutionary perspective, I elaborate the Conflict Systems Neurobehavioral (CSN) Model of brain architecture that I first developed in my doctoral research at Stanford (1974). About the same time, unknown to me, MacLean was independently developing his tri-level concept.

Upon discovering MacLean's work, I later adapted the CSN Model to rest upon a critically clarified and updated version of his tri-level brain platform. Both the CSN Model and MacLean's tri-level concept proceed from the major evolutionary spurts that took us from primitive vertebrates to mammals, then to primates, and ultimately to our human status.

The dual motive basis, self- and other-interest, of the CSN Model rests firmly on the fundamental taxonomic fact that we are mammals. Mammals have both self-preserving neural circuitries from their ancestral vertebrate heritage combined with later evolved other-preserving, nurturing, life-supporting circuitries underpinning family and social life.

These archetypal circuitries generate conflicting impulses between self-preservation and affection or self- and other-interest. Their conflictual interaction has been tuned by evolution as a physiological homeostatic dynamic, much like other essential organic processes (temperature regulation, blood pressure, glucose, etc.) that keep us within survival, and at best optimal, limits.

A dynamic set of global-state neural algorithms, that sum the inputs from the lower circuits, express the conflict and resulting homeostatic reciprocity between earlier self-preserving circuitry and later affectional or other-preserving circuits. Our higher brain centers developed, in part, in response to the special problems of social adaptation created by our conflicting neural network architecture.

The understanding and management of the resulting conflict becomes possible with the development of newer brain structures that also permit the emergence of social exchange, voluntary choice, language, and abstract thought.

The dynamic algorithms of our neural architecture, constituting essentially a brain designed for social exchange, are expressed in three ways: (1) graphically, (2) by precise verbal description and, finally, (3) by a mathematical equation representing their homeostatic, interactive social dynamic. The neural dynamic pervades all aspects of our lives.

The second part, made up of seven chapters, explores the applications of the CSN Model with its neural equation to the dynamics of social exchange from sharing in primitive families to the gift economies of anthropology, to transactional economics and free enterprise. The market could never have evolved or continued without the second primary motive of Empathy. We would not know what to do or how to do it to respond to the needs of others.

Without Empathy we would lack the neural equipment to be engaged—we simply would not care.

The market evolved out of family giving and sharing motivated by the dynamic of our archetypal neural circuits—the tug-and-pull between the dual primary circuits of self-preservation and affection, Ego and Empathy, or self- and other-interest.

The omission of Empathy as a balancing primary motive in the structure and behavior of the market is not only inaccurate scientifically, it has produced, or facilitated, the negative side effects cited in the first paragraphs of this introduction.

The omission of Empathy has skewed market behavior toward greed and cynicism, damaging public trust in the commercial market system, and, at the time of this writing, contributed to bringing the American economy to a state of almost unprecedented virtual collapse.

The omission has further given our very valuable free enterprise system an inaccurate and unfavorable press among developing nations as fundamentally materialistic, exploitative, and noncaring.

We need to correct both the inaccurate science as well as the accompanying negative side effects.

The chapters making up part three apply the findings in physiology and evolutionary neuroscience, as expressed in the CSN Model, to the issues of social stratification, political choice, and global trade. The neural dynamic drives the tendency to reciprocity expressed at the foundation of our social and political structures, as well as their projection into the global arena made both virtual and urgent by the new information technology and the global challenges facing us.

The dual motive approach also permits the fusing of Eastern management thinking emphasizing Empathy and social responsibility, with Western emphasis on self-interest and individual initiative. Both emphases are shown to be half right— each overemphasizing one side of the social exchange equation.

Overemphasis on Empathy or collective responsibility suppresses the individual initiative necessary to creativity. Overemphasis on Ego or self-interest leads to greed and suppresses social responsibility. The proper emphasis is in the Dynamic Balance of the two archetypal circuitries.

The CSN Model and the equation of our consilient social brain provide a dynamic framework for explaining and predicting the necessary movement toward a global society, especially in the age of high technology.

The closing chapter foresees a fundamental paradigm shift to a dual motive model, based upon the new findings, that is suitable for globalization and sustainability.

PART ONE

LEGACY
AND
FOUNDATIONS

2

LEGACY AND FOUNDATIONS

All science builds on what has gone before. Rarely are there dramatic changes that take us in entirely new directions. The same is true for the Conflict Systems Neurobehavioral (CSN) Model that underpins emergent Dual Motive Theory. In developing it, I learned from and was inspired by prominent scholars who went before. Chief among these were Abraham Maslow and Paul MacLean.

MASLOW'S HIERARCHY

I was early inspired by Maslow's theoretical structure represented in his famous hierarchy of needs. In Maslow's concept, usually expressed as a pyramid, human needs are organized from bottom to top as follows: physiological needs (hunger, thirst), safety needs, belonging or social needs, esteem needs, and the self-actualizing need.

Maslow theorized that these needs were emergent: That is, as we satisfied our basic needs of hunger and thirst, our safety needs would then emerge. As we satisfied our newly emerged safety needs, the next level, the belonging or social needs, would come into play. Next came esteem needs, and finally, as these were satisfied, the self-actualizing need at the top of the hierarchy emerged (Maslow 1943, 1970, 1968).

Maslow's hierarchy has appeared in every basic text on psychology and behavior for the past five decades. It also appears in most texts on organizational behavior. Its influence has been widespread as a behavioral scheme of ready and easy reference. It has also been popularized in casual and impressionistic writing about motivation. Maslow's well-known concept represents one of the earliest comprehensive efforts to develop a model of the human biological inheritance.

Maslow's hierarchy, despite attempts to clarify it, has, however, serious shortcomings that limit its utility for conceptualizing the genetic inheritance. Firstly, it lacks an evolutionary perspective. The hierarchy of needs is presented as a given, disconnected from the evolutionary process which produced it.

Secondly, the concept of hierarchy is not fully developed. It does not allow sufficiently for interaction of the levels of hierarchy and does not account for those cases that violate the normal priority of needs (Cory 1974: 27–29, 85–86; Corning 1983: 167–172; Maddi 1989: 110–118; Smith 1991).

Maslow's hierarchy has also been criticized for being culture bound, fitting neatly with particularly the US concept of material achievement and success as a steady stair-step progression of higher development (Yankelovich 1981). It thereby tends to ignore or diminish the great accomplishments in thought, morality, and service to humanity of many of the great figures of human history (Maddi 1989).

Maslow's hierarchy, with its almost exclusive focus on the individual, affords little insight into the dynamics of social interaction. In its rather long history, despite some attempts, it has failed to become a major influence in socialization or political theory (Zigler & Child 1973: 33–35; Knutson 1972: 168–172, 261–263. Davies 1963, 1991, has made the most consistent effort to apply Maslow's concepts to politics).

THE MISMEASURE OF
MACLEAN'S MODULAR CONCEPT

MacLean's triune brain concept is one of the earliest modular concepts of the brain. Although, as recently as 1992, it has been acknowledged to be the single most influential idea in brain science since World War II (e.g., Durant in Harrington 1992: 268), it has largely been overlooked by cognitive psychology.

Faulty Reviews in Key Journals

This anomalous situation—in which the pioneering modular statement of brain organization coming from neuroscience itself and providing a natural match with aspects of the modular cognitive approach—has been brought about by a couple of seriously flawed reviews of MacLean's work that appeared in the influential journals *Science* (1990) and *American Scientist* (1992).

The effect of these faulty reviews has been to deny the use of MacLean's very significant research and insights to the researchers in the cognitive psychological as well as the social science community, who relied upon the authority of these prestigious journals.

In fact, Steven Pinker, a popular academic writer, bases his unfortunate, mistaken rejection and virtual caricature of MacLean's thought solely on a reference to the review in *Science* which is the most prejudicial and grossly inaccurate of the two (Pinker 1997: 370, 580). If Pinker had done proper scholarly due diligence and studied MacLean's work closely, he would have discovered that it provided a foundation supportive of much of his own thinking.

The detailed and documented rebuttal of these reviews is reported in Cory 1999, 2000, 2002, 2004.

A Resurgence of Interest

A considerable, well-deserved, and important resurgence of interest in MacLean's work has occurred in very recent years. For example, see Damasio 1999; Lieberman 2000; Cory 1999, 2000, 2004; Cory and Gardner 2002; Panksepp 2002; Lambert and Gerlai 2003. The latter scholars edited an entire issue of the journal *Physiology and Behavior* devoted to MacLean in which leading scholars discussed the importance of his work to modern neuroscience and medical physiology; see also, Morgane et al. 2005; Wilson and Cory 2008; Newman and Harris 2009.

It is also significant that the development of molecular genetics in recent years has brought new support to MacLean's concepts. Molecular genetics, like MacLean, supports the remarkable conservation of evolved brain architecture from our ancestral vertebrates.

As Tom Insel, Director of the US National Institutes of Mental Health (NIMH) significantly and appropriately stated in a New York Times obituary, MacLean's research opened the door for neuroscience to "ask big questions about consciousness and philosophy, instead of the more tractable questions about vision and movement."(NYT. January 10, 2008). Such overdue and well-deserved acknowledgment of MacLean's pioneering work is indeed welcome.

MacLean's concepts of the limbic system and the tri-level modular brain, when properly represented, are soundly grounded in evolutionary neuroscience, and with some clarifications, are the most useful concepts for linking neuroscience with the more highly integrated concepts of the social sciences. The presentation that follows here is adjusted to accommodate criticisms that raise valid questions.

THE INTERCONNECTED, THREE-LEVEL BRAIN

In a thoroughgoing, encyclopedic summary of the previous fifty years of brain research, MacLean (1990) documented the human brain as an evolved three-level, interconnected, modular structure (Figure 1.1).

MacLean, unfortunately, and perhaps overdramatically, contributed to the misunderstanding of his own triune brain concept by presenting it graphically as "three-brains-in-one"—as if there were separate, independent parts combined loosely together. The *three-brains-in-one* plus the well-known accompanying graphic, was popularized by Carl Sagan (among others) in his *Dragons of Eden* (1977). The overpopularization led to simplistic interpretation and confusion in both the popular and scholarly communities.

Not 3 Brains in 1: But Interconnected Neural Circuits from Different Periods of Our Evolution

When understood properly, which MacLean attempted to clarify in his 1990 classic, the tri-level structure includes—rather than separate brains—essentially interconnected neural circuitry from major periods of human evolution.

The tri-level structure includes a component of self-preservational circuitry reflecting gene-based continuity as conserved from our ancestral stem reptiles. We split off from the stem reptiles, as did the dinosaur ancestral line, during the Permian and Triassic periods, between 250–300 million years ago. It is appropriate to call this conserved ancestral circuitry the protoreptilian or early vertebrate neural complex.

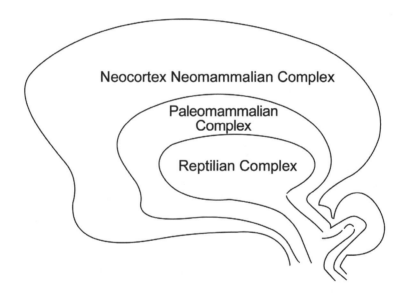

Figure 1.1. MacLean's Triune Brain, as Modified by Cory. In this figure, I have attempted to clarify MacLean's triune concept by modifying his original graphic. As represented here the three brain divisions do not constitute distinct additions (or brains) but rather modifications and elaborations of probable preexisting homologues reflecting gene-based conservation and phylogenetic continuity.

The tri-level structure also included a later modified and elaborated mammalian affectional neural complex, and a most recently modified and elaborated neocortex representing the higher centers of the human brain.

THE EVOLUTION OF INTERCONNECTED TRIALITY

As brain evolution continued in the branching vertebrate line leading to humans, simple protoreptilian or early vertebrate brain structure was not replaced.

As noted earlier, in keeping with what we have learned recently from gene molecular studies, evolution always builds upon preexisting structures. Genes reflect continuity. They don't just pop out of nowhere to create new structures. They usually experience minor variations that lead to modification and elaboration of existing structures.

In control genes, however, which direct the activity of other genes, minor modifications may occasionally lead to significant change—even the appearance of new species (see Gehring 1998 & Pollard 2009).

The protoreptilian structure, then, gave us the substructure and DNA or gene-based continuities (called homologues) for later brain development. It did this while largely retaining its basic character and function. The mammalian modifications and neocortical elaborations that followed reached the greatest development in the brain of humankind.

We must understand the qualitative differences of the three interconnected levels to appreciate the dynamics of human social experience and behavior.

The protoreptilian, or ancestral vertebrate, neural circuits in humans mainly do the same job they did in our ancestral vertebrates. They run the fundamentals, or daily master routines, of our life-support operations: blood circulation, heartbeat, respiration, basic food getting, reproduction, and defensive behaviors.

These were functions and behaviors also necessary in the ancient ancestral reptiles as well as earlier amphibians and fishes. These earlier vertebrates had to do these things to stay alive, reproduce, and become our ancestors.

The next developmental stage of our brain comes from rudimentary mammalian life. This set of circuits is also known collectively as the limbic system. These limbic tissue-clusters developed from gene-based continuities and homologues pre-existing in the protoreptilian neural complex. They included significant elaboration of such physiological structures as the hypothalamus, the amygdala, the insula, the hippocampus, the thalamus, and the limbic cingulate cortex.

Behavioral contributions to life from these modified and elaborated paleomammalian structures or limbic system included, among other things, the mammalian features (absent in our ancestral vertebrates) of warmbloodedness, nursing, infant care, socially interactive play, and extended social bonding. These new characteristics were then neurally integrated with the life-support functional and behavioral circuitry of the protoreptilian tissues to create the more complex form of mammals.

The neocortex, which MacLean called the neo- or "new" mammalian brain, is the most recent stage of brain modification and elaboration. This great mass of bi-hemispherical brain matter dominates the skull case of higher primates and humans. It gained its prominence by elaborating the pre-existing gene-based continuities present in the brain of earlier vertebrates.

Gradually—perhaps more precipitously in the gap between chimpanzees and humans (see Pollard 2009)—it overgrew, encased, and interconnected with the earlier ("paleo") mammalian and protoreptilian interconnected neural tissues. It did not, however, replace them.

As a consequence of this neocortical evolution and growth, these older brain parts evolved greater complexity and extensive interconnected circuitry with these new tissue clusters. In that way, they produced the behavioral adaptations necessary to life's increasingly sophisticated circumstances.

REFINING AND DEFINING
HUMAN UNIQUENESS

The unique features of our human brain were refined over a period of several million years in a mainly kinship based foraging society where sharing or reciprocity was necessary to our survival. Such sharing and reciprocity strengthened the adaptive evolution of the now combined mammalian characteristics of self-preservation and affection (e.g., see Humphrey 1976; Isaac 1978; Knauft 1994; Erdal & Whiten 1996; Boehm 1999).

Ego and Empathy, self-interest and other-interest, are key features of our personal and social behavior. To connect these features to MacLean's concept we need, at this point, a behavioral vocabulary rather than a neurophysiological one.

We need a vocabulary that will express what the presence of our protoreptilian self-preserving mechanisms and our paleo-mammalian affectional brain structures mean for our day-to-day, subjectively experienced, behavioral initiatives and responses to one another and the world we live in. I will draw the behavioral vocabulary from analogy with information and computer technology.

THE SELF-PRESERVING AND
AFFECTIONAL PROGRAMMED CIRCUITRY

Our early vertebrate or reptilian ancestors were cold-blooded, and they did not have brain structures for any extended parental caring. Their care of offspring was, in most cases, limited to making a nest or digging a hole to lay eggs in. The eggs were then left to hatch on their own.

The eggs and hatchlings were easy marks for predators. Further, some reptiles, not knowing their own offspring, would cannibalize them. It was not much of a family life. But the reptiles continued to exist because they produced large numbers of eggs—enough to make sure some offspring survived to reproduce again and continue the species line.

This basic reptilian neural network, plus a group of neural structures clumped together at the forward end of the brain stem and called the basal ganglia, essentially make up our human brain stem. From the mainly survival-centered promptings of these ancestral circuits, as elaborated in our human brain, arise the motivational source for egoistic, surviving, self-interested subjective experience and behaviors.

Here we have the cold-blooded, seemingly passionless, single-minded, self-serving behaviors that we have generally associated with the present-day lizard, the snake, and that most maligned of fishes, the shark.

And intuitively, we call our fellow humans who behave this way such names as snakes, geckos, and sharks.

Here is a world revolving almost exclusively around matters of self-preservation. The protoreptilian brain structures, then, will be called, following our high-tech vocabulary, our self-preservation programming or circuitry.

But we humans are mammals. We not only got the self-preserving circuitry of our early vertebrate ancestors, we got also the programmed circuitry for infant nursing, warmblooded, passionate, body-contacting, playful, and social behaviors that we share with the lion, the wolf, the primates. The motivational source for nurturing, empathetic, other-interested experiences and behaviors arises from such circuitry.

Here is a world in which nearly single-minded self-preservation is simultaneously complemented and counterpoised by the conflicting demands of affection. The early mammalian modifications, then, will be called our affectional programming or circuitry.

OUR EVOLVED BRAIN
AND BEHAVIORAL CONFLICT

These core behavioral programs within us are built up of many contributing subroutines of our neural architecture. Neuroscientist Jaak Panksepp calls such core programs global-state variables since they sum up the effect of many subroutine circuits. He states that a network doctrine is needed to grasp such system-wide emergent dynamics (2002: xiv; see also Schulkin 2002).

These global-state circuits act as dynamic factors of our behavior. They are energy-driven by our cellular as well as overall bodily processes of metabolism, or energy production, as mediated by *hormones, neurotransmitters, and neural architecture*. And each is an inseparable part of our makeup, because each is "wired into" our brain structure by the process of evolution.

The degree of gene control, however, does vary. Older brain parts, like the brain stem and parts of the limbic system, long established and necessary for survival, are under tighter gene control. Other more recent tissues, especially the higher centers of the neocortex, depend a lot on development and experience.

We are set up for behavioral conflict simply by the presence of these two global-state energy-driven modular programs in our lives—up and running, perhaps, even before birth. Their mere physical presence sets us up for a life of inner and outer struggle, as we are driven by and respond to their contending demands.

Conflict is more than an externally observed, objective ethical, moral, or decision-making dilemma, as much modern science tends to see it. We also feel it very strongly within ourselves.

That is, inwardly or *subjectively*, we get feelings of satisfaction when we can express our felt motives. On the other hand, we get feelings of frustration when we cannot express our self-preservation or affectionate impulses in the behavioral initiatives and responses we wish to make.

Behavioral tension then arises. We experience such behavioral tension as frustration, anxiety, or anger. And it arises whenever one of our two fundamental behavioral programs—self-preservation or affection—is activated but meets with some resistance or difficulty that prevents its satisfactory expression.

This subjective tension becomes most paralyzing when both circuits are activated and seek contending or incompatible responses *within a single situation*. Caught between "I want to" and "I can't"—for example, "I want to help him/her, but I can't surrender my needs"—we ambivalate or agonize.

Whether this tension arises through the blocked expression of a single impulse or the simultaneous but mutually exclusive urgings of two competing impulses, whenever it continues unresolved or unmanaged, it leads to the worsening condition of behavioral stress.

THE BLESSING OF TENSION AND STRESS

The evolutionary process by which these two opposite global-state promptings of self-preservation and affection were combined in us gave us a great survival advantage. Their combined dynamic binds us together in social interaction and provides us with a wide range of behavioral responses to our environment—a range much wider than species lacking our dual motive circuitry.

Our naturally conflicting programs are a curse, then, only to the extent that we fail to recognize them as a blessing. Our self-preservation and affection circuits allow us a highly advanced sensitivity to our environment. They keep our interactive social behaviors within survival limits by giving us the ability to understand and appreciate the survival requirements of others.

Ironically, the accompanying behavioral tension—*even the stress!*—is an integral part of this useful function. It allows us to more quickly evaluate our behavior and the effect it is having on ourselves and others.

Behavioral tension serves as an internal emotional compass that we can use to guide ourselves through the often complicated and treacherous pathways of interpersonal relations.

Behavioral stress tells us that we are exceeding safe limits for ourselves and others, and even for our larger social, economic, and political structures.

At this point we have the fundamentals of our behavioral dynamic. But if we are to manage this conflicting circuitry, we need to add another element. We need a certain level of consciousness. Maybe we should best think of it as self-aware consciousness.

CONFLICT OR CHOICE: THE MULE'S DILEMMA

Self-aware consciousness gives us the ability to talk about and generalize our internally felt motives.

If all we had were the conflicting programs of self-preservation and affection, we would be among the animals whose behaviors are run automatically by instinct. We would be driven by the urgings of fight or flight, or bondedness, and the decision would be made for us by preset homeostatic neural priorities.

With self-conscious awareness, however, we face the dilemma of choice. Perhaps, every so often, we would, nevertheless, be like the conflicted mule of southern farmland tradition, who looked back and forth between water and hay, unable to move or make a choice. We, too, might be caught in the conflict of those urgings, unable to make a decision.

What gives us the power to rise above the mule's dilemma—to overcome it? What makes the difference between instinctual conflict and the power of choice? These questions take us to the next chapter.

3

THE CONFLICT SYSTEMS NEUROBEHAVIORAL MODEL

Scientists don't know everything. And they are not really sure about a lot of important things. However, what scientists do have, if they are worth their salt, is an open mind. They question—and should question—everything.

A mountain of research, however, some old some very recent, has established beyond doubt a couple of fundamental characteristics of the human brain. First, the brain is a physiological organ. Second, it is an organ evolved for social interaction. I will look at both characteristics in more detail.

THE HUMAN BRAIN: A PHYSIOLOGICAL ORGAN

Like other organs of the body—hands, feet, heart—the brain developed over many millennia to its present form in *Homo sapiens sapiens*. It evolved out of accumulated mutations—including mutations of the highly influential master control genes that can in some instances produce dramatic change by single mutations (Gehring 1998; Pollard 2009).

Such mutations were confirmed by natural selection—that is, they generally helped us survive and reproduce—in the genetic information repository of our DNA. The brain, then, develops in each individual under the prescriptive guidance of DNA that, despite a considerable amount of developmental and experiential plasticity, assures a high degree of fidelity in the replication of fundamental brain architecture.

The main features of our brain, like the main features of our human body plan (head, trunk, arms, legs), are expressed in common across our human species.

THE SOCIAL NATURE OF THE BRAIN

Physiologically, the human brain is also an organ supporting *social* life. The social brain concept necessarily emphasizes both the self-preservation (self-interested) and affectional (other-interested) mammalian components necessary to social interaction.

The *social brain* is an organizing concept heralded in a number of recent publications—*The Evolutionary Epidemiology of Mania and Depression* (Wilson & Cory 2008), *Attachment and Bonding: A New Synthesis* (Carter, et al. 2006), *Textbook of Biological Psychiatry* (Panksepp 2004), *Foundations in Social Neuroscience* (Cacioppo, et al. 2002) and *Handbook of Affective Sciences* (Davidson, et al. 2003; see also, Cory & Gardner 2002).

Slightly earlier but related volumes include *Descartes' Error: Emotion, Reason, and the Human Brain* (Damasio 1994), *The Integrative Neurobiology of Affiliation* (Carter, et al. 1997) and *Affective Neuroscience* (Panksepp 1998). Recent years have thus brought great advances in detailing the many complex and interrelated pathways of interactive social circuitry in the brain.

The genes specifying social circuitry were selected over millions of years of evolutionary history in small kinship groups that required a cooperative interactive dynamic for survival. In fact, our survival strategy as an emerging species was not only hunting and gathering but essentially **sharing** of the fruits of these activities. These dynamic social circuits motivate human social interaction and social exchange at all levels of our lives today. (e.g., see Humphrey 1976; Isaac 1978; Knauft 1994; Erdal & Whiten 1996; Boehm 1999).

BACK TO CONSCIOUSNESS

Keeping in mind the physiological and social nature of the brain, let's return to the question of the previous chapter—consciousness or the mule's dilemma.

As scientists we don't know for certain whether kindred mammals—cats, dogs, mules, elephants, dolphins, chimpanzees, and others—with paleo-mammalian brain structures, with self-preservation and affectional circuitry, just act on preset neuronal priorities. Or whether they experience conscious conflict and must choose among such conflicting behavioral priorities.

We may suspect that these mammals do have conflict. Or we may protest from the perspective of *homo arrogance* that they do not. It's a tough question for scientists. Science has not yet developed good interviewing techniques for these other mammals.

There is, however, absolutely no doubt about us humans. We certainly do. We can reflect and generalize not only upon our choices, but upon the meanings they have for our personal lives as well as our species' existence and significance.

And it is in that capacity to reflect, to self-consciously experience, generalize, and decide upon the tug-and-pull of our conflicting urgings, that we come to third stage of brain development in MacLean's model. That is, the neomammalian or "new" mammalian brain structures—what I call the executive programming or circuitry.

IT'S TIME FOR CONSCIOUSNESS

We still do not fully understand the neural circuitry that produces consciousness.

For most of the twentieth century scientists avoided taking up the question. It was simply too difficult and there were no good tools for studying it. In the last couple of decades, however, new techniques like brain imaging have been developed.

Although the emerging circuitry producing consciousness is still unclear, I follow the position here that there is no *homunculus*—meaning from the Latin, "little artificial person"— or other Cartesian dualistic process involved.

Such ideas as a little observer inside our heads have plagued writers on consciousness for centuries. It still does today. Even hard-nosed scientists occasionally get caught up in it. After all, there has to be someone in there to see and experience what is going on.

DESCARTES' MISCHIEVOUS LEGACY

The French Renaissance philosopher, René Descartes (1596–1650), left us a legacy of mischief when he separated body from mind in the 17th century.

Descartes, with his famous phrase *cogito ergo sum*—I think therefore, I am—saw the only certain reality as mind. Mind, as the only certain reality, thus became separated from the body, to include the brain. Body and brain, these physical or material manifestations, from Descartes' view, had a more dubious reality status. Descartes' split of mind and body at that time also fit well the church's doctrine of the soul as existing separately from the body. Descartes, in the early Renaissance, was unable to detach himself from the church tradition.

Descartes, then, bequeathed us the duality of mind and body that still haunts us today when we try to come to grips scientifically with the question of consciousness.

Like Descartes, we all *know* we have consciousness. But we, as scientific moderns, cannot stand firmly and convincingly on his *cogito ergo sum*. The assertion from intuition simply doesn't meet the standards of empirical evidence that we demand today.

On the other hand, it is pretty easy to prove that bodies and brains have reality.

SELF-AWARE CONSCIOUSNESS AS NEURAL

There are lots of people thinking about consciousness these days. Some come from philosophical, even religious perspectives. We, as scientists, however, must come from a verifiable or at least potentially verifiable perspective. And from that perspective the neural substrate of consciousness is still a matter of considerable speculation and debate.

Nevertheless, it seems that our expanded and elaborated neocortex (or isocortex), anchored in and interconnected with our earlier mammalian and protoreptilian brain systems, is part of the "dynamic core" of neural structures that nobelist Gerald Edelman and colleagues see as necessary to our *self-aware* or *self-reflective* consciousness (Edelman 1992; Edelman & Tononi 2000).

As well, our elaborated neocortex provides us with the evolutionarily unique and powerful ability to use verbal and symbolic language. We can, thus, create concepts and ideas by which to interpret our consciousness. We can describe the feelings, motives, and behaviors that arise within us and in response to our social and environmental experiences.

It is with this so-called executive circuitry or programming, then, that we acquire the ability to name, to comment upon, to *generalize*, and to *choose* between our contending sets of behavioral impulses.

Self-preservation is commonly called, at a high level of cognitive integration, "egoistic" or "self-interested" behavior.

We call affection, at an equally high level of cognitive integration, "empathetic" or "other-interested" behavior.

Empathy allows us the critical social capacity to enter into or respond emotionally to another's self-interest as well as other emotional states.

THE CONFLICT SYSTEMS
NEUROBEHAVIORAL (CSN) MODEL

The Conflict Systems Neurobehavioral (CSN) Model is introduced in Figure 3.1.

Although the positioning of Empathy and Ego in Figure 3.1 (facing the reader) is primarily for illustrative purposes only and is not intended to suggest a definitive lateralization, there is evidence to suggest that the right hemisphere is favored somewhat for emotion and the left for more analytical self-preserving behaviors (e.g., see Damasio 1994; Tucker, Luu, & Pribram 1995; Brownell & Martino 1998; Henry & Wang 1998; Stuss & Knight 2002).

However, the total experience of emotion is not lateralized but involves dynamic interactions between forward and posterior regions of both hemispheres as well as subcortical (limbic) structures (Heller et al. 1998; Morgane et al. 2005). Therefore, such complex, highly integrated capacities as Ego and Empathy should more safely be thought of as engaging the interaction of both hemispheres (Beauregard & O'Leary 2008; Decety & Ikes 2009).

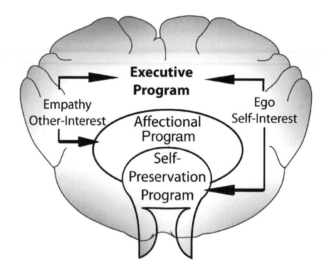

Figure 3.1. The CSN Model. A simplified cutaway representation of the brain showing the behavioral programs and the derivation of Ego/self-interested and Empathy/other-interested motives and behaviors. I should note that earlier models, e.g., Freud (id, ego, and superego) postulated three-part conflictual models. Freud, however, was unable to tie his model to brain circuitry and it remained ungrounded in neural science because brain research had simply not advanced to that point (Cory after MacLean, see Cory 1992, 1999, 2000ab, 2001ab, 2002, 2004, 2006ab).

In other words, our executive programming, especially our frontal cortex, has the capability and the responsibility for cognitively representing these ancestral limbic and protoreptilian brain connections and inputs and making what may be thought of as our moral as well as rational choices among our conflicting, impulsive, and irrational or nonrational motivations.

This self-conscious, generalizing, choosing capacity accompanied, of course, with language, is what differentiates us from even closely related primate species and makes findings in primate behavior, although highly interesting and unquestionably important, insufficient in themselves to fully understand and account for human behavior.

EXECUTIVE CIRCUITRY
AND NEURAL NETWORKS

The frontal neocortex has long been recognized to be involved in executive functions. However, the more inclusive concept may be that the neural substrate of executive functions is a neural network that includes the synchronized activity of multiple regions, both cortical and subcortical.

Our early vertebrate and limbic circuits are interconnected neural network circuits that *subjectively* generate and drive specific, and *objectively* observable, behaviors. These core motivational (and emotional) circuits are connected largely through the thalamocingulate gateway to the executive frontal circuitry as well as possibly other neocortical regions. In these higher regions, they are respectively represented as self-preserving Ego and species-preserving Empathy cognitions (e.g., see Berridge 2003; cf. Saarela 2006; Tankersley, et al. 2007).

The neural substrate for self-survival Ego mechanisms likely proceeds from circuits in the basal ganglia and brain stem (protoreptilian or ancestral vertebrate complex) through connections with the amygdala, other limbic structures (early mammalian complex), and probable other subcortical circuits, such as the insula, which add emotion or passion, ultimately to be gated into the frontal cortex by thalamocortical circuitry (see Jones 2007; Sherman & Guillery 2001; Devinsky & Luciano 1993.)

Likewise, the mammalian nurturing (affectional) substrate and its associated motivation, a fundamental component underlying Empathy, may originate in the septal and medial preoptic limbic areas. It may, then, proceed through hippocampal and amygdaloid circuitry, the insula, as well as other limbic structures.

Ultimately, and in turn, the affectional circuitry will largely be gated into the orbital and frontal cortex by neuromodulating thalamocortical circuits (to include the cingulate cortex), where the conflict with egoistic inputs is resolved in the executive or global workspace of conscious self-awareness.

The Gating of Dual Motives

As noted above, the dual motives of self-survival and affection are gated into the frontal executive by a structure known as the thalamus. The neuromodulating and gating of *affect* as well as cognition by the thalamocortical circuitry is a function well known to medical neuroscience. The role of the thalamus as the gating structure of the myelinated cables passing from the subcortical motivational circuitries, into the frontal cortex, has long been established (e.g., see Devinsky & Luciano 1993).

It was these fiber tracts that were cut in the well intended, but now notorious psychosurgical procedures of the 1930s through 1950s. Lobotomies, luekotomies, and other similar procedures were deliberate efforts to disconnect the frontal cortex from the lower archetypal motivating circuitries. The objective was to reduce anxiety, violence, and other unwanted behaviors.

The procedures were largely effective in achieving their objective. They regularly produced what medical science, euphemistically called "flat affect." That is, reduced or no Ego and Empathy. Some critics to this day complain that the current drugs used in treating such symptoms have the same intention and effect—deactivation of the emotional and motivating circuitries (Breggin 2008).

The psychosurgical practices of the 1930s through 1950s provide some of the clearest physiological evidence for Dual Motive Theory. The archetypal neural circuitries, their thalamo-cingulate gating mechanisms, and their frontal connections were known facts of physiology. The work done on humans had previously and since been confirmed by experiments upon other primates (Fulton 1951; O' Callaghan & Carroll 1982; Valenstein 1986, Housepian 1998; Pressman 1998).

Ego and Empathy Clarified

As noted earlier, Ego, as used here is not the Ego of Freudian psychoanalysis although there are some similarities. Ego, as indicated in Figure 3.1, is defined as deriving from self-preserving circuitry. It closely matches the standard definition of Egoism in philosophy and as referenced in literary terms such as "self-focused," "self-absorbed," "self-interested," or "narcissistic."

Empathy, on the other hand, includes the affectional feelings of sympathetic attachment reinforced by cognitions added in the course of neocortical assessment and representation (e.g., see Hoffman 1981, 2000). Empathy and sympathy, despite their rather distinct meanings in medical-psychiatric settings, are otherwise and especially in recent citations, more often posited inclusively (Eisenberg 1994; Batson 1991).

Recent research has further indicated that Empathy has both emotional and cognitive components activated by different but overlapping areas of neural circuitry (Singer 2006; Blair 2003). This overlapping is summed in the CSN Model, with its varying mixes of Ego and Empathy across a spectrum of behavior.

In addition, there is the contentious issue of the actual presence and accurate function of Empathy-inducing *mirror neurons* in humans. As neuropsychologist Alison Gopnik (2007) reminds us, despite all the enthusiastic press coverage, no one at present knows for sure if humans even have mirror neurons.

The numerous fMRI studies can't provide any definite answers. Unlike the single neuron electrode studies in monkeys, fMRI doesn't measure the electrical activity of individual neurons. Such studies give information about the oxygen use of sections of the brain with many hundreds of thousands of individual neurons.

Such complex capacities as Empathy, in real life situations rather than narrowly conceived research designs, must necessarily draw on many brain areas.

For the reasons cited above and to indicate the most inclusive and customary use of the term suggesting other-interest/other regard plus shared affect and sympathy, the variant *Empathetic* is used as distinct from the more specific term, *empathic*.

The Electrochemical Physiology of Dual Motives

Although it is beyond the scope of this chapter to deal with the as yet incompletely understood detailed electrochemical physiology of such egoistic/empathetic conflict, it is appropriate to acknowledge that such behavior is made possible, in part, by the complex electro-chemical excitatory and inhibitory interactions among groups of interconnected neurons and neural networks. A more detailed discussion is contained in Chapter 3 of Wilson and Cory (2008).

The role of hormones and neurotransmitters must also be acknowledged in any complete analysis.

For instance, from the egoistic perspective, testosterone is associated with competitiveness and power urges. Serotonin levels in humans seem related to confidence and self-esteem.

On the empathetic side, oxytocin, arginine vasopressin, and prolactin are important to pair bonding and maternal as well as paternal caring behavior. Opioids (endorphins and enkaphalins) seem important to positive social relationships. Donaldson and Young (2008) have recently reviewed the social bonding effects of oxytocin and vasopressin. The authors note that these ancient mammalian neuropeptides display a marked conservation in gene structure and expression.

THE MAJOR RANGES OF
RECIPROCAL, CONFLICT BEHAVIOR

The two master archetypal programs of self-preservation and affection that have been wired into our brain structure operate dynamically according to a set of behavioral rules or algorithms.

We experience the workings of these algorithmic rules internally. We also express them externally in our interpersonal behavior. We need to understand the workings and applications of these algorithms to grasp the role of conflict, tension, and stress in our personal and interactive lives.

EMPATHETIC RANGE	DYNAMIC BALANCE	EGOISTIC RANGE
self-sacrifice	compromise	power-seeking
submission	fairness	domination
giving	sharing	seizing (taking)
responsiveness	justice	assertiveness
supportiveness		competitiveness
others-over-self		self-over-others

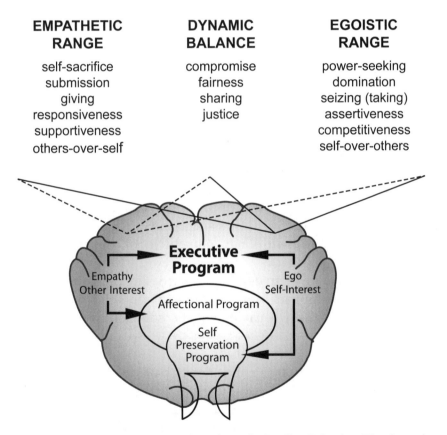

Figure 3.2. The Major Ranges of Reciprocal, Conflict Behavior. The dynamic of the model, the tug-and-pull of Ego and Empathy, allows the expression of the mix of motive and behavior as a range or spectrum. The usual dichotomizing of self-interest and altruism is seen only at the extremes of the spectrum. For a neural network modeling of the dynamic see Levine & Jani (2002).

The major ranges of the CSN Model (Figure 3.2) show graphically the features of this Ego-Empathy dynamic. In the display, both internally felt as well as expressed objectively in interpersonal behavior is divided from right to left into three main ranges. From right to left, they are the egoistic range, the Dynamic Balance range, and the empathetic range.

Each range represents a varying mix of egoistically and empathetically motivated behaviors. The solid line stands for Ego and pivots on the word "Ego" in the executive program of the brain diagram. The broken line stands for Empathy and pivots on the word "Empathy" in the diagram.

The Egoistic Range

The egoistic range indicates behavior dominated by our self-preservation circuitry. Since the two behavioral programs are locked in inseparable unity, Empathy is present here, but to a lesser degree.

Behavior in this range is self-centered or self-interested. It may tend, for example, to be dominating, power-seeking, or even attacking, where Empathy is less. When Empathy is increased, Ego behavior will become less harsh. It may, then, be described more moderately as controlling, competitive, or assertive.

As Empathy is gradually increased, the intersection of the two lines of the diagram will move toward the range of Dynamic Balance. That is, Ego behavior will be softened as Empathy is added.

But the defining characteristic of the egoistic, self-interested range is *self-over-others*. Whether we are blatantly power-seeking or more moderately assertive, in this range we are putting ourselves, our own priorities, objectives, and feelings, ahead of others.

The Empathetic Range

The empathetic range represents behavior weighted in favor of Empathy. Ego is present, but is taking a back seat. When Ego is present minimally, empathetic behavior may tend to extremes of self-sacrifice and submission.

When Ego is increased, empathetic behaviors are moderated. We can then describe them as supportive, responsive, or any of a variety of "others first" behaviors. As the influence of Ego is gradually added, empathetic behavior will approach the range of Dynamic Balance.

In the empathetic range, the key phrase to remember is *others-over-self* or others first. Whether we are at the extreme of self-sacrifice or more moderately responsive, we are putting the priorities of others ahead of our own.

The Dynamic Balance Range

The range of Dynamic Balance represents a working balance between Ego and Empathy. At this point our behavioral circuitries are operating in roughly equal measure. I speak of "working," "rough," or "dynamic" because the tug-and-pull between the two programs continues ceaselessly.

The dynamic nature of the neural architecture means that "perfect" balance may be a theoretical point, unattainable in practice. Our more balanced behavior tends to express equality, justice, sharing, and other behaviors that show respect for ourselves and others. In fact, respect for self and others is the keynote of the range of Dynamic Balance.

Energy or Activation Level
Escalation and De-escalation

The extent to which the circuits of self-preservation and affection are out of balance, or pulling against each other is a measure of behavioral tension. We experience this behavioral tension both internally and between ourselves and others in any relationship or interaction.

But that is not all.

Excessive, unmanaged, or unresolved tension engenders behavioral stress along a range of behavior. But the amplitude of escalating or de-escalating energy we invest in the interaction or the relationship is an equally important factor affecting behavioral stress and its multiple physiological manifestations.

Much of this arousal occurs automatically by activation of the HPA (hypothalamic-pituitary-adrenal) axis. Nevertheless, it is also under cortical control to a significant degree. We can put more energy into activities and responses for which we feel enthusiasm—less into others.

In highly competitive sports or contests, qualitative differences in energy are easily observed. In intellectual contests, like chess, the energy may be intense, but less obvious.

Such arousal level—or escalation/de-escalation—is applicable across the Ego-Empathy spectrum, giving us two essential axes of social behavior. Gray (1987) has indicated that the brain may moderate behavior for both inhibition and reward-seeking. Witter and Groenewegen (1992) and Gloor (1997: 325–496), report a comparator role for the hippocampus, a prominent limbic structure, in the routing of internal and external stimuli in relation to previous affective experience (cf. Iidaka, et al. 2003).

The Ego-Empathy and escalation/de-escalation axes, thus, are two of the most essential axes of social behavior expressed in the reciprocal algorithm. For a graphic representation of these axes, see Wilson and Cory (2008: ch. 10).

From the descriptions of these two axes given above, I can put together the reciprocal algorithms of our social behavior. These algorithms are detailed in the next chapter.

4

THE GLOBAL-STATE ALGORITHMS
OF RECIPROCAL BEHAVIOR

Although unfamiliar to many of my generation, the word *algorithm* has come into popular parlance with the rise of computers and information technology. In a sense it is a buzzword, a word of currency and sophistication. When you use it, you let everyone know that you are "in the know"—technologically "cool," perhaps. Let's look deeper.

ALGORITHMIC ORIGINS

Because of its recent and current celebrity, some people think of algorithm as a new word. Some even see it as a possible acronym put together from parts of other words.

Looking back into the history books a couple of millennia, however, we find that the honors must go to a Persian mathematician of the ninth century. His name is recorded as Mohammed al-Khowarizmi. Through twists and turns of fate plus the vagaries of translation, his name has come down to us in the present form that the venerable Persian would probably not recognize today.

But al-Khowarizmi gave us the formal procedures for solving standard problems of arithmetic: addition, subtraction, multiplication, and division. Procedures or processes that every schoolchild takes for granted today. At the time, however, it was a significant achievement.

Algorithm, then, originated as a way or method of solving math problems, usually by breaking them down into simpler sequential steps. Its usage, however, has now become extended. In computer science we use the word to describe the various step-by-step procedures for solving problems so that they can be programmed into computers.

Some writers, however, have taken the meaning even further. David Harel of the Weizmann Institute of Science in Israel, for instance, applies algorithms to human decision-making in most areas of life.

Harel sees algorithms applicable not only in business, science, and technology, but also to such ordinary things as looking up a telephone number, filling out a form—even cooking. Algorithms have, in fact, been compared to recipes that provide a step-by-step process for making dishes for the family dinner.

Algorithm, then, has become a flexible term that can tame many variable processes. That is why I have chosen to use it in describing the interactive dynamic of our neural architecture.

In an earlier 1992 publication, *Rescuing Capitalist Free Enterprise for the Twenty-First Century*, I called the neural dynamic the laws of reciprocal behavior. This was, of course, by analogy with the laws of the physical sciences.

Although the laws of physics and the interactive dynamic of our neural architecture are undoubtedly linked (see Cory 2000, 2009), the neural dynamic as the product of organic evolution is more variable. This variability makes the use of the word *laws* somewhat misleading.

Algorithm offers the better choice to reflect the variability of the neural dynamic. I will return to this subject in more detail in a later chapter.

THE ALGORITHMIC NEURAL DYNAMIC

From Figure 3.2, representing the major ranges of behavior, we saw the dynamic of our neural architecture displayed graphically. Here, I will supplement that visual reference by a precise verbal description of that global-state, interactive dynamic.

From the dynamic interplay of Ego, Empathy, and activity or escalation/de-escalation level come a series of algorithmic rule statements.

The first rule describes the egoistic range:

1. Self-interested, egoistic behavior, because it lacks Empathy to some degree, creates tension within ourselves and between our selves and others. The tension increases from low to high activity levels. And it increases as we move toward the extremes of Ego.

Within ourselves, the tension created by the tug of neglected Empathy is experienced as a feeling of obligation to others or an expectation that they might wish to "even the score" with us.

Within others, the tension created by our self-interested behavior is experienced as a feeling of imposition or hurt, accompanied by an urge to "even the score."

Children often reveal the dynamic of such behavior in a clear, unsophisticated form. Imagine two children playing on the living-room floor. One hits the other. The second child hits back, responding in kind. Or the children may not hit each other at all.

One might instead call the other a bad name. The second child reciprocates, kicking off a round of escalating name-calling. One child may eventually feel unable to even the score and will complain to a parent to intervene. Most of us have experienced such give-and-take as children. Surely, we have seen it countless times in our own children and grandchildren.

Similar behavior is embarrassingly observable among adults. It can be seen in husband and wife arguments, bar fights, hockey games, political campaigns, even in sophisticated lawsuits. The rule operates not only in such highly visible conflict situations, but also in very subtle interactions—in the small behavioral exchanges, the ongoing give-and-take of all interpersonal relations.

Expressive of the underlying conflictual excitatory/inhibitory dynamic of the neural architecture, we can say that

The reactions that build in ourselves and others do so potentially in proportion to the behavioral tension created by the egoistic, self-interested behavior.

That is, the harder I hit you, the harder you hit me in return. Or the fouler a name you call me, the fouler a name I call you in return. Or perhaps with more sophistication, I resolve the tension in me by an act of visible "superiority." I ignore you—although I *could* call you an even fouler name, if I chose. Such behavior can, of course, have tragic consequences if the reactive behavioral tension or stress is turned inward (e.g., recent teenage suicides related to bullying).

The second rule describes the empathetic range—behavior on the other side of the scale:

> 2. Empathetic behavior, because it denies Ego or self-interest to some degree, also creates tension within ourselves and others. This tension, likewise, increases as activity levels increase and as we move toward the extremes of Empathy.

> Within ourselves, the tension created by the tug of neglected self-interest (Ego) is experienced as a feeling that "others owe us one" and a growing need to "collect our due." This tension, especially if it continues over time, may be experienced as resentment at being exploited, taken for granted, not appreciated, or victimized by others.

> Within others, the tension created is experienced as a sense of obligation toward us.

> The reactions that build in ourselves and others, again, are in proportion to the behavioral tension created. And again, the unmanaged, or excessive tension is experienced as behavioral stress.

When we do things for others—give them things, make personal sacrifices for them—it can make us feel righteous, affectionate, loving. But we *do* want a payback. That's the tug of self-interest. It can be very slight, hardly noticeable at first. But let the giving, the self-sacrifice, go on for a while, unacknowledged or unappreciated (that is, without payback to the Ego), and see how we begin to feel.

The tension, the stress, starts to show. We complain that others are taking advantage of us, taking us for granted, victimizing us. Self-interest cannot be long short-changed without demanding its due. We may eventually relieve the stress by blowing up at those we have been serving—accusing them of ingratitude, withdrawing our favors, or kicking them out of the house. Or we may sandbag the stress, letting it eat away at our dispositions, our bodies.

On the other hand, when we do things for others, they often feel obliged to return the favor in some form to avoid being left with an uneasy sense of debt. Gift-giving notoriously stimulates the receiver to feel the need to reciprocate.

Think of the times when you have received a holiday gift from someone for whom you had failed to buy a gift. Sometimes the sense of obligation prompted by the empathetic acts of others can become a nuisance.

The third rule statement describes the range of Dynamic Balance; that is, the relative balance between our contending motives:

3. Behavior in the range of Dynamic Balance expresses the approximate balance of Ego and Empathy. It is the position of least behavioral tension. Within ourselves and others, it creates feelings of mutuality and shared respect.

For most of us it is an especially satisfying experience to interact with others in equality, with no sense of obligation, superiority or inferiority. To work together in common humanity, in common cause, is to experience behavioral Dynamic Balance.

Of course, there are many versions of the experience of Dynamic Balance: the shared pride of parents in helping their child achieve, the joy of athletes in playing well as a team, the satisfaction of coworkers in working together successfully on an important project.

RECIPROCITY THROUGH CONFLICT

These algorithms of behavior operate in the smallest interactions, the vignettes, of everyday personal life. The dynamic of behavioral tension provides that for every interpersonal act, there is a balancing reciprocal. A self-interested act requires an empathetic reciprocal for balance. An empathetic act, likewise, requires a balancing self-interested reciprocal. This reciprocity goes back and forth many times even in a short conversation.

Without the reciprocal, tension builds, stress accumulates, and either confrontation or withdrawal results. If not, and the relationship continues, it becomes a tense and stressful one of inequality or domination/submission, waiting and pressing for the opportunity for adjustment.

These, then, are the basic interpersonal algorithms of our three-level brain. These algorithms show how we get to reciprocity through conflict. They shape the conflict and reciprocity, the give-and-take, at all levels of our interactive, social lives.

Overemphasis on either self-interest or other-interest, exercise of one program to the exclusion of the other, creates tension and stress in any social configuration—from simple dyadic person-to-person encounters up to and including interactions among members of the workplace, society at large, social groups, and entire economic and political systems.

THE SCALE OF INCLUSIVENESS

The reciprocal algorithms of neural architecture, the tug-and-pull of Ego and Empathy, apply at all levels of social exchange.

However, the intensity of empathetic bonding tends to vary with proximity and related factors creating a varying scale of inclusiveness. The scale of inclusiveness is an important factor in fully understanding the nature of human bonding created by the Ego/Empathy dynamic.

The Family Connection

A basic feature of our evolutionary development is that we evolved to full humanity in small family kinship groups. Our neural architecture is, therefore, designed primarily to work most effectively in such small face-to-face, closely knit groups. Empathy bonds us most tightly and securely in the family. Ego is reigned in by love and care for parents, children, mates, cousins.

And we feel the depth of love and passion most keenly to those in close physical proximity—those we live and work with on a daily basis. With distance the intensity of Empathy tends to become increasingly rarefied or thinned out.

In Africa, our brain developed over millions of years in such small group circumstances. Dynamically balanced, essentially egalitarian, social behavior characterized such groups.

A leader, or Alpha, did not dominate through brute Ego force, as some traditional lore would have it. The leader emerged as the one who could engage alliances and provide the most in wisdom, survival skills, and affection. Providing such is the essence of mammalian Empathy.

Our survival strategy as a species, thus, was sharing, reciprocity—not domination and submission. All this, and the neural circuitry supporting it, was essentially cast in DNA/protein concrete—hard-wired—long before we entered into larger social groupings. Long before we developed agriculture and settled down. Long before we grouped into early cities and kingdoms, creating civilization.

And long before the barely five to ten thousand years ago (a very short and recent time in our human development), when we created writing and made recorded history possible.

Present-Day Mismatch
And the Importance of Socialization and Education

Our evolution of Ego and Empathy in small family groups means that this architecture is in somewhat of a state of mismatch with our current mass impersonal environment.

Empathy for others weakens as they are more distant from us—creating the scale of inclusiveness. We feel Empathy most strongly for family and those most close to us, less to those more distant.

This scale of inclusiveness is a consistent and perennial problem for larger societies. It is only resolved by socialization or education that extends and universalizes the existing architecture beyond the confines of family and small groups.

Historically, we have sensed this mismatch and attempted intuitively to overcome it by appeals to kinship terms. Secularly, we have used such terms as the family of man, brotherhoods, sisterhoods, mother- or fatherlands.

Without the basic architecture, such appeals would be groundless. They are clearly intuitive efforts to extend and universalize the fundamental Ego and Empathy dynamic.

PREDICTABILITY AND THE CSN MODEL

The scientific worth of a model is often said to be its ability to make predictions.

Given an appreciation of the algorithmic rules of behavior and the scale of inclusiveness, the CSN Model meets that standard. Each of the algorithmic rule statements can be phrased as a testable prediction.

As a homey example, try behaving in an egoistic, domineering manner toward a family member or friend. That is, if you dare to risk the consequences.

The CSN Model predicts that both you and the family member or friend will experience behavioral tension and will report such feelings. This has been tried many times and has produced consistent results. It's really not recommended. If, on the other hand, you prefer to try empathetic, serving behavior, especially over a period of time, you may find the model's predictions of behavioral tension likewise hold.

Despite the qualifications of the scale of inclusiveness, the CSN Model's predictive and explanatory powers go far beyond such straightforward, intuitive proximal examples. The predictive power will be explicit in the extraordinary range of its explanatory power demonstrated in the succeeding chapters of this book.

5

THE HOMEOSTATIC REGULATION OF OUR SOCIAL NEURAL ARCHITECTURE

Living things, from the single cell on up, have remarkable regulating mechanisms. They must. If they didn't they would fall apart. They would simply die and breakdown into their many component parts.

In physiology, this ability to regulate, to keep all parts working together within set limits, was first described by Claude Bernard, a French physiologist of the 19th century. However, it was Walter B. Cannon, an American physiologist, who gave these regulating processes the name "homeostasis."

The year was 1929, and the name stuck. The word Cannon chose comes from two Greek words. *Homeo* means similar, and *stasis* means standing. As used by Cannon, and other scientists who followed him, homeostasis does not mean something rigidly set in concrete, unshakable, or immovable.

It describes a condition that varies yet at the same time is relatively constant. For the organism, it describes a condition that is kept within survival limits. When the homeostatic limits are exceeded the mechanism either self-corrects, or the organism gets dysfunctional. That is, it either gets out of whack, sick, or dies.

Like all other creatures, our human vital processes are homeostatic. Built-in controls keep them generally within healthy and, ultimately, within survival limits.

Familiar examples are our body temperature which must be kept within a rather narrow range around 98.6 degrees Fahrenheit. Above that we have a fever. Below that we risk hypothermia. Our body must act to correct both indicated conditions to stay healthy or alive. Another example is our blood pressure which varies rather widely to accommodate our changing levels of physical activity. Nevertheless our blood pressure must remain within limits or we're in for big trouble.

The list of homeostatically controlled physical processes is very long indeed. I could go on and on. Practically every bodily process is regulated within certain varying limits. Even the hormones and neurotransmitters that mediate behavior within our neural architecture are regulated homeostatically. When the regulation fails, ours moods, our feelings, and ultimately our behaviors get out of sorts.

A huge pharmaceutical industry exists to help us keep our bodily and behavioral processes in relative homeostasis—from blood pressure medications, to diet pills, to mood regulators.

These homeostatic processes, from the vital activities of the smallest cell up to the integrated functions of our body as a whole, can all be described by algorithms. They can likewise be represented by mathematical equations. Despite sometimes mind-boggling complexity, they all function within necessary survival limits.

HOMEOSTASIS, CYBERNETICS, AND INFORMATION THEORY

The discovery and study of homeostasis in the vital processes of living organisms led to the science of control systems, cybernetics, and information theory.

Biological systems gave us both the model and the inspiration for these technological advances. The computer or information revolution depends upon modeling of our physical regulating processes.

When we build computers, software, and information control systems, we are creating partial analogs of ourselves out there. And then we're interacting with them to support our daily lives. Information, computers, controlled mechanical processes—all model the organic algorithms that regulate living processes.

Homeostatic systems, whether biological or fabricated, require certain essentials. At a minimum, they must have standards or limits, the ability to monitor and evaluate those standards and limits against performance, and the capacity to initiate corrective action. They must also have sensors to get input for comparison, and effectors that can act to carry out the needed adjustments.

The concept of feedback is one of the most important ideas to come out of the study of homeostasis and its human-made information control sciences. Feedback refers to the information for comparison and evaluation that sensors both internal and external bring us. Homeostatic systems need feedback to tell them how they are doing. When to start corrective action. When to stop it.

HOMEOSTASIS OF THE
SOCIAL ARCHITECTURE

The word homeostasis usually refers to the regulation of the internal environment of living organisms. Can we legitimately apply the concept to the workings of our social neural architecture?

Absolutely. All the elements for homeostatic regulation are present—standards, the ability to monitor and evaluate, sensors and effectors.

In fact, our autonomic nervous system through its connections with the hypothalamus has primary involvement in behavioral homeostasis. The hypothalamus is closely linked with neural structures in the both the affectional and self-preservational circuitry located in the limbic system and the brain stem (e.g., see Herbert & Schulkin 2002; Kandel, et. al. 2000: 871–997; Nelson 2000, esp. pp. 447–494; Becker, et al. 1992).

Like other bodily processes, our social neural architecture is regulated within limits. All the sensory systems of our body feed information into the monitoring neural centers. Many cues—from happy, sad, angry facial expressions to vocalizations of tenderness, frustration, surprise, and anger—are genetically wired and fine-tuned through development and experience. The muscles of our body act to carry out adjustments to our social as well as physical environment.

What we experience as behavioral tension is the generic regulator.

Behavioral tension tells us when we are deviating from balance. Behavioral stress warns us that we're exceeding safe limits (e.g., see Przewlocki 2002).

The behavioral spectrum set out in Chapter 3 illustrates the necessary behavioral range and limits. The algorithmic rules of reciprocity in Chapter 4 describe the social regulatory process. The social equation formulated in Chapter 6, which follows, represents the process mathematically.

HOMEOSTATIC VARIABILITY, NEURAL PLASTICITY, AND LEARNING

Homeostatic regulations, as noted, can vary quite a bit in the ranges permitted.

Some are tighter, some are looser. Our social architecture is one of the looser kind. This is to be expected.

The brain, in its higher centers, is the most plastic of our organs. It is designed for learning—to respond to new experience. Learning plays an important role in the variability among individuals of the neural dynamic (on neural plasticity, see Kolb, et al. 2003; Shaw & McEachern 2001; Kolb 1995; Greenough & Chang 1989).

In addition, the higher executive centers can also assert a considerable control. Such control can never be absolute, but it can be strengthened or weakened by learning or experience. If this were not so, there would be no point in writing this book.

By self-consciously exercising our executive architecture we can vary the expression of our behavior across the spectrum of Ego and Empathy quite widely. As long, that is, as we can handle the behavioral tension we create in the process. That is to say, to a considerable extent, we can control the heat in our own kitchen.

BUT VARIABILITY HAS ITS LIMITS

Despite the variability our social architecture is, nevertheless, set within clear outer limits.

When we act too egoistically. When we nearly totally suppress Empathy. For instance, when we engage in attacking behavior, we approach the outer limits. And clearly somebody can get hurt or killed. Perhaps we even get hurt or killed ourselves.

Behavior at the extremes of either Ego or Empathy can be life threatening. We see examples of the egoistic extreme in street crime, gang wars, bar fights, and even in domestic violence.

We see the relentless and deadly reciprocity of extremes at a societal level—in war, in the conflict between Israel and the Palestinians, between Pakistan and India over Kashmir. The examples are countless.

On the other hand, we see the empathetic extreme when parents sacrifice themselves for their children. We also see it when firefighters rush into blazing, collapsing buildings to rescue trapped citizens.

In the summer of 2002 Empathy was demonstrated on television for all to see as extraordinary efforts were made to save trapped miners in Somerset, Pennsylvania.

HUMAN SOCIAL LIFE:
A RESOUNDING HOMEOSTATIC SUCCESS

In the face of so much violence reported daily in the news, we may seem mostly inclined to exceed homeostatic limits and create mainly death and destruction in our social world.

This, however, is a distortion—perhaps based on our natural tendency to see the disturbing exception, rather than the comforting rule. It is an illusion encouraged by mass media reporting in a global society.

Much more often the controls of behavioral tension and stress keep us well within survival limits. Mostly we cooperate, help each other out, obey the law. Mostly we live together in reasonable harmony or Dynamic Balance.

Over history, despite the emphasis on violence in the written record, cooperation has prevailed overwhelmingly. In truth, we seldom exceed homeostatic limits. The historical evidence speaks to us loudly in confirmation. Our homeostatic neural social architecture is an undeniable success. It has brought us to a population success or explosion of over six billion.

Crispin Tickell, a longtime advisor to British prime ministers and former president of the Royal Geographical Society, makes this point in a well-read article titled *The Human Species: A Suicidal Success?*

Of course this collaborative success of our social brain has created other challenges to the maintenance of social homeostasis that we must yet confront adequately—like overpopulation, exhaustion of resources, pollution, global warming.

Nevertheless, there is no denying the evidence of success so far.

6

THE ORGANIC, HOMEOSTATIC EQUATION OF OUR NEURAL ARCHITECTURE

The previous chapter discussed the homeostatic regulation of our social neural architecture. Earlier chapters presented the dynamic of our neural architecture in two forms: the CSN Model of the major ranges of social behavior and the descriptive algorithmic rules of reciprocal behavior.

Here, I will introduce a third form—the mathematical expression or equation that represents the homeostatically regulated dynamic.

If math is not your favorite subject, don't let the math I use intimidate you. I will keep it simple. I won't use a lot of the usual confusing math symbols or Greek letters. Instead I will use abbreviations of the actual English words. You won't have to hold a bunch of numerical abstractions in the frontal part of your neural architecture while you try to follow the reasoning.

Keep in mind something that is easy to forget. The math is *not* the dynamic. Nor is it the reality. Math *represents* the dynamic and the reality. Math is a tool we invented that helps us clarify and simplify. Symbols are used because they are easier to manipulate than word descriptions. They also help us to see relationships more sharply.

In the equation, I will *represent* the previous graph of the major ranges as well as the written description of the algorithms. I will try to capture very simply the dynamic of our social neural architecture.

Here goes:

$$BT = \frac{Ego}{Empathy} \text{ or } \frac{Empathy}{Ego} = \pm 1 \text{ (Dynamic Balance, approx. equilibrium, or unity)}$$

There it stands: the dynamic homeostatic equation of our consilient, social brain expressed as a dynamically balanced equation, an equation approaching equilibrium, or an equation expressing optimal homeostasis.

Pretty straightforward really.

In the equation, BT stands for behavioral tension and is a function of the ratio of Ego to Empathy or vice versa. It represents our self-preservation and affection circuitry tugging and pulling against each other.

Because of the self-correcting homeostatic nature of the dynamic—the varying tug-and-pull of forces against each other— we can make either Ego or Empathy the numerator or denominator as needed. We can do this because it is the *magnitude* of divergence or convergence between the two self-correcting forces that we are interested in expressing by the equation.

This short equation gives basic mathematical expression to the social architecture of our evolved brain structure. As the conflicting circuits of our social brain approach equilibrium, Dynamic Balance, or optimal homeostasis, behavioral tension/ stress are minimized.

I use the symbolic notation, ± 1 (plus or minus one) to represent Dynamic Balance for two reasons:

First, the plus or minus notation represents approximate, but not perfect unity, equilibrium, or Dynamic Balance. Perfect unity, equilibrium, or balance, would be 1 or unity without the plus or minus. Perfect unity is a theoretical point impossible to attain because of the ongoing tug-and-pull of the dynamic circuitry.

Second, the notation represents the minimal range for behavioral tension. Since the dynamic tug-and-pull goes on ceaselessly, there is never zero tension. Also there is never zero Ego or Empathy because they are locked together in inseparable unity in our neural architecture.

Zero is impossible as a value in the numerator or denominator because that would indicate organic death. At death the organic homeostatic equation would decompose into a Newtonian or nonorganic equation.

On the other hand, as the ratios diverge more and more toward the extremes of Ego or Empathy, behavioral tension increases. In proximity to either extreme, our behavior becomes life-threatening, we may kill or self-sacrifice. Behavioral tension gives us due warning.

As a moderate example, however, if we have an Empathy magnitude or numerical value of 8 and an Ego magnitude or numerical value of 4, or vice-versa, we can say that we have a behavioral tension magnitude of 2.

The neural dynamic works generally to keep our social behavior within survival limits. This is its most important function and that is the reason for its Darwinian selection into our genome.

On the other hand, at the level of optimal functioning, the contending algorithms, driven by behavioral tension, tend to move us toward Dynamic Balance of Ego and Empathy or self- and other-interest—that is, toward balanced reciprocity, or equality.

The equation, therefore, is very simple, but deceptively so, because it can be quite variable and can ramify in many ways.

For instance, we can experience, even control or direct, by effort of our frontal executive, a different mix of Ego and Empathy in every one of our relationships and interactions. Some of our relationships may be quite dynamically balanced or harmonious. Some may be tension-filled. Some may be quite unbalanced and stressful.

In one day—even in one hour of an exciting day—we may be jerked reactively back and forth all over the Ego-Empathy spectrum. Or we may move back and forth more self-consciously. Perhaps the average of all our relationships and interactions is a measure of our personal social health.

I will get back to this thought later in the book. In the meantime I want to point out a couple of ways the social equation is different from others you may be more familiar with. A look at history will lead the way.

A HISTORICAL NOTE ON MATHEMATICS IN SOCIAL SCIENCES

The issue of magnitudes in economics as opposed to precise numerical calculation has been acknowledged at least since the time of the French economist Jean-Baptiste Say (1767–1832).

Concerning the application of mathematics to economics, Say wrote:

The *values* with which political economy is concerned, admitting of the application to them of the terms *plus* and *minus*, are indeed within the range of mathematical inquiry; but...they are not susceptible of any rigorous appreciation, and cannot, therefore, furnish any *data* for absolute calculations. In political as well as in physical sciences, all that is essential is a knowledge of the connexion between causes and their consequences. Neither the phenomena of the moral or material world are subject to strict arithmetical computation (italics in the original).

Another French mathematician and economist, Antoine Augustin Cournot (1801–1877), considered by some to be the first to apply mathematics successfully to political economy, had thoughts similar to Say.

Cournot affirmed that simple numerical calculation of magnitudes is not the point of mathematization in economics. The purpose of such presentation is the elaboration of form and structure.

Cournot was concerned with the demonstration of functional relationships that could be expressed by the functions of calculus. He was not concerned with numerical calculation and felt some events were resistant to precise numerical calculation except in trivial situations or games of chance.

He wrote:

those skilled in mathematical analysis know that its object is not simply to calculate numbers, but that it is also employed to find relations between magnitudes which cannot be expressed in numbers....(1838: 2–3).

Later on, French economist Léon Walras (1834–1910) attempted to solve the issue by dividing economics into three classes: *pure science, applied science, and practical science.*

In the first two, mathematical formulas should be abstract and general in order to apply to all cases. Pure theory is concerned with the relationships and functions of magnitudes, not precise numerical calculation. On the other hand, in practical economics, under limited conditions, one can hope to achieve instances of precise numerical calculation.

THE NEURAL SOCIAL EQUATION: SOME DIFFERENCES

The neural social equation is not a simple reciprocal. Don't let this confuse you.

Simple reciprocals, which we see a lot of in math, merely show a proportional relationship. They compare the amount of something to the amount of something else. Or they compare a part to a whole.

Simple reciprocals have no dynamic similar to the social equation. There is no behavioral tension. On the contrary, the social equation is dynamic. It is driven by tension. The numerator and denominator tug-and-pull against each other, straining toward Dynamic Balance or equilibrium.

Don't confuse the equation with the resultant or outcome of a simple intersection of forces like you see often in the physical sciences. Such forces impact each other, but they do not varyingly tug-and-pull against each other dynamically.

The organic equation is different. It represents a homeostatic, dynamic, living process. And that difference makes all the difference in the world.

SIMPLE, BUT POWERFUL

Indeed the equation is simple. But it does what has never been done before. It captures the central dynamic of our neural architecture. It captures a vitally important living, organic algorithm in very simple terms.

It allows us to see and express relationships in many areas of our lives. Relationships we have seen only dimly and, perhaps, as fragmented up to now.

In the chapters that follow, I will show these relationships. They extend from our social relationships to the dynamics of the market to the workings of our social and political worlds.

Scientists use the words *elegant* and *beautiful* to describe such equations. There are a number of them in physics. There are none so far in the social sciences. If you choose to follow me through to the end, you too may judge it to be the elegant or beautiful equation of our social neural architecture.

7

PHYSICS VS. SOCIAL SCIENCE: SOME DIFFERENCES

The major ranges of behavior, the algorithmic rules of reciprocal behavior, the social equation—all describe *global* or *central behavior tendencies* of our social brain. That is, they don't explain all the detail about our behavior, but only the general homeostatic dynamic at a high level of physiological integration.

They also operate rather *imperfectly*. I suspect that this will be true of any behavioral algorithms or principles we try to describe at this level of integration. As Maynard Smith has observed, such variability is characteristic of organic algorithms (2002). These behavioral algorithms, then, can only approximate, but not fully match, the precision of the laws of classical physics or even quantum mechanics.

This is partly because they come about through the process of organic evolution. Organic evolution is by its very nature quite variable in its outcomes. It involves some random change and shuffling of DNA, some mixing up of the DNA-bearing gene packets themselves, all acted on in an unpredictable way by natural selection.

Even if we could track DNA changes as they happen, we could not be sure what changes natural selection would eventually choose to keep.

If the falling objects of Galileo's famous experiments acted like these organic algorithms, his findings would not be so mathematically neat and specific. Instead gravity may vary from moment to moment. Objects may fall fast at times, slower at others, and sometimes take short detours, before finally reaching the ground.

Getting to the ground would be the outcome of a general tendency to fall.

The reciprocal algorithms of our social brain, therefore, cannot operate as immutable universal physical laws but as generalized algorithms with degrees of variation. Probability gets into the calculus.

Even the early developers of the application of statistics to economics were aware of the limitations of such application. For example, William Newmarch, of Yorkshire, England, wrote in 1861 that in statistics there was no body of laws comparable to the physical sciences.

He commented that statistics as applied to man in society amounted to no more than carefully recorded observations of events that take place under certain conditions. He considered that the element of free will (or perhaps choice as presented by the dynamic of the reciprocal algorithms) would prevent the appearance in the social sciences of regularities or laws comparable to physics.

SOURCES OF PROBABILITY AND THE CSN MODEL

The CSN Model, then, because of its organic, homeostatically, variable nature, depends on probabilities for a great deal of its predictability. The idealized, or rather statistically generalized, tug-and-pull of Ego and Empathy may be further probabilized in actuality by other contributing factors.

Among such factors are: genetic variation, gender and developmental differences, individual experience and learning, as well as other environmental shaping and reinforcing influences.

In other words, *genetically speaking*, given the individual differences in genetic inheritance that we see in such obvious things as in hair, skin, or eye color, some individuals *behaviorally* may be more or less as strongly wired for self-preservation and affection as others.

But granting *gender, developmental, experiential, and learning* differences, every human being is, nevertheless, similarly wired with the fundamental brain architecture unless he/she has very serious genetic defects indeed.

WE TAKE OUR COMPATIBILITY FOR GRANTED

We generally take the commonality of our human brain architecture for granted. We interact with each other socially without questioning our general compatibility. Indeed, without a common architecture our social life would be impossible. A good deal of early childhood research backs us up.

Influential developmental psychologists like Jean Piaget of Switzerland and Lawrence Kohlberg of Harvard, operating from a behavioral perspective (rather than an evolutionary physiological one), have built and tested theories of childhood moral development. In the theories of both scholars, moral stages of development emerge much the same in all cultures when the child experiences anything approaching a normal family life.

Such generalized moral stages could not be found across cultures if they were not genetically based on the species-wide brain structure and its associated behavioral potentialities.

DEVELOPMENT AND LEARNING
INTERACT WITH OUR GENES

From the standpoint of *individual learning, socialization*, and other *environmental* factors, modifications in gene activity and expression occur in early development and throughout life.

The higher brain centers, especially, develop in an interactive social context producing some variation in gene expression. Our *individual* life experiences may facilitate, suppress, strengthen, or otherwise modify the expression of these DNA-based neural circuits.

Other environmental factors, to include the physical conditions under which we live, as well as our socially and scientifically accepted institutions and paradigms, may also shape and reinforce the expression of the evolved algorithmic dynamic. Recent research has revealed considerable plasticity in our neural development.

Individual learning, experience, or environmental factors of our individual lives *cannot*, however, *eliminate* the fundamental gene-based structure and programming of the brain.

That is, not without radical injury, surgical, or genetic intervention. And the behavioral tension of our dynamic architecture will be there to both resist the changes and to shape the experience, even shape the environment itself, in a dynamic manner. That is, we resist radical manipulation of the human genome and we work assiduously to support and create physical and social environments for our healthy gene expression.

PHYSICS, GENES, AND BEHAVIOR

Because of these factors, the behavioral algorithms are *statistical— much in* the same way as are the second law of thermodynamics and quantum theory of physics.

That is, they *generally do not allow precise* prediction of specific behavior at the basic unit of analysis—the individual, molecular, or subatomic levels respectively—but only on the aggregated basis of statistical probability.

The algorithmic rules of reciprocal behavior may, nevertheless, very well prove to be *equally* as valid and useful to social science as the laws of physics are to physical science.

They do not and cannot, however, have the immutable quality of physical laws such as gravity. As products of organic evolution and developmental processes, they inevitably involve *more probabilities* because of individual differences, genetic and learned, in the evolved basic units.

THE BEHAVIORAL WAVE FUNCTION

We can make an admittedly loose, but interesting, analogy between the inclusive spectrum of possible behaviors of the CSN Model and the particle wave function of quantum physics. The wave function of a particle is defined to include all the possible values of a particle according to probability.

Similarly, we can think of the "wave" function of behavior as including all possible internal and interpersonal behavioral probabilities (mixes of Ego and Empathy) spreading across the egoistic, empathetic, and Dynamic Balance ranges.

We could write a mathematical wave formula to represent this, but predictability on an individual basis would be challenging because of the high rate of individual variability. I will avoid the temptation of such a detour from my main undertaking and get on to developing the insights and applications of the dynamic equation of our global-state neural algorithms.

But first a few final observations. Viewed from the outside, behavior is predictable from the CSN Model, as is quantum behavior—only on a probability basis specified by the metaphorical wave function.

The behavioral "wave" function, like that of particle physics, collapses or reduces to one behavior in a decision, action, or observation. If it doesn't collapse, we see frustration, tension, and indecisiveness—ambiguous behavior stalled in uncollapsed waveform.

Upon observation by an *external* observer, the wave function
of behavior can be said to collapse to a specifically observable
behavior by the individual, and that is the end of it. But this would
be an overly simplistic "objective" perception somewhat more
characteristic of the now largely superceded perspective of radical
behaviorism.

Internally, subjectively, we experience a much more
complex process because we have conscious access to the
dynamic. We know in our conscious self-awareness the tension,
the difficulty, the struggle we go through in important issues of
Ego and Empathy conflict.

Even yet, in the surely much simpler processes of quantum
physics we still do not fully understand what set of dynamics leads
to the wave function collapse. In behavior, the dynamic lies in
the complexities of subjective preconsciousness and/or self-aware
consciousness.

For example, in physics it is not known exactly why and how
wave function collapses or reduction occurs and how eigenstates
are determined (e.g., see Hameroff & Penrose 1996: 311). The
standard Copenhagen Interpretation sees collapse as occurring at
randomly measured values when the quantum system interacts with
its environment, is otherwise measured, or consciously observed.
Stapp's well-known article on the Copenhagen Interpretation
(1972) provides a succinct presentation on this topic.

Penrose (1994) and Hameroff and Penrose (1996) introduce
a new physical ingredient they call objective reduction (OR)
which becomes guided and tuned into orchestrated OR, in which
quantum systems can self-collapse by reaching a threshold related
to quantum gravity.

PART TWO

APPLICATIONS TO THE
MARKET AND ECONOMICS

8

RECIPROCAL SOCIAL EXCHANGE AND THE EVOLUTION OF THE MARKET

Our social brain is structured for give and take—for social exchange. The graphic of the CSN Model, its descriptive algorithms, and the equation of our social brain represent a dynamically reciprocal neural architecture. In this chapter, I show how the market evolved from this dynamic.

RECIPROCITY: THE UBIQUITOUS NORM

Anthropology and sociology have long studied the norm of reciprocity. Economists have picked up the theme more recently. This universally observed norm is found in all societies, primitive and modern.

The literature on reciprocity is extensive and still growing. L. T. Hobhouse (1906: 12) called it "the vital principle of society." Richard Thurnwald (1932: 106) described it as a principle "which pervades every relation of primitive life." Anthropologist Bronislaw Malinowski (1922, 1926) and sociologist Georg Simmel (1950: 387) have considered it the *sine qua non* of society.

Harvard sociologist Talcott Parsons (1951: 21) viewed it as "inherent in the nature of social interaction." Alvin Gouldner (1960) wrote an extensive review article in the *American Journal of Sociology* citing much of the previous literature.

French anthropologist Claude Levi-Strauss (1969: 98) has referred to it as a "trend of mind." J. van Baal (1975: 12) has considered it a "part of the human condition." More recently, reciprocity has become of interest in economics (e.g., see Fehr & Gachter, 2000; Cory, 2002, 1999, 1992; Bowles & Gintis 1998: esp. Ch. 17).

So universally has reciprocity been observed that leading anthropologists and sociologists have long suspected that it must have a psychological or biological origin (e.g., see Levi-Strauss 1969 & Homans 1950; 1961: 317). That is, reciprocity must ultimately rest upon mechanisms within the human brain.

The dynamic of our evolved neural architecture provides these mechanisms. A closer look at some of the dynamics of exchange will bear out the empirically observable workings of these algorithmic processes.

The prevalence of reciprocity means that in society, everywhere we look, we find social relations of give and take. The relations are sometimes informal, sometimes formal. But spoken or unspoken, written or not, they tell each member that what is received must be returned in some form, at some time.

The tension binding these give and take relations produces the web work of obligation that holds the society together.

In evolutionary theory, scholars account for reciprocity by such concepts as kin selection, inclusive fitness (Hamilton 1963, 1964), reciprocal altruism (Trivers 1971, 1981; Alexander 1987) and game theory (Maynard Smith 1982; Axelrod & Hamilton 1981; Bendor & Swistak 1997). These accounts draw upon so-called selfish gene perspectives, which see such reciprocity as basically selfish.

More recently, however, researchers have reported widespread reciprocity in the behavior of rhesus monkeys and chimpanzees based not upon selfishness, but Empathy. Two excellent books that present the extensive evidence for Empathy among primates are de Waal (1996) and Boehm (1999).

The observation of Empathy in our primate cousins is a welcome approach that tries to escape the selfishness of traditional approaches. All these approaches, however, are based on the outside observation of behavior. They have not tried to identify or even speculate about the neural circuitry within the animal that must necessarily have been chosen by the evolutionary process to accomplish the work of motivating, maintaining, and rewarding such observed reciprocal behavior.

The CSN Model, building upon the evolutionary neuroscience of Paul MacLean, goes to the heart of the question of brain circuitry substrating reciprocity. The social brain, driven by the tug-and-pull of Ego and Empathy, is the motive source of human reciprocity. The circuitry lies within the self-preservation and affection structures of our evolved neural architecture. From these insights, we can easily understand the evolution of market exchange.

THE EVOLUTION OF THE MARKET

To understand the behavior of the modern day free enterprise market as it is shaped by the circuits of our social brain, it helps to go back to early times—to reconstruct as best we can the days before the market appeared.

The Family or Group Bond

In those times, when our ancestors consumed what they produced, the excess that they shared with, gave to, or provided for the needs or demands of the family or community was in the nature of natural affection or Empathy. The reward for the empathetic, supplying act was emotional—there was not a specific, but a diffuse value assigned to it.

It also had social effects. The givers, providers gained status in the group. The emotional and the social effects were both directly governed by the reciprocal algorithms of behavior.

Let us look more closely. The provider, say the warrior, brought meat from the hunt or the mate brought berries and fruits from the field, tanned skins, and so on, to give to the family or group. The act of providing created behavioral tension in the giver, who acting with Empathy denied Ego to some degree. This Ego denial required a response of acknowledgment—an expression of gratitude, respect, affection, or some other reaffirmation of Ego.

This providing or giving also created behavioral tension in the receivers. It was a service to their Ego, their needs or demands—to their own preservation. The tension created required an offsetting empathetic response, a thank you, an expression of appreciation or respect.

In any family or close group, even now, this dynamic flows constantly, even in the smallest activities. In the small group, the rewards, the reciprocations, are mostly not quantified, but are diffuse. They become obligations—bonds—that hold the group together for protection or mutual survival. Nevertheless, they must reach some approximation of balance, or the unresolved tension will build within the group and become disruptive.

Expressions for *thank you* and *you're welcome*, found in all known human languages, reflect this reciprocity and the behavior needed to sustain it. We call it *courtesy*. It greases the social skids. Without courtesy, daily life would be unbearable. We would have to swallow all that tension or be at each others' throats.

The Gift

From these primitive, familial exchanges, emerged the gift: an empathetic act of providing or serving that followed the same algorithmic behavioral rules that governed provision for survival. It created tension in the giver—an expectation of reciprocity—and tension in the receiver, who was bound to reciprocate.

The rewards associated with the gift were at first diffuse, unspecified, unquantified—except by some subjective measure of feeling, emotion, or behavioral tension. A gift to a warrior or chief might vaguely obligate his protection. A gift to a prospective mate might vaguely obligate his or her attentions.

In 1950, the Presses Universitaires de France published anthropologist Marcel Mauss's, pathbreaking earlier study about exchange practices in primitive and ancient societies called *Essai sur le Don*. It was most recently translated into English by W. D. Halls (1990) and given the title, *The Gift*.

Mauss was the nephew of Emile Durkheim, an influential figure in establishing the academic discipline of sociology. Mauss was not a neuroscientist, and from all indications had no interest in brain function. And considering the state of neuroscience at the time of his study more than a half century ago, knowledge of the discipline would probably have been of little or no help.

Mauss's study was done in the field. That is, he lived with the peoples he studied so that he could observe their customs and practices closely at firsthand. The quality of his fieldwork set a mid-century standard for such work among anthropologists.

Mauss's findings of pervasive reciprocity in gift-giving, in all of its varied forms, throughout these seemingly primitive societies, powerfully confirm the algorithmic dynamic tug-and-pull of Ego and Empathy of our neural architecture.

In his introduction, Mauss tells us clearly of his intent. He sets himself the task of discovering of what rule, legal or informal, compels members of ancient or premarket societies to reciprocate gifts received (1990: 3).

He seeks to identify the power resident in the object given that causes its beneficiary to pay it back. This binding power, Mauss finds expressed in powerful feelings and emotions, sanctified by ritual and even having religious overtones (cf., Godelier 1999). Gift exchange, then, is the essence of social life itself. It is no mere formality of practice.

At one point he identifies the compelling "force" as both mystical and practical (1990: 73). The "power" or the "force" Mauss seeks, but which he cannot identify in terms of neural science, is, of course, the reciprocal dynamic of our neural architecture.

The compelling power or force is no less than the homeostatically driven behavioral tension that mandates the give and take of interpersonal reciprocity.

There were serious social, economic, and political consequences attending the exchange of gifts. Generous giving brought honor and prestige. Failure to return an approximately equal gift brought a loss of status. Among the peoples he studied the failure or refusal to engage in exchange of gifts was tantamount to a declaration of war (1990: 13).

To further confirm his findings among living tribes, Mauss searched the literature of ancient peoples—Romans, Germans, even the Hindu Vedic literature of ancient India. Through their legal codes, customs, practices, and myths, he found the give and take of exchange central to the lives of all known human societies.

Such universality of practice and custom—worldwide—in all known peoples, cannot be explained away by cultural contact or dispersion. Reciprocity in all its forms is driven by neural algorithms etched into the amino acid sequences built by our genes early in human prehistory.

The anthropological literature on gift-giving has expanded greatly since Mauss's work. It continues to the present day. Such literature overlaps with the literature on reciprocity. Although the total volume of work is too extensive to deal with here, I will point out some more recent works that show the continuing interest in this fundamental social phenomenon. For example:

Titmuss (1972) examined the commercial blood acquisition system of the US with the voluntary one in Great Britain with the finding that the latter system was less contaminated, less wasteful, and less costly that the US system.

French scholars have continued their interest in reciprocity and giving following the work of Levi-Strauss, Malinowski, and Mauss. Rather than the positivist, self-interest approach of Mauss, recent scholars have taken the perspective of altruism (e.g., see, Gérard-Varet, Kolm, & Mercier Ythier 2000). Davis (2000) reports on the altruism in gift giving in sixteenth century France. Fennell (2002) is of special interest to the presentation here because she reports that empathetic, nurturing dialogue characterizes the gift even in modern society.

From Gift to Transaction

From the gift in all its varied expressions evolved the transaction—namely, the gift with the reciprocal specified or quantified.

The evolution of the transaction from the gift is widely supported by the anthropological literature (e.g., Polanyi 1957; Gregory 1982; Mauss 1990). The *Dictionary of Anthropology* in distinguishing the commodity from gift states that a commodity exchange creates a relationship between *things* (that is, it is impersonal) as opposed to gift exchange which creates a relationship between *people* (Seymour-Smith 1986: 44).

Gregory (1982) holds that commodity exchange is an exchange of alienable objects between persons who are in a state of reciprocal independence, which establishes a quantitative (i.e., specified) relationship. Gift exchange, on the other hand, is an exchange of inalienable objects between persons who are in a state of reciprocal dependence that establishes a qualitative relationship between the persons involved in the exchange (see also Barfield, 1997: 73).

Bohannan defines market exchange or the market transaction as the exchange of goods at prices governed by Supply and Demand under a free and casual contract. On the other hand, reciprocity or gift exchange is seen most clearly in kinship relations (1963: 231–232). Since kinship reciprocity precedes market transactional relations in human affairs, the latter clearly evolved from the former.

Hunt (2002) discusses human mammalian sharing in child-rearing, as well as sharing in small unit situations even in modern contexts, and other forms of exchanges or transfers. His approach has a quasi-evolutionary framework and may be compared with the approach I have chosen in this chapter. Appadurai (1986), in line with my presentation, has shifted from the standard anthropological focus on objects to the nature of the transaction itself.

A large body of evidence, then, clearly establishes the case that the transaction evolved from the gift. The transaction probably evolved in groups larger than family or extended kinship units. It is here that we begin to deal with strangers. The transaction is the beginning of the contract, perhaps of the commercial market itself.

The transaction operates, however, by the same algorithms of behavior as the gift—except that it attempts to head off the residual, unresolved behavioral tension that creates a condition of obligation or bonding.

After all, in the commercial market, we may be dealing with complete strangers. We may wish to avoid any future obligation to them from our exchanges. We have not seen these strangers before and we may never see them again.

Further, we are naturally suspicious of them. They are not family or close neighbors. We feel it wise to avoid the left over tension that might oblige us to invite them home for dinner—to share the feast as our ancestors did.

In such market transactions, then, both the gift object transferred and the reciprocal are specified to the satisfaction of giver and receiver. The exchange deal is done in equal or balanced return. There is no behavioral tension binding us socially and economically in a cycle of mutual obligation.

Nevertheless, despite these considerations, the transaction itself retains its essential mammalian characteristics. It is an act of Empathy, of nurturing, which requires a balancing reciprocal act in payment to Ego.

When we encounter its equivalent in the seemingly impersonalized market economy of today, how often do we feel the subjective experience of the transaction? We take our sick child to the physician, who with Empathy and care applies the knowledge it took ten years and a fortune to gain.

We pay the bill—that is, we make a return gift with money that represents a portion of our accumulated education and labor. The scenario is repeated in transactions with the plumber, the carpenter, the computer maker. The behavioral algorithms still apply, but the feeling, the subjective experience, has to a large degree been lost.

BEHAVIORAL TENSION
YET DRIVES THE TRANSACTION

But wait! Let the transaction go wrong, the expected reciprocals not be forthcoming, and the behavioral tension becomes immediately and personally felt. The reality of the transaction—the market—reveals itself with clarity and intensity.

Ask yourself, for instance, the following: If you responded to an ad from a local electronics store for a top of the line TV set with all the bells and whistles—at the unbelievable bargain price of $99.00. You rushed down, ad in hand, before supplies were sold out, and paid your money. You received your unopened box and hurried proudly home with it.

Pulling your prized purchase eagerly from the box in front of the waiting family, you discover that it is a cheap model with only channel and volume buttons and a set of squatty rabbit ears.

Would you feel behavioral tension at the unexpectedly unbalanced reciprocal? What would you do? Would you laugh it off? Or would you pack it back up and return it with a set of choice comments reflecting your behavioral tension in unmistakable terms? Likely, you would do the latter.

No one likes to be cheated or short-changed. And most of us will be motivated to take some action to correct the imbalance.

The small claims courts of the nation have their dockets crammed full, primarily with issues of unbalanced reciprocity in the marketplace. If we don't get satisfaction in expected reciprocity, we may very humanly harbor the behavioral tension indefinitely, hoping to get even in the future.

Our neural architecture assures this reaction.

9

ADAM SMITH, RATIONAL CHOICE, AND EQUITY THEORY

In the previous chapter, I presented the evolution of the market in terms of the tug-and-pull of Ego and Empathy. The market was created by the human social brain—by like-brains interacting with like-brains. There is simply no other possible source.

If markets were established and run on the basis of Newtonian mechanics, as once thought by most economists in the 19th century and some in the 20th century, we should expect to find them ready and waiting for us on the moon and Mars. After all, Newtonian principles apply there also. All we would have to do is move in and start using them.

The thought is, of course, absurd. Markets are the expression of human social exchange activity. And they don't exist independently of that activity.

For the last two hundred plus years, the orthodox theory of free enterprise and economics has similarly inaccurately claimed that self-interest is the *sole primary motive* of the market. How did we get it so wrong?

Open almost any basic economic textbook and you will find that we blame Adam Smith (1723–1790). Smith was a moral philosopher. He taught at the University of Glasgow, Scotland back in the 18th century.

Smith earned the reputation as founder of economics and the capitalist free enterprise system by publishing the *Wealth of Nations* in 1776—the same year the American colonies declared independence from Britain over economic issues.

The source for the venerated self-interest motive was a quote from Book I, Chapter 2 of that volume. It goes as follows:

It is not from the benevolence of the butcher, the brewer, or the baker, that we expect our dinner, but from their care for their own interest. We appeal not to their humanity but to their self-interest, and never talk to them of our own necessities, but of their advantages.

This often cited quote, however, is taken completely out of context. On the same page and on either side of the famous quote, yet never included, are two clear references to the importance of benevolence or Empathy. Just two short paragraphs above the famed quote Smith reminds us that:

…man has almost *constant* need for the *help* of his brethren (italics added).

And, immediately following the famous quote, he tells us:

Thus nobody but a beggar chooses to *depend chiefly* upon the *benevolence* of his fellow-citizens….(italics added).

When properly understood, then, Smith, in the celebrated quote, is not saying that there is only self-interest, but that there is both self-interest and Empathy and that we should show an empathetic concern for the self-interest of the butcher, the baker, and the brewer, in requesting their products and services.

That is, being competent players in the market, we should not seize their products and services unjustly, or do so beggarly. Rather we should expect to compensate their labors. In fact, Smith makes this absolutely clear—again on the same page—when he says in the line directly above the celebrated quote:

Give me what I want, and you shall have what you want, is the meaning of every such offer.

In the above phrasing, Adam Smith has virtually stated the algorithms of reciprocity, the dynamic tug-and-pull of Ego and Empathy, self- and other-interest. Both you and I get what we need from the exchange. Nobody gets ripped off. In everyday parlance in our modern times, we call this intuitively—*win-win*. Everyone gets what they want, and everyone is satisfied.

The exchange process, as Smith saw it, then, was more accurately aimed at a balance of self- and other-interest. And Smith didn't know anything about brain science or neural architecture. He was operating intuitively from common sense. After all, he had the same neural architecture we have—although he had no concept of it as such.

The evidence goes even further. Smith wrote another book—a magnum opus called *The Theory of Moral Sentiments,* which he first published in 1759, well before the *Wealth of Nations.*

The second book, almost entirely ignored for two centuries, was for Smith the more important of the two. It emphasized morality, sympathy, and fellow-feeling. Smith considered this book so important he revised it six times—the last time shortly before his death in 1790.

Smith's two volumes capture the tug-and-pull of Ego and Empathy, the algorithms of reciprocity. Their titles, in all their glory, may accurately be placed above the graph of the major ranges of the CSN Model (Figure 9.1).

How did such an historical oversight or misinterpretation occur?

I think there is a reasonable explanation. It goes partially along the following lines. The businessmen and entrepreneurs of that day were chafing under the excessive and invasive restrictions of the British mercantile system. The crown's bureaucracy was micromanaging everything, stifling trade and business in general.

The businessmen saw what they needed to break the restrictive bonds of mercantilism in the self-interest motive and in the hands off (*laissez-faire*) approach advocated by Smith. They pounced on the two like a fumbled football, and off they went. After all, they were practical men interested in making money, not in theory. The Empathy—the moral concerns—of Smith got lost in the shuffle.

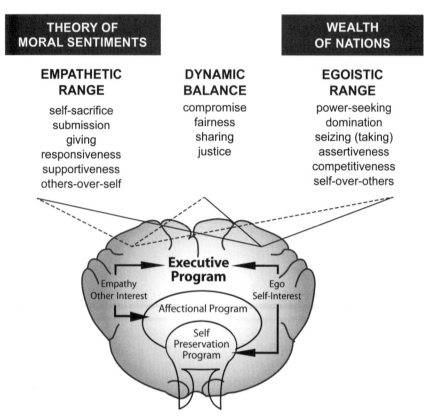

Figure 9.1. The Works of Adam Smith and the Major Ranges of Reciprocal Behavior.

The overemphasis on self-interest that followed, however, had its negative side effects. It skewed business behavior toward egoism by its denial of Empathy. It often led to excess and greed—as in the 1890s, 1920s, the 1980s, and the greed epidemic of the late 1990s, the early 2000s, and most recently the subprime economic crisis brought on, in large measure, by flagrant greed.

The excesses periodically give the free enterprise system a bad press and lead to public reaction and regulation in the public interest to counter the negative tendencies.

Adam Smith, when properly understood, got it right. The free market, as an expression of our neural architecture, depends upon the interplay of Ego and Empathy, self- and other-interest. Not just self-interest alone. A look at the everyday presentation of the business marketplace bears this out further.

EMPATHY IN THE MARKETPLACE

The overemphasis on self-interest and the lack of an adequate behavioral model have prevented us from seeing how the marketplace derives from brain structure, and how Empathy or altruism plays an equal role with Ego or self-preservation. But the role of Empathy is clearly present in the language, if not the practice, of the marketplace.

The everyday language of marketing *is* the language of Empathy. Let's take a look.

Advertisements, almost without fail, emphasize service or benefit to the customer. Customer service is, in fact, the keynote of most businesses. Every retail store of any size has a customer "service" department in a prominent location. Never once have I seen a company "self-interest" department so proudly and prominently displayed.

Almost nowhere else are we treated with more exaggerated Empathy, even obsequiousness, than in some retail businesses. In marketing, as any good salesperson can tell you, Empathy works. People respond to it.

The features-and-benefits approach to selling is built entirely on Empathy. I was told long ago when I worked as a salesperson: "When you talk features, you're bragging; when you talk benefits to the customer, you're selling." Empathy rules. Depending on the skill and sincerity of the salesperson, the genuine feeling may or may not be convincingly displayed, but the basic empathetic behavior is there.

For another example, turn on the TV set at any time of day and count the appeals to Empathy—what great benefit of health, wealth, joy, and entertainment the products and services huckstered will bring you. In the Fall of 2002, with corporate greed and a losing stock market, I listened especially to the ads of the brokerage companies. They were very revealing about the nature of their business. How they wished to have it perceived.

A leading discount broker, openly stated you must get the self-interest out of the transaction in order to properly advise the customer. A prominent nondiscount broker claimed to identify with your dreams—to make your dreams their own.

The list of companies appealing to Empathy and other-interest as their primary purpose in the market goes on and on. Even if we choose to view such ads cynically, they nevertheless indicate the crucial importance of Empathy and other-interest in the exchange process.

The act of selling, therefore, clearly demonstrates not only the role of Empathy, but also the reciprocal algorithms of behavior. The saleperson's serving behavior toward the customer creates tension in the salesperson, who, acting empathetically, denies his or her own Ego to some degree, thereby producing the expectation of reciprocity, a reward.

The salesperson's empathetic behavior also creates tension in the customer—a sense of obligation to buy. The sales process not only demonstrates these algorithms of behavior; but it depends upon them.

We, thus, see clearly the contending forces of our neural architecture at work in the daily activity of selling and buying. Anyone who focuses only on self-interest sees only one side of this socio-economic equation. The dynamic of economic exchange, when properly understood is an expression of the dynamic of our neural architecture—the equation of our social brain.

The trick or deception of assigning a self-interest motive to everything—even to the most empathetic or altruistic acts— is made plausible by the fact that the reciprocal is always there.

There is always an egoistic reciprocal to any empathetic act; and, likewise, there is always an empathetic reciprocal to any egoistic act.

The dynamic of our social brain supports the protesting observation by nobelist Amartyr Sen in his well-known article "Rational Fools." Sen writes that one can "define a person's interests in such a way that no matter what he does he can be seen to be furthering his own interests in every isolated act of choice"(1979).

The equation also exposes the most glaring and socially distorting deficit of so-called rational choice theory which attempts inaccurately to account for all exchange behaviors in terms of quantifiable self-interest.

RATIONAL CHOICE THEORY CONTRA THE HUMAN MAMMAL

Since the subject came up, let's take a brief, revealing, look at current rational choice theory in the light of our indisputable mammalian heritage.

Rational choice and exchange theory in sociology deal with the issues of power and social integration. Sociologist Peter Blau (1964) hits at the heart of reciprocal exchange when he sees its two general functions as creating bonds of friendship and establishing relationships of subordination or domination.

Of course, domination and subordination carry inevitable behavioral tension which is at the root of the underlying implicit assumption of all exchange theory—the tug-and-pull tendency toward equalization of value among all social relationships.

The work of sociologist James S. Coleman illustrates the distortion, however, that appears in the work of some of our most capable theorists when our mammalian heritage, is not fully grasped. Coleman bases his theory of action on the overt premise of rational, self-interested humans, unconstrained by morality, norms, or altruism.

He apparently is unaware of, or else assumes erroneously that we lack, our very prominent and significant limbic septal (to include our medial pre-optic area), thalamocingulate brain structures, and our orbital frontal cortex—and that we are only wired innately for self-interest when he writes:

To assume that persons come equipped with a moral code would exclude all processes of socialization from theoretical examination. And to assume altruism or unselfishness would prevent the construction of theory about how persons come to act on behalf of others…when it goes against their private interests (1990: 31–32).

The above quoted statement is, of course, patently not true. If we recognize that the programming for Ego and Empathy, self- and other-interest—although admittedly undefined by specific social content—is innate in our mammalian neurological structure, we are certainly not thereby prevented from constructing theories about socialization.

The focus of such theorizing would, of course, shift from the one-sided view of exclusively self-interested, sociopathic, half-humans to a more correctly balanced view.

Our theory could then appropriately focus on how these two innate potentialities of Ego and Empathy achieve social expression and how they are blended in balanced or unbalanced reciprocity over history in the particular moral codes and norms of any specific culture or society.

Exchange theorist Karen Cook and her associates appropriately see exchange as the ubiquitous structuring activity of societies. Drawing on a metaphor of James Coleman, Cook writes that theories of social structure alone "provide a chassis but no engine." Concerning the unique contribution of exchange theory, she goes on to claim:

A major strength of exchange theory is that in making explicit the reciprocal nature of social interaction it provides a theoretical engine of action to power the chassis that is our understanding of social structure (Cook, O'Brien, & Kollock, 1990: 164).

Cook correctly sees the reciprocal nature of social interaction as the dynamic process of social action and society-building. She remains, however, within the rational choice, self-interested framework and thereby misses the essence of reciprocity—the tug-and-pull of Ego and Empathy, concern for ourselves, and recognition and concern for the interests of others. Her "engine," being universal, inevitably implies a grounding in biology or human nature. She does not, however, provide such a grounding.

EQUITY THEORY

Equity theory, an alternative direction in sociology and social psychology, is closely akin to exchange theory. Equity theory purports to be a general theory that provides insights into social interactions of all kinds—from industrial relations to issues of justice in more general social encounters.

Walster, Walster, and Berscheid (1978) provide a thorough statement of equity theory and bring together the previously scattered research as of the year of publication. More recently, it has been extended to the most personal relationships of marriage and other relationships of intimacy.

Hatfield and Traupmann (1981:165–178) summarize the application of equity theory to intimate relationships, a focus in social psychology that has emerged in more recent decades (see also, Guerrero, et al. 2007).

Equity theory, by the very use of the term equity, reveals its implicit grounding in an intuitive perception of the neural dynamic as it tends toward balance in our behavior. Equity theory's four propositions, proclaimed apparently from faulty intuition or generalized observation, are otherwise ungrounded.

According to theorists Walster and colleagues, the four propositions require that:

1. Individuals will try to maximize their outcomes.

2. Groups will try to maximize collective rewards by creating systems of equity and will encourage member adherence. Groups will reward equitable behavior and punish members who don't conform.

3. Members in inequitable relationships will become distressed to the extent of the inequity.

4. Members in an inequitable relationship will try to eliminate their distress by restoring equity. The greater the inequality, the greater the distress, and the harder they will work to restore equity (Walster, et al. 1978: 6; see also, Donnerstein & Hatfield, 1982).

Walster and colleagues state unequivocally that equity theory rests upon what they consider "the simple, but eminently safe assumption that man is selfish" (1978: 7).

Except for the fact that the theorists remain in the rational choice, self-interested framework, their propositions, as asserted, are expressive of the reciprocal algorithms of behavior. The dynamic is also run by behavioral tension as reflected in the distress experienced by members.

The apparent logical inconsistency of proposition 1, maximizing outcomes, with proposition 4, restoring equity, is glaring under the assumption that man is selfish and seeks to maximize. If man selfishly seeks to maximize, why should she/he be satisfied with merely restoring equity rather than seeking to reverse the situation to one of dominance in his own favor?

This logical inconsistency of the propositions becomes resolved when the tug of Empathy is added to self-interest. According to the reciprocal algorithms of behavior, Empathy is what permits us to settle, without excessive distress, for a position of equity rather than a reversal of the inequities of the relationship which would be required under a concept of maximizing.

I might reiterate with confidence, then, that reciprocity, proceeding from the evolved structure of our human brain, is the basic structuring dynamic of our social lives.

Anthropological and social research have convincingly shown that reciprocity underpins our most primitive and basic social relations, from family interactions, to gift exchange, to the foundations of more complex economic life. It continues to do so in a less obvious, but no less pervasive manner, in our modern systems of exchange.

10

THE INVISIBLE HAND
AS A NEURAL ALGORITHM

This chapter takes on an icon of economic lore—the Invisible Hand. As a staple of economic theory, the Invisible Hand appears in every economics textbook.

It also appears in many books on free enterprise and business. Television talk shows even take note of it. Libertarians, conservative Republicans, and even Democrats invoke it—sometimes reverently and mysteriously. It is generally traced to Adam Smith.

Actually it goes back a little further. No one knows exactly who first thought it up, but the principle is probably first clearly anticipated by the Englishman, Bernard de Mandeville (1670–1733).

In 1714, Mandeville published a work called the *Fable of the Bees* in which he argued that individuals in pursuit of their own purely selfish goals, nevertheless, unintentionally produced benefits for society. This is known as the doctrine of "unintended consequences." It is the forerunner of the Invisible Hand.

Seemingly repelled by Mandeville's excessive emphasis on human selfishness in the already famous *Fable*, Adam Smith sought a more balanced interpretation.

Smith's teacher and predecessor at the University of Glasgow, Scotland, Francis Hutcheson, as well as his friend, the famed British philosopher David Hume and others of his circle, followed more in the footsteps of philosopher John Locke (1632–1704). They believed that mankind had an innate concern or sympathy for others—a concern that led to a moral sense. Smith states his position in the ongoing debate in his *Theory of Moral Sentiments* (1759).

Section 1 Chapter 1 of his moral masterwork, opens with the following paragraph:

How selfish soever, man may be supposed, there are evidently some principles in his nature, which interest him in the fortune of others, and render their happiness necessary to him, though he derives nothing from it, except the pleasure of seeing it…like all the other original passions of human nature, [it] is by no means confined to the virtuous and humane, though they perhaps may feel it with the most exquisite sensibility. The greatest ruffian, the most hardened violator of the laws of society, is not altogether without it.

Thus, Smith described fellow-feeling or sympathy as he called it. And such is Empathy as I call it.

As noted in the previous chapter, Smith, our economic forefather, then, saw not one but two great natural motives somehow rooted in human nature—self-interest, the desire to accumulate wealth and better one's personal circumstances, and sympathy or fellow-feeling, the source of benevolence and morality.

Smith, we know, had no access to the findings of modern neuroscience. He knew nothing about brains or neural architecture. He sensed these two motives as somehow built into the nature of human beings by the Invisible Hand of Deity.

Smith felt that given freedom from government restriction, which was very extensive and invasive at that time, the dynamics of human nature in pursuit of wealth would produce more wealth and a better distribution of it than any deliberate system statesmen could devise. But unlike Mandeville, he saw the benefits proceeding from both self-interest and sympathy.

In Moral Sentiments he writes further on:

[the rich] are led by an *Invisible Hand* (emphasis added) to make nearly the same distribution of the necessaries of life, which would have been made, had the earth been divided into equal portions among all its inhabitants, and thus without knowing it, advance the interests of society.

Here we have the idea of *unintended consequences* clearly expressed by Smith as the *Invisible Hand*. In other words, left to operate freely, the dynamics of human nature, driven by the principal motives of self-interest and fellow-feeling, will somehow work to create an approximate equality of distribution, at least at the level of the necessities of life.

Smith could see how fellow-feeling may work effectively to provide moral stability and provisioning among neighbors, but he was troubled when he tried to visualize its working at the higher level of nations and among nations.

To fill this gap, then, and following the thinking of some of his predecessors and contemporaries, he invoked the aforementioned *deus ex machina*, or miracle machine, of the Invisible Hand.

It was essentially an undefined, semi-mystical concept taken more on intuition or faith than any empirical evidence or observation. Among nations as among individuals, Smith saw divine intervention providing a corrective when human nature or natural law fell short of the job.

Smith went on from there to develop his famous economic principles of Supply and Demand as the dynamic forces that drive the marketplace. These principles, now inappropriately elevated to the status of laws, have served as the foundation of economics up to the present day.

In fact, the Invisible Hand is now taken to be the natural outcome of the workings of the so-called laws of Supply and Demand. Even Alan Greenspan, former head of the Fed, and economic psychologist in residence for the nation, can be heard to invoke the laws of Supply and Demand and by implication, the Invisible Hand.

DEMAND AND SUPPLY:
EXPRESSIONS OF THE SOCIAL BRAIN

Let's go back for a moment. From the evolution of the market traced in Chapter 8, we can easily see that Demand and Supply are expressions of our dynamic neural architecture. Ego demands. Empathy provides or supplies.

Without Empathy there could be no market. We wouldn't know what to offer or how to offer it to respond to the demands or needs of others. We probably wouldn't even care to be bothered.

When Ego and Empathy meet in Dynamic Balance, *fairness* and *cooperation tend* to emerge in exchange activity. When Ego (Demand) and Empathy (Supply) intersect freely in the market-place, we *tend* to have equitable exchange. Since the evolved algorithmic dynamic works imperfectly, I use the word *tend*.

Figure 10.1 sums up the discussion of the evolution of the market I began in Chapter 8. The figure also illustrates the emergence of the economic concepts of Demand and Supply as an expression of our neural architecture. Demand expresses our egoistic, survival-centered needs. Supply or providing proceeds from Empathy and is fundamentally an act of mammalian nurturing. Let's go over it in more detail.

In the sharing, egalitarian culture of early kinship hunting and gathering bands, the reciprocal obligation, mandated by our neural architecture, was, like in the smaller family unit—not specified, but diffuse. That is, the obligation was not clearly quantified, but had a general somewhat formless effect of social bonding and obligation.

The emotions of gratitude, affection, respect, esteem, and prestige evoked or expressed in the exchange were the biological glue that held such units together for survival. Such emotions, of course, are expressions of our Ego/Empathy neural dynamic.

As I proceed to the level of social organization that we call a tribe, the mandatory exchange of gifts takes on a qualitative change. The reciprocal is no longer diffuse but becomes anticipated.

A roughly equal return gift kept the balance of prestige and obligation roughly equal. Behavioral tension was minimized. An unequal exchange, however, left a residual of unsatisfied obligation or behavioral tension. Unequal exchange led to contests of status and power always underpinned by the dynamic corrective tendency of behavioral tension.

THE GIFT ECONOMY VS. THE MARKET ECONOMY

It is perhaps at the tribal level that we find what anthropologists describe as the *gift economy*.

The gift economy was a total social system of gift exchange in which the distribution of goods and services was open to public scrutiny. Judgments of fairness and equity were community-shared—there for all to see. Gift exchanges, and their balance or imbalance, defined the essential structure of the society.

Gifts were the sources of prestige, honor, and came to be backed up even by social sanctions of ceremony and religion. Canadian researcher David Cheal sees that the gift economy of today is based mainly upon a feminine perspective of relationships and love (1988: 183).

This may very well hold true for early societies. Cheal's point is reinforced from an extreme feminist viewpoint by Genevieve Vaughan (1997).

Whatever the faults of Vaughan's one-sided emphasis, she accurately sees giving as based on mammalian mothering. The mammalian affectional architecture from which Empathy arises is, of course, shared by men as well as women.

The exchange market, in keeping with the scale of inclusiveness, evolves as distance from the family and its sharing relationships increases and the relationship factors become rarefied, thinned out, or depersonalized.

This finding of giving as based upon mammalian affection goes against the widespread image of the bullying, overpowering alpha male who ruled by sheer physical power. Physical power may have given an edge, but prestige, status, and leadership in the gift economy were based upon the capacity to give away more than other contenders.

The gift economy is the forerunner of the commercial or transaction economy.

The evolutionary sequence summarized here roughly conforms to the standard anthropological literature and follows the presentation in Chapter 8. Economic historian Karl Polanyi (1957) advanced the argument of a transformation from a gift economy to a market economy.

Anthropologist Marshall Sahlins most fully developed this theory in his *Stone Age Economics* (1972). Sahlins made the important point that the difference between gift exchange and commodity exchange should be viewed as a continuum not as a bipolar opposition.

Gift exchange, as indicated in Figure 10.1 and the supporting presentation, tends to be between people who are kin. As the kinship distance lengthens—in keeping with the scale of inclusiveness—the transactors become strangers, and commodity exchange emerges (see Sahlins 1972: 185–276). Commodity exchange is characterized by impersonal relationships, no desire for social bonding characteristic of kinship exchange, and specified or quantified reciprocals.

Changes in the manner of social exchange, thus, mark this transition and justify our calling them differently. But what are some differences that distinguish the two?

There are at least three.

First, in the gift economy you get the gift whether or not you can reciprocate equally. The relationship is much more personal, bonded, and inclusive. You are not left to starve or die of exposure because you cannot return an equal amount of valued goods.

Of course, you make payback in loss of status and residual obligation to your benefactor. There is no free gift.

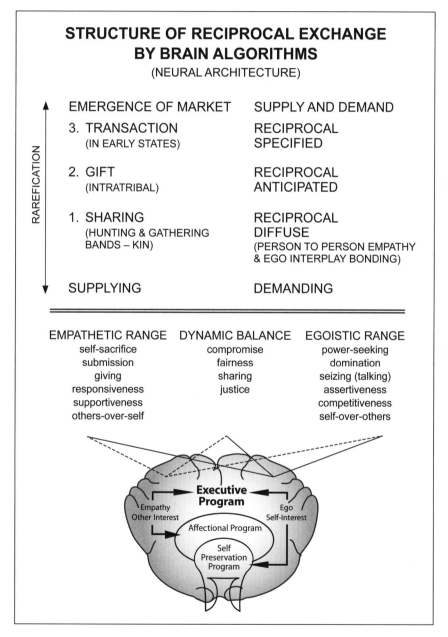

Figure 10.1. Evolution of the Market Shaped by Neural Architecture.

As we move to the transaction, however, the relationships become more impersonal, probably deliberately so.

This brings us to the second difference. In the transaction economy the reciprocal is specified or quantified. You don't get the gift or object of exchange in the first place, if you can't produce the specified reciprocal. The exchange just doesn't take place. If you can meet the specified reciprocal, of course, then well and good. The exchange does takes place.

The third difference follows from the second. That is, the transaction involves no gain or loss of social prestige. It carries no residual obligation or behavioral tension. It's a clean deal with minimal social effects.

Gift economies and market economies to a great extent existed side by side over much of human history.

The patron-client relations of the great feudal systems were primarily an extension of a gift-exchange economy. They were bound by residual obligations between patrons and clients underpinned by the behavioral tension of unequal exchange.

In such a system when the patron could no longer provide, he/she lost the support and loyalty of the clients. Sometimes the breakdown of the social exchange relationship was marked by violence and bloodshed.

In the Middle Ages the emergence of the towns, the merchant class, and the transactional market economy challenged the feudal patron-client power structure. And there were considerable tensions between the two.

By the modern age the transactional, market economy had prevailed. Of course, the gift economy never went away. It still functions on a less visible scale among isolated social groupings, as well as among families and groups, even in the most highly developed commercial economies.

THE INVISIBLE HAND IN THE STRUCTURE AND BEHAVIOR OF THE MARKETPLACE

As Figure 10.1 illustrates, in the transactional or commercial market, the dynamic tug-and-pull of Ego and Empathy becomes expressed as Demand and Supply. The behavioral tension driving toward a proper reciprocal balance between Demand and Supply in the marketplace accounts for the basic motive force for the Invisible Hand.

Scholars have previously accounted for the hand's illusive dynamic in various ways. Early thinkers, beginning with Smith saw in it the workings of Deity or natural law. Later scholars, with more sophistication, appealed to Newtonian mechanics or other inappropriate physical processes. Some just gave up on the question, but still quoted it on faith.

Such variables as history, culture, and institutions, of course, play their part. And they do so importantly. They give the market its unique expression in any social context. The hand can't do it all by itself.

To grasp the functioning of the Invisible Hand in the marketplace, it helps to keep a clear distinction between structure and behavior.

Structure

The Invisible Hand, as driven by our neural algorithms, tends to work despite the one-dimensional overemphasis on self-interest in classical economics. This is because the *very structure* of the market itself is the *institutionalized product* of the Ego/Empathy dynamic of our evolved brain structure.

Our basic self-survival Ego demands are rooted ultimately in our ancestral protoreptilian or vertebrate neural complexes.

Contrastingly, the act of providing or supplying, is fundamentally an act of mammalian nurturing.

The market exchange system originated from this dynamic. The market could never have evolved or been maintained on the basis of Ego or self-interest alone. Without Empathy we would not know how or what to do to respond to the needs of others.

Behavior

Behavior, in individual choices and transactions within the above institutionalized structure, may vary considerably in the mix of Ego and Empathy motives on both the Demand and Supply sides.

Nevertheless, even in the most Ego-skewed (or self-interested) market behavior the overall tendency of the market will be toward a Dynamic Balance of Ego and Empathy. Individual and collective actors, whether seemingly motivated primarily by self-interest or not, will be compelled by the very market structure itself—to survive in the market—to perform the *structural equivalent* of *Empathy*.

That is, they will be required to provide (Supply) a proper service or product to fill the needs (Demand) of others or be driven out of business by competitors willing and able to do so. This is the source of the unintended consequences aspect of the Invisible Hand—referred to by Adam Smith himself as well as modern economists.

On a level playing field, left to its own dynamic, the Invisible Hand, stripped of its ghostly demeanor, will tend to come forth. The architecture of our social brain drives it. The dynamic equation of our social brain represents it.

The Invisible Hand largely expressed itself more fully in the small social units of primitive humankind. The interplay of Ego and Empathy in face-to-face groups led to a generally egalitarian sharing of resources and power.

Primatologist Christopher Boehm in his study of the origins of egalitarian behavior notes that all known foraging societies were egalitarian. He comments that one of the great mysteries of social evolution is the change from egalitarian to hierarchical society (1999: 88).

Anthropologist, Mary Douglas (1990), writing in the foreword to Marcel Mauss's *The Gift*, makes the same point. She observes that the mandatory reciprocal nature of giving, present in pre-market societies, functioned as the equivalent to an Invisible Hand.

As the size of social units expanded, however, and the division of labor grew increasingly defined, the natural tendency could be obstructed in many ways. The very complexity and distances of the modern market block the natural tendency at many points. Such obstructions permit inequalities that would be unheard of in the small, largely kinship group environment of our evolutionary adaptation.

The concept of unintended consequences or the action of the Invisible Hand in early social exchange and in the evolved structure of the modern market is made possible by our evolved neural architecture. The idea comes to us intuitively and naturally based on the dynamic of our social brain—the Ego/Empathy dynamic playing out within each of our skulls as well as between us in social interaction.

The intuitive doctrine of unintended consequences or the Invisible Hand launched a determined research program to scientize it. This program called general equilibrium theory has been the core of modern economic theorizing from Adam Smith to the present day. The next chapter will take a closer look at the evolution and status of general equilibrium theory.

11

GENERAL EQUILIBRIUM THEORY: FROM NEWTONIAN TO ORGANIC DYNAMICS

The publication of Adam Smith's *Wealth of Nations* (1776), spurred a movement to further refine his concepts. Additionally, scholars sought to move economics from the status of a moral science to that of a positive or objective science.

The model chosen was, of course, physics. The monumental work of Isaac Newton (1642–1727) with his laws of gravity and the motion of heavenly bodies, was the natural inspiration. Economists sought to discover the natural clock-like laws of the universe that drove the market to equilibrium—like the forces of physical nature and the dramatically precise mathematical calculus that had been developed to describe them.

The main challenge, then, was to account for the anticipated market equilibrium in terms of the equilibrium of natural force vectors. The Invisible Hand was, ambitiously, to be moved from the vague status of a divine intervention or intuited but ill-defined force of human nature or natural law into the status of a mathematically definable set of natural force vectors comparable to those of physics.

This search for the underlying regularities of the Invisible Hand, seen as resulting from the interaction of Demand and Supply, became known as general equilibrium theory or GET. For the most comprehensive historical analysis of the Invisible Hand and general equilibrium theory consult Ingrao and Israel (1990).

GET: OFF ON THE WRONG FOOT

Neuroscience was not yet developed at this time. Thus, the model of the physical sciences was the only one available short of the prevailing philosophical speculation about human nature, natural law, or the mystical attributes of the Deity.

Furthermore the Newtonian system and methodology were overwhelmingly venerated as the standard of true science in the intellectual circles of the day. This veneration held in England and also on the continent of Europe.

It was impossible to know at that time that the foundation of the market was in the organic algorithms of our social brain—like brains interacting with like brains—not in the mechanical laws of physics.

GET, thus, got off on the wrong foot to a long and tortuous history. But it couldn't be helped. There was no equivalent or acceptable alternative available.

The effort to find the universal physical laws driving the market to equilibrium occupied economists and mathematicians over the next 200 years. Almost every conceivable approach was tried without producing satisfactory results. The efforts continue to this date with at best some limited success but with mostly discouraging outcomes.

The largely vain search has led some theorists to suggest that a new approach or paradigm may be needed. The proper model, the CSN Model, based in neural architecture did not become available until the full emergence of evolutionary neuroscience in the closing years of the 20th century.

I will briefly trace the main developmental features of GET up to the present. In doing so I will omit much historical detail but hopefully still provide an appreciation of where GET came from and where it stands today.

LÉON WALRAS AND
THE FULL ESTABLISHMENT OF GET

Equilibrium thinking had long occupied the minds of many European scholars. The effort to Newtonize the concept of the Invisible Hand, therefore, shortly shifted from Adam Smith's Scotland to continental France.

Montesquieu (1689–1755), historically associated with the doctrine of the separation of powers so fully expressed in the American constitution, was early concerned with exploring the equilibrium of social forces in keeping with the Newtonian paradigm.

The French economist Léon Walras (1834–1910), however, is the one credited with putting GET effectively on the economic landscape. Drawing upon the partial work of a number of important predecessors, he put together a set of equations for all the markets of an economy.

These equations were to be solved simultaneously to achieve an economy-wide equilibrium. It was an ambitious project, modeled after Newtonian mechanics, in the belief that the laws of economics, like the laws of physics, could be expressed precisely in mathematical form.

Walras not only followed the model of Newtonian mechanics, he also followed Plato's concept of universals. Citing Plato, Walras held that the purpose of science is the study of universals; the only difference among the sciences is with the facts their practitioners select for their study (Walras 1954: 61).

The Platonic approach created a further distortion. Universals, of course, do not hold in evolved systems, because of the inherent variability I discussed in Chapter 7. Walras, as well as his followers in GET, was putting too great of a demand for precision upon a variable organic dynamic.

Especially important in Walras's system was his development of the utility theory of value. Previous scholars like

Ricardo and Karl Marx believed that the amount of labor put into a product determined the value. Walras held that not the labor but the utility or satisfaction that the product yielded to buyers in the market was the proper measure of value.

The prices, then, that people were willing to pay, marked the level of utility for buyers and these prices changed continuously as they groped for a stable equilibrium between sellers and buyers in the market guided by natural underlying market forces. A stable equilibrium of price vectors became the aim of GET.

AXIOMATIZATION AND
THE TOP DOWN FORMALIZATION OF GET

The bottom-up approach of Walras and his followers, attempting to match the success of physics, failed to produce the desired results.

The mechanical model, then, later gave way to the top-down modeling of mathematician John von Neumann and mathematical economist Oskar Morgenstern. In 1944, they published their jointly authored *Theory of Games and Economic Behavior.*

This work launched a new impulse toward axiomatization. This was matched by a somewhat parallel effort by economist Paul Samuelson of Harvard in his *Foundations of Economic Analysis* (1947).

Axiomatization involved the building up of a system or model economy by proposing, without necessity of proof, a set of principles that dictated the direction of movement within the model system. Such a system, then, may or may not have any connection with reality. It was primarily an effort to determine under what conditions a system *could* work.

The new approach was inspired mainly by developments of uncertainty in modern quantum physics. The uncertainty principle, articulated by German physicist, Werner Heisenberg, revealed at the quantum level—the particle-wave duality plus the fact that both the momentum and the position of a particle could not be determined simultaneously.

The precise measurement of momentum and position was a process fundamental to the Newtonian system. The findings of quantum physics shook the previously unshakable foundations of straightforward Newtonian mechanics.

With uncertainty produced at the foundations of physical science, it was plausible and justifiable to move to a top-down posture of formal modeling in economics. Formal modeling was an attempt to impose some certainty on what had now become an uncertain reality.

The new approach, in turn, led to the top-down axiomatic approach of French economist Gerard Debreu and American economist Kenneth Arrow. What the bottom-up approach failed to achieve, the top-down approach tried anew.

The modeling and axiomatic approaches made little attempt to connect with real economic systems. Their purpose was to try to capture the illusive pattern of intuited market forces from the top-down by rigorously structured highly simplified models of possible economies.

The pursuit of the question of a market equilibrium produced by the intuited Invisible Hand became formally divided into the three categories of *existence, uniqueness*, and *stability*.

Existence required a general equilibrium of sorts. *Uniqueness* required that the equilibrium settle at one overall set of prices. *Stability* required that the market forces themselves drive inevitably toward equilibrium—and not away from it into disequilibrium.

All three aspects were considered to be essential to the proof of GET.

The axiomatic formalization of Arrow and Debreu, published jointly in the journal *Econometrica* in 1954, applied the new methodology to the earlier but recently updated GET theory of John Hicks. Hicks, who spent time at both the London School of Economics and Cambridge published his *Value and Capital* in 1939.

These efforts, and some follow-on ones using the same approach, did achieve demonstration of the *existence* of GET under very general assumptions inherently fundamental to the basic Walrasian theory.

On the additional problems of *uniqueness* and *stability*, however, the results have been disappointingly unsuccessful. Nevertheless, failure did not deter the committed.

Formalization continued apace. In the continuing formalization process, however, form has taken precedent over content. Models have become more and more divorced from reality and equally from empirical verification.

GET TO THE FUTURE:
THE ASSISTED FREE ENTERPRISE MARKET

The over-formalization of GET and the limited success at the end of the past century led Michio Morishima, a theorist at the London School of Economics, to judge the world of GET to be in fact a dream world not workable in the context of actual society (1992: 70–71).

Morishima stated that GET economists, including specialists in von Neumann mathematical modeling, had sunk into excessive mental estheticism. He predicted a poor future for GET in the 21st century unless economists could forgo the delights of mathematical display and proceed to build models based on reality.

My own evaluation, based on the recent findings of the foundation of the market in the dynamics of evolved brain structure, is that the further pursuit of *uniqueness* and *stability* are probably exercises in futility.

The neural algorithms, although providing the intuitive basis for the search for laws and patterns, are too weak and variable— too subject to blockage and frustration in the complexities and distances of the greater market—to ever assure us of getting to an unassisted equilibrium that is unique or stable.

Our challenge is, therefore, to pragmatically assist the market to reach these goals of meeting the needs of society with a minimum of inequalities and the accompanying social (behavioral) tensions.

Of course, the motivation to do so is likewise an expression of the Ego/Empathy dynamic represented by the equation of our social brain.

We will achieve the sought after dynamic equilibrium in the society-wide market of the future only by an Empathy/Ego-motivated intentional, pragmatic assist to the market forces which themselves emerge from our neural architecture. Such assistance to the market will probably require wisely limited regulation to avoid stifling the incentives that challenge us to produce the societal wealth for the benefit of us all.

The *assisted* free enterprise market can lead us into the future and serve the purpose of a global democratic society.

FROM NEARLY FULL CIRCLE: THE RETURN TO MORALITY

When the study of economics eventually shifts to its proper organic foundation in the dynamic of our neural architecture, it will have come nearly full circle from the days of Adam Smith.

From its origins as a moral or normative science, through its failed transition to a purely positive science, the new economics will emerge as a mixed positive-normative science that may serve us properly into the globalized future.

When that happens the dynamic architecture of our social brain will provide the guiding framework.

12

THE NEURAL BASIS
OF PRICE THEORY

From here I take the analysis to greater depths. I've shown that the neural dynamic of the social brain drives the dynamic of market evolution, the interplay of Supply and Demand, and provides the motive power of the Invisible Hand and general equilibrium theory.

So far this is pretty impressive.

But these are large-scale generalities. How does the social brain dynamic stack up when we get down to the nitty-gritty of microanalysis? Let's take a look at price theory—one of the most well-worked and established branches of economics.

THE CLASSICAL APPROACH AND
THE SCHIZOPHRENIC DUALITY OF THE MARKET

The foundational premise of traditional price theory is that self-interest is the only primary motive of economic exchange. Theorists present and interpret Demand curves, Supply curves, and the combined form, illustrating their intersection at the equilibrium price, from a self-interested viewpoint.

Two functions: Demand and Supply. One motive: self-interest. The presentation is fine. The interpretation is schizophrenic.

The two functions, Demand and Supply, are themselves the motives of our social brain, Ego and Empathy, given new names from an economic vocabulary. In reality we have two primary motives disguised as functions—with one disguised to the point of denial.

The disconnect from reality in economics, like the disconnect from reality in the mental condition, is not harmless.

It creates problems. The denied motive of Empathy asserts itself from under the covers as an amorphous irritant.

Economists have to deal with its effects while denying its existence. I will return to this later on in the chapter. Right now let's take a look at the various single motive curves and see if the duality shines through.

The Demand Curve

The Demand curve claims to represent one economic function. With a little effort, however, two motives can be clearly distinguished. The declining curve represents the quantity of something that will be demanded or purchased at different prices. At high prices a smaller amount will be demanded. As prices go down the amount demanded will go up. We see two elements, then, quantity on the x-axis, price on the y-axis.

When we look closely, we can easily see that this represents a give and take relationship. For instance, if the figure on the next page is my Demand curve, it tells the world that if I must *give* $5 for a unit of a product, I will *take* only one. However, if I only have to give $1 for a unit, I will *take* five of them. Clearly, I both take and give in the possible transactions this curve represents.

Take and give are just different words expressing the motives of Ego and Empathy, self-interest and other-interest. If I take something, I expect to reciprocate out of respect or Empathy for the other person's interest. That is, I am not going to steal it. If I were to cheat or steal—show no Empathy for the other's interest—the Demand curve would be meaningless.

The Demand curve, then, clearly shows the dual motives assumed in the transaction but denied in the theory and interpretation. There is not self-interest only, but also Empathy or other-interest.

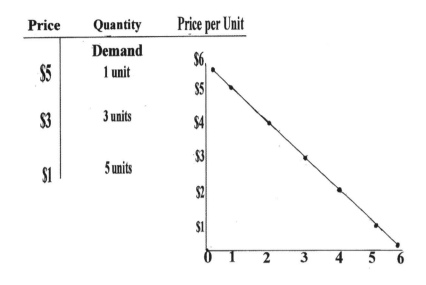

Price	Quantity
	Demand
$5	1 unit
$3	3 units
$1	5 units

So much for the Demand curve. But does the dual motive show up in the other economic curves? Let's take a look at the Supply curve.

The Supply Curve

The Supply curve represents the giver, provider, or supplier's viewpoint. I put all three words in—*giver, provider, supplier*—to show the continuity of meaning.

Sometimes we loose this continuity when we shift words around. We get the impression we're talking about something new when we're really saying the same thing. This shifting and loss of continuity happens all the time when we cross the boundaries of academic disciplines.

I can also add another word to the list—*seller*. Of the now four word list, *seller* maintains the continuity but adds the special meaning of the transition in market evolution from the gift to the transaction. When we use the word *seller*, we clearly know for the first time that we have a transaction—an exchange with the reciprocal *specified*.

We know that the giver, provider, or supplier—as a seller—expects to be paid a price for the product provided. The reciprocal is not diffuse but is now specified. The shift in market evolution, as discussed in earlier chapters, is clearly marked historically by the shift in words. History repeats itself every time we subliminally make this word choice.

The Supply curve represents how much this giver or provider, now becomes seller (we know the historical shift has taken place because we see the prices on the y-axis), will provide at the prices indicated.

The Supply curve goes up because the seller is willing to provide or sell more as the price gets higher. That is, at $5 per unit, the supplier would be willing to provide five units. On the other hand, if the price were $1 per unit, the supplier would be willing to supply only one unit.

As in the Demand curve the dual motive comes through clearly on close inspection. The provider-seller performs the empathetic structural role, the role of mammalian nurturing. His/her Ego is reaffirmed by an expression of gratitude, a thank you, in the form of a payment specified by the price. Good job. Well done.

The give and take, Ego and Empathy, of the Supply curve are there for all to see. Not one primary motive of self-interest, but two primary motives working together.

Both the Demand and Supply curves, then, when we properly interpret them, confirm the hidden duality of the transaction. But what about the combined curve—that great artifice of price theory that brings Supply and Demand together? What does it say about duality?

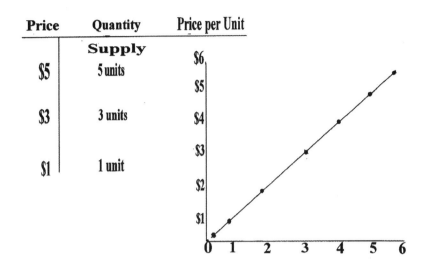

Price	Quantity	Price per Unit
	Supply	
$5	5 units	
$3	3 units	
$1	1 unit	

Market Equilibrium

Nowhere to hide! Piece of cake. Of the three, the combined curves show most clearly the duality of the market.

Both supplier and demander, giver and taker, are overtly represented. True, they were always there in the Demand and Supply curves, but now they're out in the open.

The driving motives of Ego and Empathy are revealed in all their splendid duality. To claim that self-interest is the only primary motive, as mainstream economic theory does, is clearly a flat denial of reality.

In standard price theory, the intersection of the two curves is said to represent the equilibrium price. Demand and Supply equal each other and the market is said to clear.

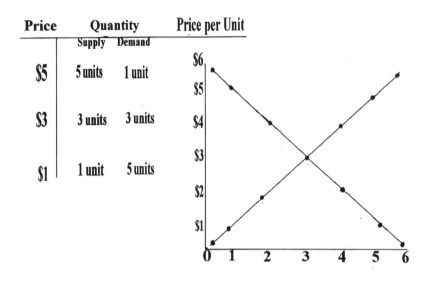

Price	Quantity		Price per Unit
	Supply	Demand	
$5	5 units	1 unit	
$3	3 units	3 units	
$1	1 unit	5 units	

Dynamic Balance: Pinned and Pegged

On close inspection, however, the illustration says more. It represents the function of our dynamic neural architecture, the tug-and-pull of Ego and Empathy, in balance.

The dynamic tug-and-pull has been pinned down, fixed artificially at a moment in time by price—the specified, impersonal reciprocal.

On the grand scale of the market as a whole, the illustration can be said to represent the Invisible Hand as attested by such economist luminaries as Walras and Alfred Marshall, among many others.

The Expanded Social Equation

The entire process, then, at a microlevel of analysis, clearly shows the shaping power of our dynamic neural architecture. Let's crank in the expanded social equation to cover the dynamics of

Supply and Demand as they reach equilibrium in price theory:

BT = EP (equilibrium price) = $\underline{\text{Demand}}$ or $\underline{\text{Supply}}$ = ±1 (approx equilibrium,
$\qquad\qquad\qquad\qquad\qquad$ Supply $\qquad$ Demand $\qquad\qquad$ or Dynamic Balance)

The Homeostatic Equation
and the "Haggle" Range

Behavioral tension (BT) as it approaches Dynamic Balance is the same as or equal to equilibrium price (EP) as Demand and Supply reach equilibrium. Demanders and suppliers are experiencing minimal behavioral tension or, in other words, they are willing to deal—to complete the transaction at a common price.

The plus or minus (±) 1 in this application of the equation not only represents the homeostatic, never stationary, tug-and-pull of the Ego/Empathy dynamic, it also captures the negotiating approach to equilibrium price traditionally seen in small markets, such as flea markets or bazaars.

In such markets buyers and sellers almost always haggle over prices and eventually narrow the range from which both may be satisfied and agree to consummate the transaction.

Of course, in the larger markets prices are often artificially fixed within the normally anticipated "haggle" range of Demand and Supply. But even here, adjustments are often made by the device of sales and clearances.

The Homeostatic,
Self-Correcting Market Dynamic

Another interesting point is that the homeostatic dynamic allows for the reversibility of numerator and denominator. This reversibility represents the self-correcting tendency of the two interacting forces, Ego and Empathy, Demand and Supply, toward a homeostatic equilibrium.

It is not a Newtonian, but an organic process.

As in other homeostatically-regulated physiological processes such as temperature, blood pressure, and others, this reversibility is made possible because the convergence or divergence from unity is what is of interest. With reversibility the ratio between Supply and Demand can reveal in a single equation relationships of disequilibrium in prices as well as magnitudes of excess Demand or excess Supply.

Price Theory: An Expression of the Social Brain

Price theory is an expression of the social brain. The social equation mathematically represents not only the dynamic of our neural architecture, of Supply and Demand, as well as the Invisible Hand—it is the foundational calculus for price theory.

Further, it cures the schizophrenic condition produced by the faulty interpretation of self-interest as the sole primary motive. The social equation allows us to see clearly the duality of the market. It heals the split between motives and functions in price and market theory.

A BONUS: PRICE BECOMES AN ENDOGENOUS VARIABLE

As if the healing of schizophrenia were not enough, we get a bonus effect from the foregoing analysis.

In economics price is treated as exogenous. Exogenous means that price itself is outside the frame of analysis. Economists don't know where price comes from or why it changes. They just take it for granted—as given.

That means that in standard economic theory, Demand and Supply curves are related *only* at the equilibrium price. Price, as an exogenous variable draws them together, but remains unaccounted for.

Tâtonnement, Groping, and the Auctioneer

This lack of explanation is troubling to economic theorists and they often introduce an artificial device to make things sound sensible. Some use the French concept of *tâtonnement* or "groping" to characterize the indeterminate sourcing of price. For example, Walras used the *tâtonnement* or groping process to explain the upward and downward movement of prices which solved his set of equations bringing Demand and Supply into equilibrium (Walras, 1954: 170).

Others introduce the fiction of an auctioneer that calls the various prices across the span of the market and notifies both the suppliers and demanders when equilibrium is reached so that they can take advantage of it.

Needless to say, it's a rather awkward, if not humorous, set of devices—not designed to inspire confidence except, perhaps, in the minds of the most committed devotee or true believer.

Enter the Social Equation

The social equation, however, changes price from an exogenous to an endogenous variable. It connects the dynamic of neural architecture with price theory and demonstrates the continuing relationship between Demand and Supply that exists at all other points on the Demand, Supply, and combined curves.

BEHAVIORAL TENSION: MOTIVATING PRICE CHANGE

We can now identify behavioral tension as the source of motivation for change that brings Demand and Supply into price equilibrium.

At all points outside the equilibrium point demanders and suppliers are unable to get the reciprocity they expect and want.

Result? In keeping with our reciprocal neural algorithms, these market participants experience behavioral tension. This behavioral tension is what motivates buyers and sellers to change their behavior to bring price into equilibrium.

Therefore, all points on the Demand and Supply curves that do *not* match the equilibrium point are clear indicators of behavioral tension. This, again, effectively confirms the dynamic unity of neural architecture with economics.

Of course, this change brought by the social equation only explains the motivational source for price changes. The problem of communicating the changes to buyers and sellers across the greater market remains.

13

NEURAL ALGORITHMS
AND CALCULUS IN PRICE THEORY

Continuing the analysis, I take up in this chapter some simple applications of calculus used in price theory. Calculus is loved by some, scary to many. I may be going back on my promise to keep the math simple. So I don't blame you if you choose to skip this chapter.

If you hang in there, however, I think you'll find it worth doing. I will demonstrate further the important linkage between our dynamic neural architecture and the market. I will also show you how clarifying that linkage brings new insights. Together we can see relationships that were invisible before—hiding there in the shadows—like the duality of the market that was obscured from view by the faulty assumption of the sole self-interest motive.

With a little background in basic algebra I think you can follow the math. I will assume you are staying with me and plow right ahead.

SOME CALCULUS IN PRICE THEORY

Standard texts on price theory tell us that Demand and Supply are represented as *functions* that convert prices to quantities. So what are these things called functions?

Functions are mathematical devices that are defined by what they do. In this case, functions take numbers in one group and assign them to numbers in another group. Economists use the mathematical notation of functions to *represent* the relationship which they *perceive* to exist between Demand and Supply:

$D(P) =$ Quantity demanded at price P

$S(P) =$ Quantity supplied at price P

The notation D(P), when used to indicate a function, does *not* have the usual algebraic meaning of multiply D by P.

And it is not read that way. As a function, it is read D of P or D at P. And D at P assigns a specific number demanded at P which amounts to a specific price. The number assigned is the quantity demanded at that price.

S(P) is read and treated the same way. S at P assigns a specific quantity supplied at a specific price.

From functions we can move to *derivatives*.

Simply put, derivatives are rates of change. They are indicated by placing a prime marker at the upper right of the symbol for function.

The derivative, or rate of change, for the Demand function D then is indicated by D'. It is read D prime. The same holds for the Supply function. S' is read S prime. When expressed with the parenthetical P for price, they are read as follows: D'(P) reads D prime of P. S'(P) is read S prime of P.

Derivatives as used in price theory are expressed as follows:

The fact that the Demand curve slopes downward is expressed by the inequality

$$D'(P) < 0$$

The above is read D prime of P is less than zero. A rate of change (derivative) less than zero means that the value of the rate of change is negative.

Therefore price is declining (as reflected on the y-axis) and so the curve slopes downward. The curve also moves forward along the quantity demanded line (x-axis) marking the increase. The net effect is to illustrate or *represent* the standard relation believed to exist between price and quantity demanded—as price declines the quantity demanded increases.

The fact that the Supply curve slopes upward is expressed by the inequality

$$S'(P) > 0$$

The above is read S prime of P is greater than zero. A rate of change (derivative) greater than zero means that the value of the rate of change is positive.

Therefore price is rising (as reflected on the y-axis) and so the curve slopes upward. The curve also moves forward along the quantity supplied line (x-axis). The net effect is to illustrate or *represent* the standard relation believed to exist between price and the quantity supplied—as price increases the quantity supplied increases.

Equilibrium price is the price at which the functions D of P and S of P are equal to each other. This is *represented* by the notation

$$D(P) = S(P)$$

Equilibrium quantity is the common value that must be identified as the quantity both demanded and supplied at the equilibrium price or point on the graph. On the graph presented in Chapter 13, the common value is about 3 units at the equilibrium price of $3.

HIDDEN RELATIONSHIP REVEALED:
PRICE AS INDICATOR OF BEHAVIORAL TENSION

When treated in the standard manner outlined above, Demand and Supply are related *only* at the point of equilibrium—the equilibrium price. As in Chapter 12 analyzing the Demand, Supply, and equilibrium curves, price is an exogenous (originating outside) variable that brings Demand and Supply together but remains essentially unexplained. In the calculus used above, Demand and Supply are treated separately prior to their intersection at the equilibrium point.

The calculus model used in standard price theory, then, does not represent the relationship that we discovered earlier in Chapter 12—that behavioral tension exists at all other points. The equation of our social brain expressing the dynamic of neural architecture again reveals this hidden relationship. I repeat for effect:

$$BT = EP \text{ (equilibrium price)} = \frac{\text{Demand}}{\text{Supply}} \text{ or } \frac{\text{Supply}}{\text{Demand}} = \pm 1 \text{ (approx equilibrium, unity,) or Dynamic Balance}$$

This extension of the neural social equation, applied also in Chapter 12, means, of course, that all other points (prices) on the Demand and Supply curves are indicators of behavioral tension. Behavioral tension, then, equates to price; or, said another way, price is an indicator of behavioral tension. With the new insights, of course the Demand is, likewise, an indicator of behavior tension.

Price or behavioral tension *not* in equilibrium is what motivates demanders and suppliers to alter prices in the direction of equilibrium.

Price at equilibrium indicates minimal behavioral tension and so is acceptable to both demanders and suppliers.

The plus or minus ($\pm$)1 indicating approximate or approaching equilibrium maintains the representation of the tug-and-pull homeostatic dynamic of the neural architecture. At the same time it represents the possible range of acceptable prices as buyer and seller haggle to reach agreement.

In this case the equilibrium price can be the single price arrived at out of an equilibrating range of prices. Such is the essence of any negotiating process in the market, no matter how formalized. The give and take negotiating that leads to an acceptable price is seen clearly in domestic flea markets and in many similar institutions (e.g., bazaars) around the world. In our larger, impersonal markets, of course, the price may be arbitrarily fixed. But here, too, the price is often effectively negotiated within a range by such devices as sales or clearances.

Price, therefore, by linking with the dynamic of neural architecture now becomes an endogenous variable. That is, it becomes a variable that we can explain or account for within the now extended frame of analysis.

14

APPLICATION OF THE BASIC HOMEOSTATIC EQUATION TO ECONOMICS

In the previous two chapters I analyzed the standard curves of economics as well as some simple calculus of price theory in terms of our neural dynamic. This chapter will further demonstrate the application of the basic organic, homeostatic equation to economics.

DEMONSTRATION: UNIT CHANGE ABOVE/BELOW EQUILIBRIUM PRICE

In the illustration below, I have arbitrarily assumed an equilibrium price and units of price, Supply, and Demand.

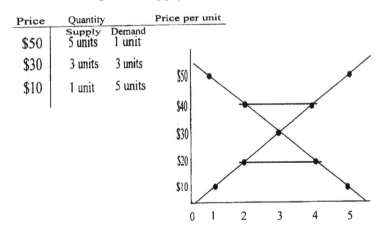

Price	Quantity	
	Supply	Demand
$50	5 units	1 unit
$30	3 units	3 units
$10	1 unit	5 units

In applying the organic equation, units of change or the first order derivative must be used, rather than the actual numerical value. Solving for EP ± 1 we go above or below the EP by an unit increment of 1. Demand and Supply as used in this demonstration, of course, refer to quantities demanded and supplied.

Thus:

BT @ EP + 1 = $40. At P $40 <u>Supply</u> = <u>4</u> numerically or <u>2</u> units of magnitude

  Demand   2   1

BT @ EP − 1 = $ 20. At P $20 <u>Demand</u> = <u>4</u> numerically or <u>2</u> units magnitude

  Supply   2   1

Since we are representing an organic homeostatic algorithm (in contrast to a point reduction force vector of Newtonian mechanics) in which the opposing forces (circuits) constantly tug-and-pull against each other in countering deviations from homeostatic equilibrium, a decrement in one is counterbalanced by an increment in the other.

Therefore, there is no change in magnitude of divergence or behavioral tension at equal increments above or below EP.

The Constant Case

The previous example represents a special case chosen to demonstrate the application of the equation in easily under-standable fashion. In this simple case both the unit magnitude and numerical value have the same ratio. More complex applications require additional recourse to calculus and rely upon the unit magnitudes of divergence.

For example, in all cases where price and quantity increments or units are constant, the rate of change is constant as represented by straight line curves of Demand and Supply, the unit change between Demand and Supply will likewise remain constant. For each unit price change above or below EP, the unit change between Demand and Supply will be two.

Like two cars driving away from the same place in opposite directions at the same speed bound by an elastic counterforce, for each unit of time the distance increases by two units of distance.

The Elaborated Equation

This can be represented by the following elaboration of the basic equation to calculate divergence from balance and to derive values to be substituted into the original equation:

$$BT = \frac{d(D\leftarrow\rightarrow S) \, @ \, EP \pm X}{r(D\leftarrow\rightarrow S) \, @ \, EP} = \, ?$$

The letter d refers to the difference, differential, unit difference, or rate of change.

The double arrows $\leftarrow\rightarrow$ indicate that Demand and Supply are interconnected and the magnitude of their divergence is a fundamental measure of the homeostatic, self-correcting function of BT (behavioral tension) as one circuit acts to counter the other in deviations from homeostatic equilibrium.

Thus, a value decrement in one is countered by a value increment in the other. No loss in magnitude of BT occurs. The unit magnitude of divergence between them is what is of interest as a measure of BT.

The letter X represents the specific value of EP plus or minus.

The letter r denotes the ratio between Demand and Supply at EP which by definition is unity or 1.

In simple terms, then, BT equals the unit differential between Demand and Supply or vice-versa at values of EP plus or minus 1 or more, divided by the ratio between Demand and Supply, or vice-versa at EP, which is, by definition of equilibrium, unity or 1.

As a Function
The constant rate of change can be expressed as a function.

That is, BT = f(x) @ EP ± ?; f(x) is the unit differential between D & S, or S & D, or f(x) is d(D← →S), which represents an increment of 2 at every unit of price above or below EP as D & S increasingly diverge.

The following table results as divergence begins:

$$f(x) \text{ at } EP \pm 1 = 2$$

$$f(x) \text{ at } EP \pm 2 = 4$$

$$f(x) \text{ at } EP \pm 3 = 6$$

$$f(x) \text{ at } EP \pm 4 = 8$$

$$f(x) \text{ at } EP \pm 5 = 10$$

Substituting the values of the table into the elaborated equation:

$$BT @ EP = \frac{1}{1} = 1$$

$$BT @ EP \pm 1 = \frac{2}{1} = 2$$

$$BT @ EP \pm 2 = \frac{4}{1} = 4$$

$$BT @ EP \pm 3 = \frac{6}{1} = 6$$

$$BT @ EP \pm 4 = \frac{8}{1} = 8$$

$$BT @ EP \pm 5 = \frac{10}{1} = 10$$

Inserting values into the original basic equation approaching equilibrium:

$$BT = \frac{Demand}{Supply} \text{ or } \frac{Supply}{Demand} \text{ at } EP \pm 1 =$$

At equilibrium with no divergence:

$$BT @ EP = \frac{D}{S} \text{ or } \frac{S}{D} = \frac{1}{1} = 1$$

For positive values of EP above equilibrium, Supply is the numerator.

To adequately represent the ratio, Demand, then, is arbitrarily held constant at 1 as the units diverge between Demand and Supply:

$$BT @ EP + 1 = \frac{S}{D} = \frac{2}{1} = 2$$

$$BT @ EP + 2 = \frac{S}{D} = \frac{4}{1} = 4$$

$$BT @ EP + 3 = \frac{S}{D} = \frac{6}{1} = 6$$

$$BT @ EP + 4 = \frac{S}{D} = \frac{8}{1} = 8$$

$$BT @ EP + 5 = \frac{S}{D} = \frac{10}{1} = 10$$

For negative values of EP below equilibrium Demand is the numerator.

To adequately represent the ratio, in the negative case, Supply, then, is arbitrarily held constant at 1 as the units diverge between Supply and Demand:

$$BT @ EP - 1 = \frac{D}{S} = \frac{2}{1} = 2$$

$$BT @ EP - 2 = \frac{D}{S} = \frac{4}{1} = 4$$

$$BT @ EP - 3 = \frac{D}{S} = \frac{6}{1} = 6$$

$$BT @ EP - 4 = \frac{D}{S} = \frac{8}{1} = 8$$

$$BT @ EP - 5 = \frac{D}{S} = \frac{10}{1} = 10$$

The Nonconstant case

When the conditions of constancy do not hold—rates of change are not constant—the determination of BT and the unit differences of Demand and Supply will require more complex mathematical operations, to include averaging processes. This, however, does not affect the validity of the organic equation's application to economics.

Interim Summary

Based upon the integration of the neural dynamic with Demand and Supply, we can conclude:

That all points on the Demand and Supply curves *not* at equilibrium represent points of behavioral tension. And it is this behavioral tension that *motivates* demanders and suppliers to change their behavior toward the equilibrium price.

Without such an organic motivating, self-correcting force the market could never come to equilibrium on its own except by accident or randomly.

At all prices, as long as the first order derivative, or rate of change is constant, or the slope is a straight line, and the units are of equal increments, the ratio between the unit differentials or Demand and Supply at EP $\pm$ 1 will be 2:1 or a magnitude of divergence of 2.

The ratio of divergence from EP will increase by an increment of 2 for each unit change of price. At EP ± 5, for example, the unit differential between Supply and Demand, or vice versa, will be a magnitude of 10. This is the fundamental measure of behavioral tension in the market.

When the rate of change is *not* constant, the determination of differential magnitudes will become more complex and will require an averaging process.

Price adds *significance* and acts as an amplifier of BT. As a general proposition, as price increments rise or fall, the magnitude of BT also rises or falls. That is: generally, buying a house or car carries more significance than a loaf of bread.

Of course, this can vary subjectively with the situation of each party to the exchange.

DIFFERENCES IN REPRESENTING
THE ORGANIC, HOMEOSTATIC EQUATION

Representing an organic, homeostatic algorithm, such as that of our social neural architecture, with a constant counterbalancing tug-and-pull of two forces or circuits, requires some modification in mathematical representation.

The magnitude of convergence or divergence from equilibrium is what is of interest, not the numerical value.

Equal increments above or below the equilibrium point represent the *same* magnitude of behavioral tension because one force makes up for the other.

That is why Demand and Supply may be inverted in the equation to represent the magnitude of divergence more accurately.

This magnitude is the fundamental calculus of behavioral tension in the market, amplified or diminished by *price* as an indicator of significance.

EXTENDED APPLICATION
OF THE ORGANIC EQUATION

Up to this point economics has lacked the conceptual apparatus to meaningfully and mathematically ask the question of socio-behavioral tension in the market.

The very question of motivation for change toward equilibrium has been largely begged, brushed over simplistically, or left as an implicit assumption.

The degree of socio-behavioral tension or stress in the market is, of course, of great importance to behavioral and socio-economics as well as to sociology and political science in general. The organic social exchange equation provides a framework for addressing this important issue.

I have now completed the excursion into mathematical analysis.

The outcome of this excursion provides confirmation that the dynamic of our neural architecture shapes the exchange process. And the application of the social equation, expressing that dynamic, clarifies much that has previously been obscure in the analysis of Demand and Supply in standard price theory or microeconomics.

15
THE FALLACY OF SELF-REFERENCE

After completing the microanalysis started in Chapter 12, I want to make a short detour. I think the detour topic is timely and important.

I want to acknowledge the well-known animal behavior or ethological phenomenon of defense of territory in the face of change. Both aspects—resistance to change and defense of territory are common among academicians as well as other higher primates. And economists are no exception.

When I examined the fundamentals of price theory, I exposed an unacknowledged schizophrenic duality lurking in the shadows. The schizophrenic condition was resolved by linkage with the dynamic of our social brain. The expansion of the social equation represented mathematically the linked relationship between the neural and market dynamics.

$$BT = EP \text{ (equil price)} = \frac{\underline{Demand}}{Supply} \text{ or } \frac{\underline{Supply}}{Demand} = \pm 1 \text{ (approx equilibrium, unity,) or Dynamic Balance}$$

In spite of the convincing demonstration, economists will likely be reluctant to accept it. I know. I have presented the material at numerous economic conferences. Economists, like other creatures, don't like change and they defend their territory. And, in this case, they have marked their territory meticulously.

NAIVE AND NATIVE SKEPTICISM:
I SEE IT BUT IT'S IMPOSSIBLE!

Returning by air from one such academic conference, a fellow economist who had attended my presentation, was seated a couple of rows ahead. He looked back, saw me, and asked to look at my paper again. Obligingly, I produced it.

He studied it intently during a thirty minute leg of the flight.

Finally, he handed it back to me saying, "I think it's accurate as far as the psychology or neuroscience, but it's not possible to apply it to economics."

Déjà vu. The response reminded me of when my mother and father took us kids to visit New York for the first time back in 1946. At that time the Empire State Building was famously the tallest building in the city if not the world. My eleven-year-old younger brother, who was always the skeptic, stood with the family on the sidewalk in front of the building and gazed up at the towering structure almost disappearing into the low clouds.

After a few studied moments, he muttered profoundly: "That's impossible!" Here was my first experience with the skeptic's denial of barefaced reality.

TERRITORIAL DEFENSE AND *HOMO ECONOMICUS*

As noted above, economists, of course, are very human in their dislike of change and their defense of territory. Their pet concept *homo economicus*, or economic man, has been a proud icon of the discipline— of their territory. They rush to defend it when it appears threatened. The core of *homo economicus* is rational, self-interested man.

Economists take considerable pride in the explanatory power of this venerable concept. Like true believers they try to extend its reach beyond economics into other social science disciplines. They even take pride in turning such venerated human institutions as marriage and child-rearing into the self-interest calculus of *homo economicus*.

In Face of the Evidence

In recent years, the evidence for Empathy and cooperation among humans, has accumulated dramatically. This has caused some embarrassment for economists subscribing faithfully to *homo economicus*. Reacting to criticism of the exclusive emphasis on self-interest in the face of evidence for Empathy, cooperation, and even altruism, economists have compromised.

The Grudging Acknowledgment

They grudgingly acknowledge the interlopers, but don't give them full status. Self-interest remains the only primary motive. The "softer" human qualities—soft-headed some might say—are called preferences or tastes.

Let's take a look at the problems this half-hearted compromise creates.

BY SLIGHT OF HAND
SELF-INTEREST VIA SELF-REFERENCE

It's an old magicians trick! Economists maintain the primacy of self-interest while accommodating other motives by a *slight-of-hand* shift in perspective.

They do this by shifting from *self-interest* to *self-reference*. Unlike the magician whose job it is to deceive us, this is probably an unconscious defensive stratagem on the part of economists.

Nevertheless, it amounts to a logical fallacy.

The Fundamental Fallacy

The confounding of *self-reference* with *self-interest* is, in fact, a fundamental fallacy of the entire traditional economic approach. The fallacy allows the subsuming of all motives under the rubric of self-interest and obscures the roughly equal role of Empathy.

Taking the individual as the starting point, microeconomic theory mistakenly *transforms* this individual or self-referential *perspective* into an all-inclusive *motive* of self-interest. From this logically unwarranted transformation any other motive is, thus, obscured or swallowed up in self-interest.

Accordingly, Empathy—and its derivatives of cooperation and altruism, even love—cannot be considered true motives. They must, therefore, be trivialized as tastes or preferences— indistinguishable in significance from such banalities as coffee, tea, or milk.

Fallacy Revealed

But as revealed in Chapters 12 through 14, under the sweeping searchlight of the social brain dynamic, the hidden duality of Ego and Empathy is clearly exposed in every Demand curve and every Supply curve, especially when both are combined to show price equilibrium. The dual roles, then, are always present implicitly if not explicitly.

The demander performs the egoistic role. The supplier performs the empathetic role.

EMPATHY AS A PREFERENCE OR TASTE: THE DISTORTIONS THAT FOLLOW

Economic theory has not yet come to terms with the new findings from evolved brain structure that I have been presenting so far. It's new stuff and many economists are probably still totally unaware of its existence.

So mainstream economics currently proceeds happily on its way from the self-reference perspective to treat self-interest as the only primary motive. Empathy is treated as a taste or preference.

The distortions accompanying such treatment are numerous. I have summarized the most important ones below:

1. Empathy becomes optional. One may have such a taste or preference or not. This is distorting because Empathy is *not* optional. Empathy is a fundamental motive of our neural architecture roughly equal with self-interest or Ego. It proceeds from the very large, very visible, and very identifiable mammalian neural structures.

2. Empathy is trivialized. Empathy, as a preference or taste, is indistinguishable from a taste or preference for Hummers or Mercedes or for slippers or sandals.

3. It distortingly forces a rational self-interested perspective.

4. It misconstrues the real nature of the market.

5. It obscures the dynamic shaping effect of the Ego/Empathy interplay in all social exchange.

6. It is not consilient with evolutionary neuroscience—a more fundamental science.

All together, the above six shortfalls add up to serious error.

A discipline, claiming devotion to the scientific method should display some uneasiness about such a gap between theory and fact. Economists should, perhaps, wake up to the new reality—forego their defensiveness and inertia to change, and meet the new challenges presented head-on.

I think the changes will do little damage to the discipline as a whole and will equip it to move more hopefully into the 21st century.

Escaping the morally challenged straitjacket of sole self-interest should be refreshing to economists as well as the rest of the world.

IN THE FACE OF ECONOMIC CRISES:
SOME QUESTIONS

In the face of recent economic crises we have an obligation to confront some pressing questions. Examples of such questions may be:

Should we continue educating our economists and business leaders in the fundamentals of self-interest?

Should we cling to a theory that provides subtle justification for corporate greed?

Should we continue to promote a theory that mistakenly presents our very valuable free enterprise system to the developing world, in the throes of globalization, as a heartless, materialistic expression of human selfishness?

Especially, do we really need to hang on to a theory when that theory is no longer scientifically justifiable?

16

THE WISHFUL THOUGHT
OF FRIEDRICH HAYEK

Recently, I walked into the office of the Department of Economics of a major state university.

In the course of conversation the chairperson informed me that her department was Austrian. I asked what she meant by that, having in mind the old institutional theorists of Austria. She replied—Hayekian.

I was a bit taken aback. I had always thought that academic departments should be diversified. Nevertheless, the point as made was understandable. At the beginning of the 21st century the thought of Austrian born Friedrich Hayek (1899–1992) is most influential among theoretical economists in the Western world. He represents the standard model of economics, par excellence.

In keeping with the new findings linking neural architecture with economics that were explored in the previous chapters, it is relevant to take a close look at Hayek's influential thinking.

A MAN OF HIS TIME

Hayek was a man of his time. *The Road to Serfdom*, his 1944 classic, made the case against socialist command economies. He argued that socialism, as collective or government ownership of the means of production, is not only unproductive, but also intrinsically not free.

Hayek felt that individual freedom could not exist under central planning and that private property is essential for both economic productivity and political freedom.

Later works essentially expanded on Hayek's original line of thought. *Law, Legislation, and Liberty*, published in three volumes by the University of Chicago Press (1973, 1976, & 1979), developed his concept of the spontaneous order of the free market. In *The Fatal Conceit* (1988), he attacked the assumption of socialism that the spontaneous institutions and practices of the market can be done away with in creating a command economy.

In the years following the collapse of the Soviet Union, Hayek's position has become, in large part, conventional wisdom.

Hayek spent many of his years in the United States, principally at the University of Chicago where he interacted with numerous prominent economic thinkers. He received the Nobel Prize for economics in 1974.

SPONTANEOUS ORDER VS. THE INVISIBLE HAND

Of special interest here is Hayek's concept of spontaneous order. On the face of it, the concept sounds similar to Adam Smith's Invisible Hand. Hayek saw this similarity and acknowledged it.

The two concepts, however, are significantly different. Hayek's spontaneous order was an order based on the rule of law. Individuals could exchange and interact with each other freely, limited only by the rules of civil society.

There was no place in his spontaneous order for the role of sympathy, fellow-feeling, or benevolence as Adam Smith saw it. In fact, Hayek saw such moral feeling as injurious to the production of wealth and its equitable distribution. Hayek's spontaneous order was the Invisible Hand without the reciprocal of Empathy.

Or was it? Let's take a closer look at Hayek's thinking, especially since it is so widely accepted today.

MORAL INSTINCTS:
IMPEDIMENTS TO THE MARKET SYSTEM

Unlike Thomas Hobbes, Hayek acknowledges that we are not just self-interested but also have moral instincts. He sees these moral instincts, however, as unhelpful in the spontaneous order.

In fact, he insists that the moral instincts that we inherited from the face-to-face societies of our primitive ancestors are the chief obstacle to the moral approval of the market system that creates our wealth. This somewhat counterintuitive contention by Hayek deserves some inspection.

Moral Instincts:
As Primitive Necessity

According to Hayek, these moral instincts, driving concern for the visible needs of others, were necessary to the survival of the group in primitive times. Such moral instincts required that we consciously try to benefit others.

Self-interest as Market
Rule of Conduct

The market system, on the other hand required that we concentrate on our own self-interested gain in order to achieve unknowingly and unintentionally, the best outcome for others. This market rule of conduct conflicts with our inherited moral instincts because we cannot see the benefit to others of our own self-interested efforts in the impersonal market.

Conscious Pursuit of Social Justice:
As Destructive Mirage

The moral discomfort we feel, then, leads to the idea that we must consciously act to bring about social justice. This idea, in turn, interferes with the proper functioning of the market and is conversely destructive of the wealth necessary to provide benefits to all.

From this Hayek concludes that the conscious pursuit of social justice is a mirage and destructive of the spontaneous order under which the unrestricted free market will take care of social justice automatically.

IMPLICIT EMPATHY:
LAW AND THE RULES OF CIVIL SOCIETY

Hayek denies a role for Empathy—or, as he sees it from his mid-20th century, moral instincts—in the free enterprise market.

But does his system, in fact, omit Empathy as a necessary component of the market?

To answer this question, we need to get past the rhetoric—past the obvious—to the basic reality. When we do this, we see that Hayek builds Empathy implicitly into his system.

As a constitutional theoretical lawyer, Hayek lays the requirement for the free enterprise market in the rule of law combined with the rules of civil society. Both are implicit expressions of Empathy. Both mandate concern for the interest of others or all.

Law, of course, empathetically enforces and guarantees protection of everyone's private property, requires people to keep their word in the form of their contractual agreements, and demands they avoid cheating, committing fraud and other criminal behavior inherently harmful to others.

The rules of civil society empathetically require courtesy, consideration of others, and playing by the established fair play rules of the game.

Hayek, then, implicitly and apparently unknowingly, sets, by law and civil behavior, the essential empathetic framework within which the supposedly unrestricted free market must work. Indeed, owing to the scale of inclusiveness, no vast market system could work without them.

Hayek, thus, sets fair rules and assumes fair outcomes. Given this setup, Hayek clearly feels we should not waste our energies worrying individually about social justice. The system, as defined, will take care of that by itself—if we just go for it, egoistically.

In other words, given the right framework, we can proceed to behave like sociopaths in the market, with the assurance that all will work out well for the good of us all.

A *NOT SO SPONTANEOUS* ORDER

From within the framework of the rule of law and the requirements of civility, Hayek assumes a spontaneous order will proceed. Actually, within the framework so defined, it would be stretching the point to call any emergent order *spontaneous*. At best it would be a guided or facilitated order.

Hopefulness and Wishful Thinking

Hayek's case is, therefore, a hopeful one based, in part, upon implicit assumptions and wishful thinking. We can understand and appreciate his motivation as a reaction to the abuses if not horrors of National Socialism in Germany and the failure of command, centrally planned economies under communism.

Nevertheless, his position is, at best, a theoretical, if not an ideological one. There is very little evidence to support the positive and relatively balanced outcomes that he anticipates from an unrestricted market, bound only by the minimal rule of law and civility. And because of the harshness involved in establishing such a market no government has yet been able politically to implement such a system.

Although the evidence is clear that a relatively free market (there has never been a completely free market) does produce more wealth than centrally planned or centrally controlled ones, there is no evidence to show that the unfettered market achieves, on its own, anywhere near an equitable distribution or even the elimination of poverty.

There are just too many obstructions—among them the very scale of inclusiveness itself—that prevent the natural tendency from achieving its ideal equilibrium state.

Resolving the Hayekian Conflict

However, the conflict Hayek sees between the market and our inherited moral instincts can be resolved with a proper understanding of his own implicit assumptions coupled with a grasp of the evolutionary structure of the market as the institutionalized expression of our neural architecture.

Just knowing that the productive, supplying side of the equation is fundamentally an expression of mammalian nurturing should relieve the moral discomfort somewhat.

Moreover, paying close attention to one's productive enterprise—that is, insuring quality of product and service, being trustworthy and honest in business relationships, having concern for consumer safety and welfare—is not simply self-interest.

It is, rather, the combined expression of self-interest and Empathy that is necessary to a proper working of the free enterprise market system. The essential Empathy component, may be implicit and obscured as in Hayek's system; or it may be explicit as in the acknowledged dynamic of our social exchange neural architecture.

MARKET STRUCTURE
AND MARKET COMPETITION

It is, also, important at this point to keep in mind the real nature of market competition. Competition can be properly understood by holding in memory the distinction made in Chapter 10 between market structure and market behavior.

In the institutionalized market structure—especially in the ideal of the perfectly competitive market (PCM)—expressing the dynamic of our neural architecture, behavior is different toward competitors than toward customers. This critical distinction is often forgotten or not grasped in the first place.

In the mammalian structure of the market, suppliers and producers *compete*—not with customers or buyers—but with each other to *serve* or *provide* for the needs of the *customers or buyers*. The very structure of the PCM requires or forces this as a fundamental posture.

Providers or sellers don't *compete* with the customers to see if they can delude, outfox, or rip them off. Although this is a flawed posture that some seem to fall into. They compete with other providers.

To repeat—market competition, then, is not between providers and customers. It is between sellers and providers, to better serve the demands of customers—and, of course, to receive in reciprocity the reward or profit they well deserve for so doing.

STRUCTURAL EMPATHY
AND BEHAVIORAL EMPATHY

Empathy always plays its reciprocal role in the market. That role may be structural, behavioral, or both.

In the PCM, confronting the relentless fact of market competition, suppliers—to survive in the market—*must* perform the *structural* equivalent of Empathy.

They *must* do so even if they do not feel Empathy as a personal motivation. That is, in the face of competition from other suppliers, they must provide the best possible product or service at the lowest possible price to meet the needs of the customers. If they fail to do either, they will eventually be driven out of business by competitors who do both.

On the other hand, however, if suppliers perform their services with concern for quality, care for the well-being of the customer, with a sense of social responsibility, and with a commitment to fair play, they express Empathy in behavior. Empathy in market behavior builds trust and in the long run reduces the costs of market transactions.

Empathy in behavior may also act as a limiting influence on the runaway corporate greed we see so flagrantly practiced in the market.

At least the acknowledgment of Empathy's primary motive status would undercut the moral rationale for greed implicitly provided by the emphasis on self-interest as a sole primary motive.

This faulty overemphasis on self-interest characterizes Hayek's so-called spontaneous order as pervasively as it does mainstream economics.

The free enterprise market, when properly understood, then, does *not* conflict with what Hayek calls our inherited moral instincts (Empathy), but provides the opportunity to consciously and intentionally satisfy them.

CREATIVITY, INNOVATION, AND THE FREE ENTERPRISE MARKET

A proper grasp of the dynamic nature of the competitive free enterprise market leads to a better understanding of one of its most important features—its remarkable creativity.

Creativity

As providers or suppliers seek, under terms of full and relatively free competition, to better respond empathetically to the needs, wants, and desires of the buyers, they each seek differential advantage in so doing. The natural outcome is a process of continuous innovation and creativity.

The very institutionalized Ego/Empathy dynamic structure of the ideal market not only forces but also incents this posture. In a dynamic, competitive market, those providers who fail to innovate fail to survive. Competition among suppliers and providers is essential to the innovative, creative process.

Creative Destruction and Innovation
Whither Go'ist?

Economist Joseph Schumpeter coined the term *creative destruction* to characterize this constantly innovative aspect of the economy of capitalism (Schumpeter 1942). Creative destruction and creative innovation are but two sides of the same coin.

Lacking an understanding of the true nature of the market as the expression of our neural dynamic, Hayek, however, was unable to grasp the essential structural role of Empathy in the creativity of the competitive market.

Schumpeter, writing in 1942, saw the capitalist entrepreneur always seeking new commodities, new technologies, new sources of Supply, and new organizational forms. This process brought large scale change if not upheaval. The great advances brought by computer and information technology seem to bear out Schumpeter's vision.

Additionally, Schumpeter saw an inevitable tendency toward socialism propelled by this dynamic innovative, destructive aspect of capitalism. It remains to be seen if he eventually proves right on that score.

Creativity and innovation continue to be at a premium in the competitive high-tech environment.

Creative Destruction, Sustainability, and Inequality

Of course, as Schumpeter recognized, there are dangerous side effects to this unrestrained innovation and creativity. We face the rapid depletion of resources, the pollution of the environment, global warming—even international conflict.

There is also the problem of inequalities. Such effects might provoke political intervention that stifles the productivity of the system. How to cope adequately with such side effects constitutes one of the greatest challenges facing the free enterprise system in the new century.

This takes us back to the problem of Hayek's spontaneous order.

PRAGMATISM VS. IDEOLOGY: RESPONDING TO MARKET FAILURE

Despite the wishful thinking of Hayek's poorly comprehended *not- so-spontaneous order*, the market fails. And in recent decades, dramatically so.

With the variability of the tug-and-pull of Ego and Empathy within the market structure, the scale of inclusiveness, and other disrupting factors, the market notably falls short of achieving its anticipated or predicted equilibrium states.

In the vast markets of today, there is more than ample room for market failure and the creation of undue suffering and inequality—even the persistent poverty we see existing among riches.

Such market failure permits the creation and accumulation of undesirable and destructive levels of socio-behavioral tension. To cope with this I believe we must take a pragmatic approach, not an ideological one.

In any countermeasures, however, we must keep the market sufficiently free to incent for production and the creative growth of wealth. At the same time we must assist the market where it fails to provide adequately or achieve an acceptable level of equitable distribution.

Our responses to market failure should be pragmatic and situational, not ideological, or based upon wishful thinking with little evidence to back it.

Hayek's naïve concept of spontaneous order, which excludes, presumptively if not actually, both the structural and behavioral role of Empathy, fails before the new evidence from evolutionary neuroscience.

The structure of the market, as the expression of the interplay between self-preservation and mammalian nurturing, provides the basic dynamic for the intuited Invisible Hand. The neural dynamic is the causal underpinning for the emergence of any spontaneous order. Empathy, or our moral instinct, properly understood, constitutes the necessary reciprocal for any market to exist.

Hayek's concept of spontaneous order is, in the final analysis, no improvement on Adam Smith's intuitive concept of the Invisible Hand. It is, in effect, a step backwards, modified somewhat by law and civility, to the earlier position of Mandeville in his *Fable of the Bees*. (See Bianchi [1992] for an interpretation of Hayek's debt to Mandeville).

17

MODELING EQUILIBRIUM WITH BEAUTIFUL MINDS, BEAUTIFUL EQUATIONS

This part ends with application of the social brain dynamic to economics with a look at a more popular theme. We were captivated by the story of Nobel prize winner John Nash. Our fascination derived more, perhaps, from the human interest story than the mathematical achievements themselves.

A Dose of Mystique and Weirdness

The book and the movie *A Beautiful Mind* played upon the mystique of mathematics as well as the popular fantasy that insanity and genius are closely related. We like to believe in the mysterious. And we also like to think that those who are different from us are a bit weird. Both mystique and weirdness played together to capture the popular imagination.

But mystique and weirdness contribute nothing to understanding. They, in fact, get in the way. Mystique emerges from superstition; weirdness from ignorance. Neither have a legitimate place in science.

And neither help to clarify the nature of the so-called Nash equilibrium. Nash himself did not grasp the underlying dynamic necessary to such an equilibrium. In fact, the fundamental nature of the Nash equilibrium remains unclarified to this date.

Dangling in Space

As it stands the Nash equilibrium is simply a concocted mathematical structure without inherent roots. It dangles unanchored out in mathematical space tethered only tenuously to reality by the statement of arbitrary and not justified conditions, assumptions, and axioms, accepted as given and not subject to challenge—constraints called forth from the depths of a source unknown.

Why then has it drawn so much attention in the social sciences?

THE MYSTIQUE OF MATHEMATICS

The answer is: Partly because of the mystique about mathematics. Partly because of its perceived utility.

Representation vs. Reality

Math has been exceptionally useful in physics. What we require in physics is a good mathematical *representation* of a physical reality so that we can manipulate it and perhaps eventually control it. The key word here is representation.

Mathematics *represents* the reality. It is not the reality itself. And it does not have the same authority.

Anything that can be systematically discriminated—time, space, speed or change can be disassembled and reassembled tautologically, following the patterns of our neural network architecture, by clarifying, refining, and reinvoking the same relationships that held in the initial discriminations.

In such cases math can be made to have application to the real world.

But then the mystique makers take it further. Captivated by the seeming ethereal uniformity of brain-discriminated and created units of representation—their so-called symbolic beauty—many have seen math as existing independently of the human brain that creates it.

The Platonic Romance

Such persons see the elements of math as platonic universals having an existence in the universe independent of humans or anything else. Perfect forms in themselves. Forms themselves existing without substance but strangely applicable to all substance.

It is quite a romance, this platonic math—this math of pure forms. But pure forms are one thing, utility in reality another. The success of math in representing, describing and quantifying the forces and processes of real life physics is quite impressive. It is also understandable.

Dancing Among Arbitrary Discriminations

There is, thus, an inherent duality in our perception of math.

On the one hand, in applying math to physics as well as our daily lives, we are playing back and forth across the patterns of our neural architecture upon our own arbitrary units of discrimination. The fact that the units seem inherent in our neural architecture leads easily to the platonic illusion.

On the other hand, math has proven of great heuristic tool for clarification of the relationships among matter-energy, time-space. This is an accomplishment of substance—not the speculative and highly dubious platonic math of pure and empty form.

Math need not dangle, disembodied and unanchored, devoid of meaning but esthetically beautiful, in empty space. Math can lead us to something of value, some dynamic reality.

But the mystique of math combines the two, the empty speculation as well as the discovery and description of substance. The success of math in quantifying the discriminations of physics has inspired envy and mimicry by the social sciences.

And the social sciences have imported not one but both aspects of the mystique indiscriminately.

MATHEMATICAL MYSTIQUE AND THE SOCIAL SCIENCES

The social sciences have thus become pervaded with mathematics.

Not necessarily meaningful mathematics. But math for the sake of math. Entire journals are dedicated to such exercises. Almost all journals are infected by them. No matter how insignificant the research questions, if the math is presented in good form, the article is almost always judged on just that alone.

The result is an outpouring, an overwhelming cascade of the trivial, transient, and ephemeral. Snapshots in time of shifting, moving, amorphous, and dubious variables with no long term or generalizable significance. Mathematical manipulation of trivia almost totally lacking in social, economic, or political utility. Form without substance.

Appeal of the Nash Equilibrium

Why then has the Nash equilibrium captured the imagination of so many and been so widely called upon?

Because it is expressed in terms of formal math, thus indulging our fascination with mystique? Probably.

But also equally probably because it is innately, subjectively appealing. Why the subjective appeal? What social reality, if any, does the Nash equilibrium connect with that makes it intuitively appealing to us?

If it does connect, we should be able to see its outcomes, its applications. We should also be able to discover the dynamic upon which it turns gropingly in the yet unpenetrated shadows of causality.

Pre-gravity and the Nash Equilibrium

Consider this: we know the cause of the force of gravity. Before we knew the cause and properly described it, we just knew that things fell off other things in an earthward direction. They always fell down. They never fell up, except temporarily when impelled by an identifiable force.

We are still in the pre-causal-gravity-stage of understanding the Nash equilibrium. Nash's formalized artifice seemingly grasps at a social phenomenon—not as clear cut as gravity—but we think we see something like it occurring out there.

We follow Nash through elaborate formal symbolism to try to frame the elusive dynamic—to prove our subjective intuition of its importance and reality. Yet we haven't the foggiest idea of why it does what it does. We have no grasp of the causal dynamic.

Where should we look?

THE CLUES IN THE CONDITIONS, ASSUMPTIONS, AND AXIOMS

Perhaps we should look first at the triad upon which Nash's formalization is based: the conditions, assumptions, and axioms.

These are the givens. They are not to be questioned. They are asserted—the framework that the dynamic must work within to achieve the equilibrium.

But where do they come from?

Anybody's guess. The mathematician doesn't justify them or explain them. Like the first premises of the French renaissance philosopher, René Descartes, they come from intuition or common sense without having to be established or justified.

By postulating the triad, the mathematician, gropingly seeks to see if she or he can corral the intuitive, vaguely apprehended causal dynamics. This approach has heuristic or exploratory value. It can lead to eventual discovery and definition of the causal dynamics. But it is not a very scientific or objectively empirical beginning.

Rather, it is a highly subjective one. Nevertheless, in the conditions, assumptions, and axioms may lay clues to the unarticulated, indeed not understood, dynamic. What are they saying or suggesting about the dynamic—which amorphous unspecified force—they are trying to corral?

THE SOCIAL EQUATION
AS THE CAUSAL DYNAMIC

Nash equilibriums as conceived by John Nash apply to human behavioral interactions.

And Nash's modeling proceeds like standard economic theory on the explicit assumption of rational, self-interest as the primary motive.

Some game theorists have applied Nash's methodology to nonbehavioral situations in such areas as ecology, gene theory, and population biology. Such efforts draw on Nash's formalism, but they tap a different fundamental dynamic. They are at best analogous in form only. They are not and should not be called Nash equilibriums.

Nash equilibriums are always social and the social equation is the dynamic underlying the Nash equilibrium. Without the social dynamic the equilibrium—even the assumption of the equilibrium —would be impossible.

Although entirely dependent on the social dynamic, the Nash equilibrium is not based on a conscious grasp or clearly stated articulation of that dynamic.

EMPATHY AS IMPLICIT
IN THE NASH EQUILIBRIUM

The *essential* condition of a Nash equilibrium is a social exchange relationship. Or a social game as implied and treated by the terminology of formal and mathematical game theory.

And there could be no social exchange without Empathy. Social exchange requires the ability to put oneself in the other's shoes, otherwise one would not be able to appreciate or evaluate the preferences of another.

The understanding and evaluation of others' preferences are essential to a Nash equilibrium. The understanding and evaluation of others' preferences are also fundamental to any concept of Empathy. Empathy, then, is foundational to any concept of a Nash equilibrium.

It appears not to be, only because it is obscured by the formal methodology. We should not be fooled by this.

Empathy: A Foundational,
but Unclarified Assumption

Empathy, then, is a foundational, but unclarified assumption of any Nash equilibrium.

But does it sometimes appear explicitly? Yes, it does.

To see this we must go to the original statements by Nash himself, avoiding some later extensions of his work which in some cases have become so overly formalized as to be totally vacuous abstract exercises.

NONCOOPERATIVE VS. COOPERATIVE GAMES: IMPLICIT VS. EXPLICIT EMPATHY

First we have to look at Nash's distinction between Noncooperative and Cooperative games.

In both games players reach an equilibrium in which no player may improve his/her position as long as other players maintain theirs.

Noncooperative Games

In noncooperative games, no prior negotiation or agreement is assumed. Individual players just act on their own independently.

But don't be fooled. The action inevitably takes place within a *social context*. Without the social context, there is no game. The social context, then, is crucial. Preferences of others must be understood and evaluated.

And besides Nash lays on the requirement of "accepted ethics of fair play"(1951: 294). Fair play means we play by the rules and respect the rights of others. Such is the essence of Empathy. Empathy is implicit but nevertheless clearly required.

Cooperative Games

In cooperative games, prior negotiation and agreement, take place. This is the only distinction between cooperative and noncooperative games.

In the negotiation and agreement of cooperative games, the role of Empathy becomes more obvious. To bargain and reach agreement *explicitly* requires the ability to understand, evaluate, and respect other's preferences, strengths, etc.

Even when the additional condition of enforcement by a referee is added (1951: 295), this represents in itself just another agreement requiring Empathy.

Without the agreements and ethics of fair play—the implicit and necessary Empathy—the structure of both noncooperative and cooperative games, as conceived by Nash, simply collapses.

The games become impossible, except perhaps in the most trivial, inconsequential form. Solutions become random.

THE NAME OF THE GAME: ACCOMMODATING SELF-INTEREST AND EMPATHY

Both noncooperative and cooperative games then involve the estimation and accommodation of self- and other-interest (Empathy).

In fact that's what the game is all about.

Further Examples

Let's take some further examples from Nash's own words.

In an early paper (1950), titled *The Bargaining Problem*, Nash opens with the following statement: "A two person bargaining situation involves two individuals who have the opportunity to collaborate for mutual benefit." (1950: 155).

"Mutual benefit" engages Ego and Empathy. It implies a chance to balance self- and other-interest.

The game further requires equal bargaining skill, full knowledge of each other's preferences, the agreement of the two parties on what is a fair bargain, and both a give (Empathy) and take (Ego) between the two (1950: 159, 161). Empathy is, thus, clearly fundamental in this paper.

In a later paper (1953) called the *Two-Person Cooperative Game*, Nash expands on the bargaining problem. He writes:

The theory presented here was developed to treat economic (or other) situations involving two individuals whose interests are neither completely opposed nor completely coincident. The word cooperative is used because the two individuals are supposed to be able to discuss the situation and agree on a rational joint plan of action....

This statement clearly requires consideration of self- and other-interest and a consent to give and take within agreed rules.

The concept of a Nash equilibrium, as conceived by Nash, thus, rests clearly on the causal dynamic of the reciprocal algorithms of our evolved neural architecture.

In terms of the social equation, a Nash equilibrium is an equilibrium that approaches Dynamic Balance as well as optimizing utilities.

THE SHORTFALLS OF THE GAME MODEL: INHERENT BLINDNESS TO SOCIAL DANGERS

There are several shortfalls of the game model set out by Nash. Most of these Nash himself acknowledged. Some of them characterize almost all mathematical and economic modeling.

Limitations or Shortfalls

Some, but not all, of these shortfalls or limitations are:

1. The modeling is highly idealized. This is openly stated by Nash and is necessary to get where he wants to go with his modeling. Highly idealized means the modeling is divorced from the messy details of reality. It has none of the rich texture of real life situations.

2. It is totally dependent on the stated conditions, assumptions, and axioms. These are not justified but are asserted subjectively from intuition. They are all dubious in reality.

3. It doesn't deal with ongoing change. It fixes a transaction or situation artificially at a moment in time. It can't deal with change except at another artificially fixed moment in time. It can't and doesn't deal with shifting reality.

4. It draws on the causal social dynamic, but doesn't identify it. Further, it falls short of grasping the fullness or significance of the dynamic. Like most transactional analysis in economics, it is incomplete. It misses reality in truly important ways. Listed below are a few of these ways:

a. It assumes the game is complete at the chosen moment in time. It allows for no after effects.

b. It doesn't tell whether the players like their best solutions. The solutions are the best under the extensively stipulated conditions, assumptions, and axioms.

c. It obscures the effects of behavioral tension. If players are dissatisfied, feel cheated, have ambition to do better, and are motivated to change their outcomes, this means that, in reality, the game is not over! The game solution, then, just represents a snapshot in time of an ongoing process.

d. It obscures the cumulative effects of transactions. Given the human capacity for memory and the dynamic of behavioral tension, these cumulative effects are, in reality, potentially very significant.

Blindness to Dangers

The modeling lacks any predictability for cumulative behavioral tension that might motivate change or even revolution to redress the progressive, less than equal or less than dynamically balanced, so-called equilibrium solutions.

The obscuring of the behavioral tension inherent to the dynamic of social neural architecture is the most serious reality flaw in the modeling. The game of the moment is only over for the mathematician or economist who is doing the modeling.

In reality—for the rest of us—the game goes on with cumulative, potentially momentous and dangerous effects. It may even blow up in our faces. The modeling blinds us to the cumulative dangers that may confront us, economically and politically.

PRACTICAL WISDOM VS. OBFUSCATION

In sum, Nash's modeling intuits and rides upon the causal dynamic of the social architecture. It rests upon the social equation.

Subjectivity in the Guise of Formality

Nash, however, has no consciously articulated concept of such a dynamic. He tries gropingly to corral the intuited but undefined dynamic by a formal framework of conditions, assumptions, and axioms mediated by symbols—all largely subjectively based.

As constructed, the entire edifice rests, not upon empirical reality, but upon intuition and subjectivity. Only the mathematical formality gives it unjustifiably the aura of objectivity. It is not objective, but only formal.

By the time all the conditions, assumptions, and axioms are added in to force the solutions, the connection with reality is often very tenuous indeed.

The Utility of Modeling

There is, nevertheless, real utility in such modeling.

It is useful to the extent that it helps us to focus attention, identify alternatives, and to facilitate systematic thinking. In other words, it can be a helpful tool as long as we don't take it too seriously, or endow it and its practitioners with an unwarranted mystique of infallibility.

Of course, the mystique is facilitated and played upon for effect by the entertainment industry which regularly shows actors, representing geniuses, in front of chalkboards full of esoteric mathematical symbols designed to befuddle and awe-inspire the unsophisticated viewer.

PART THREE

APPLICATIONS TO
SOCIETY AND POLITICS

18

THE STIFF UPPER LIP, ORIGINAL SIN, AND WESTERN SCIENCE

In Part Three, I shift from a primary focus on the market and economics to the concerns of sociology and politics. This chapter can, therefore, be viewed as transitional.

THE "SILO" EFFECT OF DEPARTMENTED ACADEMIA

There is, of course, no real separating of the subject matter across the social sciences. Our academic disciplines, our departmented university systems, force artificial divides upon the seamless texture of society as well as their consilient unity with the natural sciences (e.g., Cory 2000: 15; Margulis 1998: 26; Dyson 1999: 2).

These artificial divides produce a "silo" effect, similar to that of the financial sector that so disastrously impacted the subprime economic crisis of 2008 and 2009 (see Tett 2009).

Often this "silo"-ed effect introduces confusion and distortion into an otherwise seamless fabric—splitting it by alternative language, definitions, and concepts that in many cases only say the same things in different ways.

So I will almost inevitably continue to draw upon the themes of economics as I make the transition into the issues of social structure and politics.

THE LARGER CONTEXT

In Chapter 9, I blamed the misrepresentation of Adam Smith on merchants eager to escape the intrusive micromanagement of the mercantilistic bureaucracy. Like all one-dimensional explanations, this was a partial explanation of a more complicated subject.

For a more complete understanding we must look to the larger social and intellectual context. This context was colored by centuries of the Judeo-Christian tradition with its emphasis on the struggle between good and evil.

The Judeo-Christian Tradition: Cosmic Good and Evil plus Original Sin

In the Judeo-Christian Tradition, which dominated the Western world across the centuries from the fall of the Roman Empire to the Renaissance, good and evil were seen as cosmic forces personified as the Deity versus Satan. Central to this dichotomous tradition was the doctrine of original sin. Humans fell to the temptations of evil Satan to be ultimately redeemed by the Deity of goodness.

The Enlightenment: Is Human Nature Good or Evil

As England and other parts of Europe emerged from the tradition-bound Middle Ages into the Enlightenment, the religious dichotomy took on a secular form. The struggle between good and evil was shifted into human nature itself. The big question became: Was human nature good or evil?

As is customary in human affairs scholars split on this issue.

Human Nature as Evil

One stream of thought, in keeping with the Judeo-Christian tradition and the doctrine of original sin, saw humans as evil.

This group was represented in part by the English philosopher Thomas Hobbes (1588–1679) who held forth in his *Leviathan* that men must submit to an absolute ruler in order to control their conflicting, self-interested motives and assure their safety in an orderly society.

Hobbes saw humans as motivated by two forces: self-preservation and the desire for conquest. On this belief, in the absence of an absolute sovereign, Hobbes saw the natural state of humans as a war of all against all.

Human Nature with Good Moral Sense

An alternative group centering around the thought of John Locke (1632–1704) saw humans as having a strong sense of moral obligation as well as self-interest. Based upon his perception of human nature, Locke argued for a limited rather than absolute form of government. Adam Smith, with his dual concept of self-interest and fellow feeling, fell closer to the position of Locke.

But the essential dichotomy prevailed in discussion. Evil was replaced with selfishness; good with morality and altruism.

Into the midst of this controversy was injected the momentous advent of Darwinian theory.

CHARLES DARWIN: SURVIVAL, SELF-INTEREST, AND ALTRUISM

With the publication of Charles Darwin's *The Origin of Species* (1859) seventy years after Adam Smith's death, the one-sided emphasis on self-interest, already running strong, was powerfully reinforced as the dominant view of humankind in the world of capitalism and capitalist economic thought.

Darwin's classic work created an intellectual revolution with its demonstration of evolution based on natural selection—with natural selection interpreted as the bloody struggle of the fittest to survive. His theory influenced almost every area of serious thought and stirred controversy throughout society.

The Misinterpretation of Darwin

Like Adam Smith, Darwin suffered from misinterpretation. "Fittest to survive," in Darwin's view, referred to reproductive success or fitness—the capacity to produce more descendants.

However, the more dramatic connotations of terms like "struggle" and "fittest" were seized upon by some zealous enthusiasts to evoke, in the words of the poet Alfred Lord Tennyson, "nature red with tooth and claw"—the personal struggle to the death for survival among nature's creatures.

This was, original sin—selfishness and self-interest—to the extreme.

Reinforcing Hobbes:
The Rise of Social Darwinism

The bloody tooth and claw interpretation of Darwin certainly reinforced the already prevalent Hobbesian position.

It led to a philosophy called Social Darwinism, which excused all forms of economic exploitation and inequality as the natural and inevitable expression of the law of evolution—"the fittest to survive."

The wealthy were judged as more biologically fit than the poorer classes. Social Darwinism thrived in the latter part of the 19th century as a justification for such excesses of industrial capitalism as sweat shops, slums, and child labor. It was abandoned as an overtly influential school of thought because of its conspicuously negative social effects.

THE MAKING OF "SCIENTIFIC" ECONOMICS

Parallel to the rise of the tooth and claw interpretation of Darwin, the nineteenth century launched the movement to a "scientific" economics.

The Moral Beginning

The academic or intellectual study of economics had previously been a moral enterprise. It was pursued primarily by moral philosophers like Frances Hutcheson, the mentor of Adam Smith, David Hume, Lord Shaftesbury, and Smith himself.

The Move to Newton:
Economics and the Emergence of "Physics Envy"

Economic thinkers, however, who were inclined toward science, had always taken as ideal the model of Isaac Newton's physics and mathematics. Newton represented the epitome of science with his model of a clockwork universe working on immutable laws of physics. The well-known "physics envy" of the social sciences which prevails even today began here.

The Emergence of "Scientific" Amoral Economics

To model their scientific version of economics on physics and math, the "scientific" economists sought to be objective in the manner of physics and quantitative in the manner of math. The normative issue of morals had no place in an objective, positivistic economics bent on aping the success of physics.

Science was considered to be value-free or value neutral. Morals, underpinned by the motives of Adam Smith and other's fellow-feeling and sympathy, were declared unscientific and eliminated from the newly evolving economic calculus.

The Marriage of Induction and Deduction in Economics

The effort to move to a positivist economics involved the marriage of both inductive and deductive approaches. The inductive component required the collection and analysis of sufficient economic data. The deductive component required identifying the mathematical equations that represented the law-like relations of economic behavior.

Induction and Statistics

On the inductive side the emerging discipline of statistics provided the main empirical thrust. British scholars Thomas Tooke (1774–1858) and William Newmarch 1820–1882) set statistics firmly on course by publishing a six volume work titled *History of Prices and the State of the Circulation from 1792 to 1856.*

This work constituted an extensive compilation and systematic ordering of empirical data for the period covered. In 1861, Newmarch commented in an address to the British Association of for the Advancement of Science that economics, by drawing upon empirical, statistical data, had ceased to be an abstract science.

Newmarch further noted that the only safe basis on which we could establish economic laws was not hypothetical deduction but careful collection and analysis of empirical facts. From the standpoint of statistics, however, Newmarch was aware of the difference between the inductive approach and the deductive one of mathematics.

He stated that in statistics there was no body of general laws such as those found in the mathematical and physical sciences. Nevertheless, he viewed statistics as a useful tool for investigating recurring phenomena (1861: 457). This view suggested, of course, that *some* deductive methodology must be applied to make sense of the inductively acquired data.

Deduction: The Jevonsian Utilitarian Approach vs. the Cartesian/Walrasian Approach of GET

On the deductive side William Stanley Jevons (1835–1892) stands out. He is, in fact, considered the father of "scientific" utilitarian economics. The utilitarian approach of the Britisher Jevons is to be distinguished from the French grand Cartesian deductive approach of GET (general equilibrium theory). GET, as represented by Walras, was discussed earlier in chapter 11.

Jevons, as appropriate to his utilitarian perspective, focused not on the grand design of GET but rather on the troublesome, but fundamental issue of defining the concept of utility.

As an accomplished mathematician, Jevons sought to develop the deductive framework that could handle the statistical data produced by the likes of Newmarch.

Jevons: The Conscious Choice to Ignore Morals in Favor of Baser Self-interest

In developing this mathematical framework Jevons made a conscious decision to ignore moral values in his economic analysis. It is important to note that Jevons did *not* deny the existence of caring, moral motives. He simply chose to eliminate them from consideration.

Jevons admittedly felt that the calculus of economics could best be built on the baser or self-interested motives of humans. He chose to give the fellow-feeling and sympathy of earlier thinkers no role in his calculus and focused on self-interest as the sole primary motive.

Jevons' deductive value choice, combined with the inductive emphasis on empirical data, resonated well with others who wished to model economics after mathematics and physics.

Effects and Aftereffects: A Historical Observation

Jevons stated his position in at least two of his publications. In the introduction to his *The Theory of Political Economy* (1888) he provided justification for his decision to exclude the higher moral motives of humanity and to concentrate on the lower self-interested ones in economics. In the same introduction he presented his case for economics as a mathematical science.

In the introduction to his *Essays on Economics* (1905), Jevons drew upon Jeremy Bentham's utilitarian philosophy (see Bentham 1789: Ch I, p. 1). He included all subjective economic forces under the utilitarian doctrine of maximizing pleasure and minimizing pain. This was matched by Freud's roughly contemporary co-opting of the same Benthamite proposition into the pleasure principle of psychoanalytic theory (Freud 1915–1917; 1920).

The All-Inclusive, Hedonic Approach: Obstructing the Interplay of Ego and Empathy

Thinking based on this principle is called the *hedonic approach*. This approach has recently been carried forward and developed by economic Nobelist Daniel Kahneman and associates in their edited volume on hedonic psychology (1999).

The very high level of generalization or integration of the hedonic approach is defensible and virtually inarguable at that particular high level. It has, however, the unfortunate effect of obscuring the dynamic tug-and-pull of Ego and Empathy since both motives can be subsumed under maximizing pleasure. After all, we are wired for both Ego and Empathy and it can, therefore, be considered pleasurable to express or satisfy either or both.

We must, however, drop to a lower level of analysis or integration than the sweeping, all-inclusive pleasure principle to appreciate the interplay of Ego and Empathy and the dynamic shaping effects of that interplay. This provides a striking illustration of a major problem inherent in the levels of analysis (reduction and integration) issue in the sciences. When the level is too high, it loses power to discriminate adequately.

In the case of economics, the effect has been profound. The hedonic level of integration (accompanied, also by the fallacious transition from a self-interest motive to an all-inclusive self-reference perspective as discussed in Chapter 15) does not permit a proper understanding of the dynamic of social exchange or the evolution of the market.

The Hobbesian Victory over Smithian Morality

With Jevons' deliberate value choice to exclude moral motives from consideration, "scientific" economics, thus, moved away from the position held by Adam Smith and adopted, for such "scientific" purposes, a position more consistent with Hobbes. It was, of course, not a truly scientific choice but a subjective value choice of convenience.

The development of the "scientific" school of economics, then, contrary to economic lore still passed on in the standard texts, was based on Hobbes view of human nature, not the view of Adam Smith.

In sum, it was clearly a choice made, not on the basis of science, but on the basis of values, convenience, and the desire to look like physics—to capture part of the reflected glory of that esteemed science.

The Ultimate Denial:
Fallacy in the Making

As frequently happens in the social sciences, what is deliberately excluded from examination comes eventually to be denied in reality.

"Scientific" economists, who followed in the 19th and 20th centuries, seemingly forgot that Jevons did *not* deny the existence of Empathy or higher motives, but rather specifically chose to exclude them to concentrate on what he personally acknowledged to be the baser motive of self-interest.

This post-Jevons transition constitutes, in effect, an instance of the naturalistic fallacy by economists. That is, they made the forbidden leap from value to fact. Jevons had made a value choice to ignore Empathy and morals in "scientific" economics. His followers moved from that value choice to a denial-in-fact of the existence of Empathy as a primary motive in the exchange process.

The effects of Jevon's choice and the associated "forgetting" were to be profound.

The Choice to Ignore Half of Human Nature: Cracks in the Foundation

So-called scientific economics chose to ignore half of human nature in building the foundations of its edifice. The inadequate foundations were, thus, faulty and unstable.

As the discipline moved into the 20th century, it began showing cracks in the faulty foundations. These cracks had to be pasted over—much like the epicycles created to explain "deviant" planetary motions by the Ptolemaic geocentric theorists prior to being swept away by the Copernican Revolution in the early Renaissance.

The Epicylic Patchwork

There are two conspicuous examples of epicyclic patchwork work of the faulty foundations of modern economics.

The first includes the treatment of fundamental empathic motives such as altruism, love, and caring as tastes or preferences, not as the true human motives that they are.

The second egregious epicycle is the extended conceptual fabrication called *enlightened self-interest*. This fabrication was an attempt to justify embarrassingly observable cooperation and other expressions of Empathy in terms of long-term self-interest.

Such examples were created in a vain attempt to hang on to the erroneous sole self-interest motive. The epicycles conceal only poorly the flaws in the self-interest centric perspective of economics.

The Negative Social Side Effects

The negative social side effects of the mistaken perspective are, of course, considerable. They include the encouragement of greed and the promotion of cynicism in society.

When everything is at bottom self-interest, such primary empathetic motives as caring, love, and altruism—the precious foundational motives of the family, the gift, and the market itself—cannot be admitted to be the genuine motives that they are.

They are dehumanized. Such motives must then be the result of fakery, or otherwise trivialized and turned to self-interested purposes. On the other hand, when the duality of the market, the tug-and-pull of self-interested and other-interested (empathic) circuitry is recognized, the flaws in the foundation disappear taking the bad side effects and the epicycles with them.

LOGICAL POSITIVISM
AND RADICAL BEHAVIORISM

The focus on self-interest gained additional allies from two related perspectives that emerged in the early 20th century—logical positivism in philosophy and radical behaviorism in psychology.

Both denied consciousness and subjectivity as valid for investigation by science. The entire focus was to be on externals—primarily on experimental methods applied to such externals that could be repeated in the laboratory.

Although good as far as it went, this focus became much more than just a useful methodology. Again, as in the case of "scientific" economics, researchers came to deny the very existence of what they declined to study.

Stiff Upper Lips and Original Sin

The externalized objective perspective fed into the original sin, tough-minded, stiff upper lipped mainstream of Anglo-American thinking. Science bought it hook, line, and sinker.

Behavioristic psychology, which denied the existence of consciousness or inner mental states, went in lock-step with "scientific" economics, logical positivism, and original sin. The result was an externalized, so-called objective concept of science that denied and tried to divest itself of all things subjective and seemingly soft-headed.

Being hard-headed, tough-minded, and stiff upper lipped meant one must focus on such human attributes as selfishness, fear, aggression, and nastiness in general. And 19th and 20th century science did just that—with a vengeance. Altruism, cooperation, affection, love were softheaded and few stiff-upper-lippers would dare consider them seriously.

THE SELFISH GENE:
ORIGINAL SIN IN BIOLOGY

All the foregoing contributed mightily to a parallel trend in biological approaches, particularly the Anglo-American approach, toward a form of objective negativism. The approach has a detached, self-deprecating, long-suffering quality about it.

Stiff-Upper-Lippers or Autistic Savants?

As previously in this chapter, I have chosen to call this mindset the stiff upper lip approach in acknowledgment of its characteristic Anglo-Saxon ambience. It bespeaks the "too painful to be endured, but I will do so nevertheless." It carries the "I can stoutly confront the difficult truth with head painfully, but resolutely unbowed" demeanor.

The practitioners of this approach were largely attracted to the cold disciplines of mathematics and game theory. They seem to utterly lack warmth in their presentations. They suggest autistic-like savants unable to connect with any emotion except the negatives of fear and aggression. Their pessimistic calculus sees little good in human nature.

Selfish Genes and Bloody Teeth

An example? Without necessarily ascribing all the above attributes to him, British mathematical ethologist Richard Dawkins comes readily to mind. In his negatively titled *The Selfish Gene,* widely read and admired by the hard nosed mathematical game theory community, Dawkins identifies himself enthusiastically with the bloody tooth and claw perspective on evolution (1976: 2).

Early on in *The Selfish Gene*, he writes with true stiff-upper-lippedness:

Be warned that if you wish as I do, to build a society in which individuals cooperate generously and unselfishly toward the common good, you can expect little help from biological nature. Let us try to teach generosity and altruism, because we are born selfish (1976: 3).

Original Sin! The biology version. We are born sinners, worms. Shades of medieval monastic spiritual masochism! But don't dispair totally. As Dawkins notes, we are redeemable, at least in theory, by training and education.

Redeemability and Dilemma

But by whom are we redeemable? And where do their credentials and expertise come from? Following Dawkin's logic, certainly not from the detached-from-human-warmth mathematical scientific community. After all, according to them, we lack the emotional neural substrate from which a sense of morality can be derived.

Who then is to save us? To be the teachers?—the funda-mentalist religious zealots who easily reject the cold logic of the scientific community. Certainly they are eager candidates. Is Dawkins suggesting this indirectly? If so—surely, he can't be serious.

We have a dilemma. How can we achieve what "science" denies we have the capacity for by nature?

The Dawkinsian Fallacy

Fortunately, we can all relax. The dilemma is a false one. Dawkins is simply wrong. Whatever the marketing advantages of such dramatic, socially-misleading titles as *selfish gene*, we will, hopefully, see less and less of such anti-social, fallacious, and inaccurate science in this new century.

Other than being simply wrong on his science, Dawkins commits a glaring fallacy of reasoning in the quoted passage. He reasons fallaciously from gene to gene-created mechanism.

The selfishness he attributes anthropomorphically to the gene, he totally inappropriately extends to the motivated behavior of the phenotype or the individual. There is no logical basis for making this jump. And the empirics contradict him.

The contradictory empirical science comes from evolutionary neuroscience, about which mathematical game theorists and likely Dawkins himself, seem appallingly uninformed.

MAMMALIAN ARCHITECTURE AND BEHAVIOR

In the emerging discipline of evolutionary neuroscience, we to go to the physical source—the evolved circuitry of our mammalian neural architecture. Here we look at what evolution *has* produced, not what we think it should have or could have produced.

We study the structure of the brain through actual physical examination. We code its responses through experiment and observation. The anatomical structure of the human brain can be and has been studied extensively and compared with the brain structures of other mammals and vertebrates.

We also explore with the new imaging techniques the neural sources of Empathy, parental nurturing, social bonding and expressions of fairness and justice. And we affirm the conservation of ancestral vertebrate and warmblooded mammalian circuitry through molecular genetic studies.

Evidence shows clearly that certain behaviors first appeared in fully-articulated, integrated form with mammals and still exist in the mammals we study today. These behaviors are nurturing: nursing, seeking contact comfort, clinging, using vocal signals—a set of behaviors that have been called affectional.

Emergent brain structures were significantly elaborated with the full appearance of these behaviors and are experimentally as well as logically held to be responsible for them. We still have a lot to learn about the interactive detail of brain structure and behavior, but the general features of the wiring diagram are well-established and indisputable.

Brain circuitry and behavior show, above all, that mammals are social animals. Humans, as the most highly evolved mammals, are the most social—and the most dependent on social life.

We humans are born in social groups, live in society, and reproduce in society. And it is obvious that we must have the behavioral equipment to make this possible—that is, our contending behavioral programs of self-preservation and affection, Ego and Empathy, along with the homeostatic rules that govern their operation. This is the dynamic expressed so elegantly by the equation of our social brain.

CONVERGING TRENDS

Parallel to the emergence of evolutionary neuroscience, but running on a separate track, were changes in the perspective of psychology. Such changes included a shift in focus from the externalized perspective of radical behaviorism to the inner workings of the mind. Also significant was the rise of an approach called evolutionary psychology.

Because these are important to the emerging insights into the social and political aspects of society, I will cover them briefly in the next chapter.

19

EVOLUTIONARY NEUROETHOLOGY AND INCLUSIVE FITNESS

A major shift of scientific interest in human behavior emerged in the last quarter of the 20th century. The previously forbidden domain of human cognition and consciousness was opened up to scientific study.

THE COLD WORLD OF COMPUTER MECHANISM: HUMANS AS INFORMATION PROCESSORS

The intrepid few who breached the gates did so, at first, very cautiously. Emboldened by the newly spectacular success of computers, the new researchers adopted the model of information-processing. It was a timid first step, anchored in the safe haven of cold, nonhuman mechanical analogy.

In their view we humans would now become reducible to a mechanical information-processing device.

From this perspective the brain was nothing but a computer, an information processor. And information processing was all that was studied.

Emotions, human warmth and caring, were excluded from the researchable. It was an essentially barren effort that soon exhausted its useful research programs, but it did open the gates to the more adventurous.

ETHOLOGY: THE STUDY OF ANIMAL BEHAVIOR

Parallel to the behavioristic tradition, popular principally in the U.S. and the Soviet Union, the study of animal behavior, called ethology, had been progressing largely in continental Europe.

European ethologists Konrad Lorenz, Niko Tinbergen, and Karl von Frisch won Nobel prizes in 1973 for their pioneering work in the new field. These ethologists did across species comparisons and proceeded from an evolutionary perspective.

They observed and described behavior. They did not, however, look into the black box of the brain and attempt to speculate on neural mechanisms.

EVOLUTIONARY BIOLOGY
TO EVOLUTIONARY PSYCHOLOGY

At the same time evolutionary biology powered by the engine of Darwin's insights proceeded on a track largely isolated from mainstream psychology, whether behaviorism or the more recent cognitive information-processing endeavor.

Despite a few heroic efforts at integration of the biological with the psychological and social sciences, the isolation remained essentially intact.

In the last two decades of the century, the evolutionary perspective and psychology finally hesitatingly married up in what became known as evolutionary psychology.

Evolutionary Psychology, Behaviorism, and the Black Box of the Human Brain

Like the behavioristic psychology before it, evolutionary psychology viewed the black box of the human brain largely from the outside.

It began speculating upon what could be within—that is, what could be there that was passed on in the evolutionary process through our genes.

Evolutionary psychology paid little attention to actual brain structure, but sometimes made elaborate speculations about presumed isolated and dedicated processing modules that dealt with specific environmental challenges that had arisen.

Such modules were likened to a swiss knife, each blade put neatly in place with imaginary precision in the manner of an equally imaginary professional engineer represented by the process of natural selection.

Such improbable speculation proceeded largely unchecked. It was, at times, reminiscent of the pseudoscientific phrenology of the previous century. Phrenology had notoriously sought to identify human characteristics through external examination of lumps on the cranium.

The unwritten command driving evolutionary psychology seemed to be "find a behavior, posit a dedicated brain module." The approach was considerably naïve and open to endless proliferation of imaginary neural components.

EVOLUTIONARY NEUROETHOLOGY

In the broad panorama of science many tracks proceeded independently at varying levels of reduction and integration—and in isolation because of our siloed university system. One of these tracks that moved outside the mainstream of emerging research on neuroscience was the evolutionary neuroethology of Paul MacLean discussed in the opening chapters.

In a sheltered laboratory of the National Institutes of Health, MacLean, a medical doctor, began a research program in the 1950s aimed at understanding evolved behavior through a study of the substrate neural circuitry at various stages of evolution. His emphasis was on certain lizards and lower mammals.

MacLean chose lizards because they resembled most closely the ancestral bridge between ancient vertebrates and mammals. His research program focused upon the neural circuitry underlying behavior with emphasis on emotion—especially those nurturing emotions and motivations that lay at the foundation of mammalian family life and that were apparently lacking in ancestral vertebrates.

MacLean's emphasis on the evolution of emotion was ahead of its time and out of step with the mainstream research in the emergent area of behavioral neuroscience. In keeping with the superficial behavioristic tradition, mainstream neuroscience lacked an evolutionary perspective and focused only on the mechanics of information-processing.

It called itself cognitive neuroscience, acknowledging, in its name, the exclusion of emotion.

When emotion was occasionally studied, it was under the limited, coldly formal information-processing aspect of "learning." When actual emotion was admitted into the chill halls of such science, it was the usual faire of fear, aggression, and human nastiness in general.

Original sin, in sublimated guise, still dominated the paradigm. Stiff-upper-lippers, real he-men, tough guys of science—with some very rare exceptions—didn't study love, nurturing, warmth, caring.

At the close of the twentieth century, the study of emotion, based in part on the long-neglected pioneering work of MacLean, combined with the dramatic efforts of a few dispersed, but bold researchers, seemed at last to gain attention.

The big challenge now seemed to be how the externalized essentially cold-blooded, gene-centered perspective of evolutionary biology and evolutionary psychology could be reconciled with evolutionary neuroscience and the study of the warm-blooded, nurturing side of humanity.

INCLUSIVE FITNESS:
THE GENETIC RECONCILIATION

The conceptual bridge came principally from the work of British scholar W. D. Hamilton.

In his kin selection model, Hamilton (1964) formalized the issue of how genes for cooperation and altruism could evolve and be etched into the human ancestral genome.

The core of this inclusive fitness model is that it weighed the effect of genes not only on the individual that carried them but also on kin individuals who shared the same genes.

Hamilton's Rule

According to what has come to be called *Hamilton's rule*, genes coding for cooperation, reciprocity or altruism could evolve if the costs of cooperative behavior to the individual were outweighed by the benefits to related individuals carrying the same genes.

Hamilton's rule is expressed varyingly as

$$rb - c > 0 \quad \text{or} \quad c < rb$$

In this formula r is the coefficient or degree of relatedness or kin, b is the benefit of the cooperative or altruistic behavior to the kin, and c is the cost of the behavior to the individual.

The equation predicts that as r increases, benefits will exceed costs and cooperation, reciprocity, or altruism would be favored by natural selection.

Hamilton's rule gives the basic formula for inclusive fitness from the external gene's eye view. It shows mathematically how it is possible for such traits as altruism and reciprocity to get into the genome.

The Essential Mechanism

Neither the concept of inclusive fitness nor the formula, however, can predict the mechanism created by the genes to sustain altruism and reciprocity. And, accordingly, Hamilton, displaying no knowledge of neural architecture, did not speculate on the actual nature of such neural mechanisms.

The formula of our social neural architecture derived from the CSN Model, however, expresses this motivating mechanism and establishes linkage with Hamilton's formula.

In other words, the equation deriving from the CSN Model expresses the function of the neural architecture that the genes actually *did* produce under the terms of Hamilton's rule.

The social brain formula can, in fact, be expressed in the same cost/benefit terms that Hamilton uses. Empathy can be considered the cost to the behaving individual, Ego can be benefit to the survival requirements of the recipient. Substituting cost and benefit into the formula, we get the gene-based operational mechanism for Hamilton's rule (see Cory 1999: 97–100).

$$BT = \frac{Benefit}{Cost} = \pm 1$$

Empathy Improves Survival Odds of Self *Plus* Others Inclusively

According to the algorithms of our social neural architecture, *any* empathetic, cooperative, or altruistic behavior will serve to improve the odds of survival of self *plus* others inclusively over purely egoistic or self-interested behavior.

This is compatible with Hamilton's rule which says that as long as the benefit to related individuals exceeds the cost to the behaving individual, the genes supporting such behavior can be favored by natural selection.

From Inclusive Social Architecture
to Love of All via Education and Socialization

Of course, once the neural mechanism, the social architecture, is in place, as it has been for tens of thousands of years, the empathetic or altruistic behavior may be extended to non-kin.

It may even be led to embrace the universe itself—by extending the scale of inclusiveness through appropriate education and socialization. All this extension can be achieved through the cognitive and emotional media that draw upon, modify, and elaborate the existing neural substrate. Such a capacity has been acknowledged by other scholars (e.g., see Buss 1999).

The factor of inclusive fitness, combined with the findings of evolutionary neuroscience of the homeostatic circuitry of the social brain, constitutes the motivated foundations for society as an expression of social exchange.

This dynamic is, of course, represented by the equation of our social brain.

20

SOCIAL EXCHANGE
AND SOCIAL STRUCTURE

From the give-and-take of the family to the give-and-take of one-to-one friendships, groups, communities, even up to nations and beyond—all societies are societies of social exchange.

Wherever and whenever individuals are in social contact there is give and take, or social exchange. The neural substrate for such exchange is the mammalian Ego/Empathy dynamic expressed by the equation of the social brain.

And to the extent that these exchanges are out of balance there is behavioral tension and inequality.

The Social Equation as a Metric
of Sociobehavioral Tension and Inequality

To the extent Ego and Empathy approach Dynamic Balance behavioral tension is reduced and inequalities are likewise. The following form of the social equation mathematically represents such social exchange relationships as they approach Dynamic Balance:

$$BT = \frac{Ego}{Empathy} = \frac{Empathy}{Ego} = \frac{Dominance}{Submission} = \pm 1$$

As the ratio diverges from ± 1 or Dynamic Balance, the equation indexes the behavioral tension in the society. The equation also allows us to conceptualize mathematically the relationship between equality and inequality.

It gives us a framework for estimating the magnitude of inequality and ultimately to quantify it ever more precisely.

SOCIAL STRATIFICATION

Social stratification represents a major concern of sociologists. A truly vast literature expresses the extent of that concern.

Stratification as Structured Behavioral Tension

In terms of our social equation, such institutionalized inequalities represent structured behavioral tension.

Most sociologists, apparently intuiting the tension through the dynamic of their own neural architecture, see the inequality of social stratification as a problem.

Some see it as an *unnecessary* evil based on exploitation of one group by another. Others see it as a necessary evil proceeding from the inevitable division of labor in any society of any appreciable size. Such perceptions are not value neutral, and they are emotionally charged.

For example: Radical institutionalist William Dugger exhibits a frank, emotionally-charged, and clearly normative position on inequality, when he writes:

We can pretend to be value neutral about inequality, but we never are. (1996: 21).

On the other hand, Friedrich Hayek worries normatively, and with evident emotion, about social or distributive justice when he writes:

I am not sure that the concept has a definite meaning even in a centrally directed economy, or that in such a system people would ever agree on what distribution is just. I am certain, however, that nothing has done so much to destroy the juridical safeguards of individual freedom as the striving after the mirage of social justice (1991: 388–389).

Such are the normative variants that our reciprocal brain structure pushes upon us, as Ego and Empathy, self- and other-interest tug-and-pull against each other within our skulls and between us in society.

And such clearly normative, value-bound variants are not dispassionate, but are emotionally charged as is equally clearly displayed in the rhetoric of both Dugger and Hayek. The value, as well as the emotional charge, reflects the behavioral tension that drives the dynamic of the reciprocal brain.

Between Dugger and Hayek: Where Most of Us Belong

Between the extremes of Dugger and Hayek, almost all will agree stratification, with its accompanying inequality, represents a source of tension even when it appears to contribute to stability.

Almost all will also agree that those on the lower levels tend to envy or resent those above and would change the situation given the chance. Likewise those above seemingly empathetically sense this tension and react to defend or rationalize their upper position in the inequalities.

What Any Fool Knows

On the one hand this is common sense. No one, given the choice, would willingly and knowingly choose to be on the short end of a significant or meaningful inequality. This is intuitive—any fool knows it.

Has Evaded Scientific Explanation

Nevertheless, we have never been able to explain it coherently or scientifically by linking it to neural architecture. We have previously intuited or postulated a sense of justice in human nature without a grasp of the dynamic. And we have justified and qualified "what is just" almost beyond recognition based on accommodation to the existing social context.

Social Context vs. Ideal Definition

The CSN Model and the social equation allow us to change that. We now have a dynamic framework that explains the fundamental tension behind the motivation, the associated dislike of inequality, and the desire for social justice.

That dynamic framework is our neural architecture driven by behavioral tension. The rest is contextual and situational.

When social justice is defined contextually, it accepts, reinforces, and justifies the existing social system.

When social justice is defined ideally, it foresees or calls for change in the existing system.

SELF-CORRECTIVE TENDENCY VS. SOCIAL STRATIFICATION

Our neural architecture evolved in small family units where the interpersonal interactions resolved the tension of inequalities.

Evolution of the Fundamental Homeostatic Logic of Equality

The logic of the evolved neural architecture tells us that while most of us will willingly accept some inequality in favor of ourselves, none of us will willingly and knowingly accept *less* than a position of rough equality on all matters of true significance.

The interactive, negotiating exchange process that goes on in small face-to-face family groups driven by behavioral tension tends, homeostatically, to come to Dynamic Balance or rough equality. Even within the family, members will tend to ally with each other to overcome or moderate efforts at domination by one member.

For example, the average dad of today's democratic societies is no match for an alliance of mom and the kids. Lesser developed societies still, however, may block such natural corrective tendencies by restrictive tradition and institutions.

Larger Groups, the Division of Labor, and the Emergence of the Scale of Inclusiveness

In larger groups this self-corrective tendency, historically, became increasingly hampered by the lack of close interaction. Both the distance of interaction and the division of labor contributed to hobbling the self-correcting action demanded by the evolved neural architecture.

Thus was created the scale of inclusiveness.

The Necessity for Rationale: From Ideology to Coercion to Force

Frustration of the neural tendency built socio-behavioral tension in the societies. The resulting inequalities and behavioral tension, then, had to be rationalized or made minimally palatable by institutions or ideology—or, ultimately, maintained by coercion or force.

Socio-political Participation and the Pressures for Equality

The somewhat steady movement toward equality in the overall social exchange system today is propelled by this homeo-statically-regulated self-correcting tendency of our neural architecture. In the United States, as well as other countries around the world, we have seen this tendency expressed in the movements toward equal socio-political participation.

In the United States, following WWII, we saw the emergence and successes of, first, the civil rights movement and then the women's movement. These have been followed by the call for equal rights by gays, lesbians, and other minorities.

Such minorities have been held in unequal states of behavioral tension by institutions, ideologies, or outright force. Their movements emerge, motivated by the pent up tension, as change becomes possible—that is, as institutions, ideologies, and force become weakened, tolerant, or otherwise subject to challenge.

A recent social thinker, Francis Fukuyama, following the German philosopher Hegel, has even gone so far to say, rather prematurely, that with the failure of communism and the breakup of the Soviet Union, Western-style political organization has become the end system of human political history.

The barriers to the natural corrective tendency, reflected in the scale of inclusiveness and other factors, then, will tend to be overcome if the relations among the components of the total social exchange system are permitted to operate freely. For further insight into why this is so, we can look to the evolutionary process of species closely related to our own.

THE INSTABILITY OF
SOCIAL STRATIFICATION
AMONG PRIMATES AND HUMANS

The emergence of evolutionary neuroethology permits new insights into social stratification.

Evolutionary neuroethology combines the study of evolutionary neuroscience with the perspective of evolutionary ethology or the study of behavior across the range of animal species. Like others, it is a Darwinian perspective.

An emphasis on the pervasive presence of social hierarchy or dominance/submissive relationships is a hallmark of the etho-logical approach in animal studies. Paul MacLean pioneered the study of brain circuitry substrating such behaviors.

The term neuroethology, which encompasses the study of both brain and behavior from an evolutionary perspective, captures this combined focus well.

An important insight emerged from these conjoined efforts. Our ancestral vertebrate circuitry common to fishes, amniotes, and reptiles (MacLean's protoreptilian complex or R-complex) which scripted self-preserving, often life and death contests for dominance, became integrated with the attachment or affectional circuitry of mammals.

The Emergence of Social Competition, Alliances, and Hierarchy

This combined circuitry permitted the emergence of social competition—the tug-and-pull of Ego and Empathy that is captured in the CSN Model. Dominance modified by affection leading to cognitively emergent Empathy became possible among higher primates and humans.

Although dominance, without engagement of affectional mechanisms, could still be a life and death, all or nothing contest, hierarchy could now be achieved through alliances, serving and preserving others by engaging affectional circuitry. Submission could be accepted and integrated into the social fabric.

Conflict Resolution and the Instability of Hierarchy

Conflict resolution, as we currently practice it in our behavioral, social, and management sciences, thus, became possible.

Of course, the behavioral tension, motivating the contests remained. The tug-and-pull of self-preservation and affection, Ego and Empathy, persisted latently or covertly to drive later changes in the hierarchy when the supporting contingencies and/or relative prowess of the contestants changed.

Thus, human hierarchies, like those of other mammals and primates, are inherently unstable because of the latent or potential behavioral tension. Depending on the degree of social, economic, or political inequalities, they must be held in place by institutions, ideologies, and/or police or military power.

In other words, social stratification is inherently unstable based upon the dynamic of our neural architecture.

SOCIAL EXCHANGE AS
SOCIAL COMPETITION GOES CLINICAL

Over the past decades there has been a growing, research, theoretical, and clinical literature that proceeds from this neuroethological perspective. Social exchange relationships, intensified by the social imbalances, get out of whack.

They cause behaviors and emotional states that bring us to clinics for help. The reciprocal algorithms and the equation developed from them provide a useful organizing concept for current thinking on hierarchy or dominance/submissive relationships in psychotherapeutic theory.

British psychiatrist John Price (1967) initiated the present effort to incorporate the concept of hierarchy into human psychotherapy from the ethological perspective by introducing his theory of the dominance hierarchy and the evolution of mental illness.

American psychiatrist Russell Gardner (1982) carried the effort forward in his ethological approach to the mechanism of manic-depressive disorder. Other scholars took up the call and contributed to more fully developing the social competition hypothesis of clinical depression.

FROM PSYCHOTHERAPY
TO SOCIAL STRATIFICATION

More recently a British clinical theorist and practioneer, John Birtchnell (1993, 1999) has developed a neuroethological approach to psychotherapy which, in his own words, "grew out of a preoccupation with the concept of psychological dependence." (1999: xi). He went on to tell us that:

The breakthrough came when I realized that dependence had two parts, one to do with getting close and one to do with being lower. Once that became clear, I could see that there had to be other kinds of relating that involved becoming distant and being upper. It occurred to me that being close, distant, upper, and lower must be the only possible ways we could relate. So that was it-everything we do has to involve becoming either close or distant, or upper or lower (1999: ix).

The hierarchical aspect of Birtchnell's theory is easily captured by the basic formula or equation of reciprocal interaction. Since, as a therapist, he focused on dependence in relating, he can be forgiven for not clearly seeing a fifth possibility in relating; that of dynamic equality—although he does allude to it later in his text (e.g., 1999: 14).

Dynamic Balance as Optimum Clinical Relationship

What should be suspect from the formula and the algorithms of reciprocity is that all relating other than Dynamic Balance or rough equality carries a potentially significant load of behavioral tension.

Any equilibrium of such unbalanced or unequal relationships should always be seen as a temporary adjustment on the way to maturity or psychological independence rather than dependence of any variety. This should be important to a therapist who assists clients to achieve more satisfying, less tension-filled, interpersonal relationships.

Clinical Issues as Social Microcosm

The clinical issues are of interest here because they capture in microcosm the issues inherent in social stratification. The clinical syndromes not only reflect the behavioral and emotional tensions of the neural dynamic in interpersonal relationships, they mirror the tensions in society at large.

SOCIETY AS AN OVERARCHING SOCIAL EXCHANGE SYSTEM

Our neural architecture evolved in the extended nuclear family. For millions of years of hominid evolution, before we reached our final species level of *Homo sapiens sapiens* some 100,000 years ago, we survived and evolved as small, kinship or family groups or bands.

The deeply binding interactive dynamic of self-preservation and affection, Ego and Empathy, preserved us from one precarious generation to the other. All aspects of our economic and political lives were bound into the family unit, driven and maintained by the social architecture.

Motivated by deeply felt and powerful affectional reward circuits, we shared with each other and cared for the young, the weak, the handicapped, and the aged. There is growing evidence that higher primates who trace back with us to a common ancestor do the same. The kinship groups were essentially egalitarian. All shared in the power and the economic necessities for survival.

Of Power and Economic Functions from Primitive Family to Modern State

This leads us to a fundamental fact of social organization. In the larger units of modern social organization the power and economic functions of the primitive family have been split. All social units, from the modern family on up, are social exchange units.

Society, at the very top, then, can be viewed as an overarching social exchange system. It occupies the place of the extended family and combines its functions.

A large-scale society like a nation-state has two essential societal level components previously combined in the primitive family unit: an economic exchange system and a politico-legal exchange system.

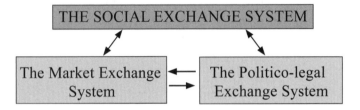

Figure 20.1. The Chart of the Overarching Social Exchange System.

Although the two systems have different jobs or functions, they work together to form the essential character of the society. Both are needed. One can't do the job of the other.

The equation of our social brain helps us to make the distinction as well as recognize the necessity for both. Let's look at the different jobs they do. The market exchange system first.

THE MARKET OR ECONOMIC EXCHANGE SYSTEM

The free enterprise market exchange system operates according to the so-called laws of Supply and Demand. Supply and Demand, as we have seen repeatedly, are not really laws but are an expression of our neural dynamic.

In the market exchange system, however, the neural dynamic or equation is constrained by the definitions of economics.

In economics, *Demand* consists of two elements: (1) *taste* and (2) *ability to pay*.

To be counted among demanders in the market exchange system, then, an individual must have a taste for a certain commodity and must also have enough money to pay for it. The economic definition, thus, excludes all those who may need commodities of necessity, like food, clothing, shelter or health care, but who lack the money to buy them.

The poor or needy, then, whether they desperately need essential commodities, or even clamor vociferously for them in street demonstrations, are excluded from the economic concept of Demand. That is, economists simply don't count them anymore. They drop out of the equation.

The concept of Supply is similarly constrained in the market exchange system. Suppliers, likewise, must meet two requirements: (1) they must be *able to sell* and (2) they must be *willing to sell*.

The ability to sell means, of course, the suppliers must be able to cover their costs of production and supplying or else they would soon go out of business. They also must be willing to provide at the prices available. Sometimes they may be willing to sell at a loss for short periods to avoid further losses, but they can't go on doing so forever because they will be forced out of business by the very structure and definitions of the market system.

The constraints of the economic definitions of Demand and Supply place limits on what the free enterprise market exchange system can do. It may produce a vast number of commodities— more than not-free systems—but it may still fail to meet the actual needs of the society. By its very structure and definitions, then, the market intrinsically may fail to meet all the needs of the society.

In fact, historically speaking, there has never been a free market system that has, without assistance, met all the needs of society. Even the best free market system, operating on its own defined principles, has failed to eliminate poverty and social deprivation. This takes us to role of the politico-legal exchange system.

THE POLITICO-LEGAL EXCHANGE SYSTEM

The politico-legal exchange system (hereinafter largely referred to as the political system) requires a different set of definitions. It must respond to the overall social exchange system.

Countering Market System Failures
Balancing Out the Social Brain Equation

In response to behavioral or social tension, the political system must act to counter failures or limits of the market system. It must balance out the social brain equation over the entire overarching social exchange system like the primitive family did over evolutionary history.

Social Demand vs. Economic Demand

Demand in the political system may appropriately be called *social Demand* as opposed to *economic Demand*.

And the definition is different. Social Demand contrasts with economic Demand on the two elements of its definition. In social Demand *taste* becomes *need*. The second element *ability to pay* is dropped. It may be replaced by *willingness and ability/disability to work* or simply, in a truly humanistic society, by presence in the community.

Complementing and Balancing
The Market Exchange System

The political system, then, complements the market exchange system and ideally balances out its failures.

The political system must readjust, by taxation, subsidy, or other method, the imbalance or failure that is an inevitable outcome of the market exchange system as defined.

Fulfilling the Charter
of the Primitive Family

Ideally, the political system fulfills the charter of the primitive family in which the neural dynamic evolved.

It cares for the unemployed, the handicapped, the aged, and others who lack the ability to qualify in the Demand definition of the market exchange system.

Civilized societies, responding to the interactive dynamic of Ego and Empathy, cannot afford to allow their citizens to lack the necessities of life. The behavioral tension created by the market failures drives this corrective action.

With Caution

Of course, for its part the political system must exercise great caution and prudence to avoid stifling the creative energy of the market system while correcting the inevitable failures, distortions, or imbalances. It is a challenging and often precarious balancing act.

Graphing and Grasping the Challenge

The equilibrium curve of Chapter 12 may be used to illustrate the essential challenge in easy to grasp terms.

Assume the equilibrium graph to represent the total social Demand for an item of necessity. This means, as a simple example, that there are six (billion, if we include the world population) items of necessity and six (billion, if world) persons comprising the society.

Under the concept of economic Supply and Demand the three items above the equilibrium point as well as the three items below the point are dropped out of the picture.

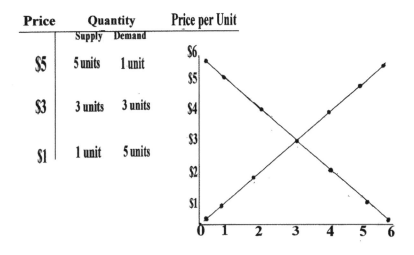

Price	Quantity		Price per Unit
	Supply	Demand	
$5	5 units	1 unit	
$3	3 units	3 units	
$1	1 unit	5 units	

The market is said to clear. All those who have the taste and ability to buy have been supplied by those able and willing to Supply. That is, we have a perfect market! It sounds great, but it is misleading.

SOCIAL DEMAND AND EXCESS PRICE

Viewed from the perspective of social Demand, things are not so good. In fact, we have a serious problem.

Assuming the excess Supply above the equilibrium point will go away or simply not be produced may get us out of difficulty on the Supply side.

But what about the three (billion?) items which represent items of necessity to three (billion?) social Demanders or citizens? Their essential needs go unmet. As a result we have substantial inequity in the market and substantial socio-behavioral tension.

Will these three, or say three billion, persons demonstrate in the streets, commit crimes, initiate an insurrection expressing this tension? Or will they instead appeal to the political system for redress to this imbalance in necessities of life? And will the political system respond? Whatever happens, we have socio-behavioral tension to deal with because of the market failure.

The social equation indexes this tension. The ratio between what is supplied in the market and social Demand is 6/3 or a behavioral tension magnitude of 2. The market in this case has met just half of the social Demand. From the perspective of the overall social exchange system, we have to deal with the behavioral tension magnitude of 2, which translates numerically into half of its citizens going without a necessity.

To further clarify things, we may introduce the term *excess price* to describe the difference between the market equilibrium price and the price we must reach to fulfill the social Demand of 6. According to the graph, a price of about $0.25 would satisfy the social Demand. Anything above that would be excess price.

So how do we get the price to that point? As a civilized society we cannot tolerate the socio-behavioral tension in the situation—that is, we cannot allow half or, for that matter, any of our citizens to go without necessities.

But we can't ask suppliers in the market system to lower the price below their ability to recover costs. The suppliers would go broke. In effect we would destroy the market.

So what do we ask of our political system?

Essentially we have two options. We may subsidize the supplier or give aid to the demander. That is, for example, we have the choice of industry subsidies or welfare payments and food stamps. Our political exchange system has been known to use both.

The equation of our social brain quickly reveals the problem as we shift from necessities to non-necessities under the contrasting definitions or constraints of the market and the overall social exchange system.

MARKET STANDARD FOR NON-NECESSITIES? SOCIAL STANDARD FOR NECESSITIES?

To satisfy the discrepancy or behavioral tension that exists between the market exchange system and the overall social exchange system, we must act politically.

We must, perhaps, apply the market standard or set of definitions to non-necessities and the social standard or set of definitions to necessities. We already do this in a fuzzy sort of way in the United States. Some of the European free enterprise societies do it much more self-consciously.

THE PREDICTIONS OF THE SOCIAL DYNAMIC

The dynamic of our neural architecture predicts that to the extent that the two subsystems—the market system and the politico-legal system—interact freely, behavioral tension and inequalities within the society will *tend* to Dynamic Balance.

Necessary Conditions

This condition of freely interacting can best be met in an open, fully participatory, and inclusive political society combined with a free enterprise market exchange system.

In such a freely functioning society the limitations or failures of the market exchange system will tend to be corrected in the politico-legal system. That is: when the market fails to produce or distribute adequately or when businesses show excessive greed or corruption, citizens will demand counteraction through legal or political processes.

A Major Challenge of an Open Society: Preventing Undue Interference or Obstruction

A major challenge facing an open, fully participatory, inclusive society is to keep the interactions between the two key systems free of undue interference or obstruction.

In the US, this is what intuitively drives most government regulation of business. It conspicuously drives such movements as campaign finance reform—which aim is to correct attempts to interfere with the normal self-corrective tendency via the political system by those holding greater power in the market system.

In sum, the inequalities generated in the market exchange system will tend, driven by behavioral tension, to be corrected in the political exchange system if allowed to work without interference. In the overarching social exchange system, then, driven by the behavioral tension of our neural architecture, things will *tend* to balance out.

INCENTIVES, PRODUCTIVITY, AND BEHAVIORAL TENSION

If there is one thing we learned from the experiments in socialism in the twentieth century, it is that incentives are required for a highly productive economy.

The varying of incentives, of course, means the creating of inequalities. This exploits the fundamental expression of our neural architecture.

We don't like inequalities. And we will strive to alter or overcome them in our own favor or at least to the point of rough equality.

Such is the engine of social competition in both the market and political sub-arenas. It is the engine that drives our free market system. It works for us.

But there are dangers to the system when the tensions or inequalities permitted for production become excessively cumulative and extreme. Our society becomes unstable. The economically or politically disenfranchised, or excluded, become motivated to change—through crime, riots, and other forms of disobedience and violence.

Ideally, to avoid excessive behavioral tension which translates into social unrest, the inqualities necessary to incent a free market economy should be held within the range approaching Dynamic Balance. Also, like the moment-by-moment, day-by-day tug-and-pull of the Ego and Empathy circuitries, the inequalities should be temporary and shifting.

If both conditions hold, the behavioral tension or inequality will be neither extreme nor cumulative in its effects. And if the market exchange system and the politico-legal exchange system are allowed to interact and self-correct freely, the overall system driven by behavioral tension will *tend* to Dynamic Balance.

Social institutions and practices which impede this self-corrective tendency—like undue influence by powerful special interest groups—will skew the dynamic to the extremes and create behavioral tension and inequalities in the society.

This, of course, translates into social discontent and unrest. The behavioral tension underlying the discontent motivates efforts toward social change in the direction of a better balance.

21

THE POLITICAL CHOICES OF THE SOCIAL BRAIN

The studies of political science and economics largely went their separate ways until recent decades.

However, a renewed emphasis on political economy reflected a change in that state of separation. It is based upon the perceived underlying unity of the political and economic sides of social life.

Although not well-defined as a subject matter, political economy logically emerges at the point on a spectrum at which the disciplines of political science and economics, coming from differing perspectives on social life, flow into each other or converge. At this point there is occurring an exchange or blending of theory and methodology.

RATIONAL CHOICE
BECOMES PUBLIC CHOICE

Indicative of this convergence has been the importing of self-interested rational choice theory into political science under the rubric of public choice. Despite the advantages of uniform theory and methods bridging the two disciplines, there is also a downside.

Importing Preexisting
Problems and Distortions

The preexisting problems and distortions are carried from economics into the public choice literature based upon the self-interest emphasis and the failure to recognize the reciprocal nature of all exchange and choice. An excerpt from an introductory text on public choice is sufficient to illustrate this claim:

> . . .chaos and anarchy do not exist in the economy. The daily . . . tasks of feeding, clothing, housing, transporting, and entertaining the population are accomplished without fanfare or centralized control. The source of this order is individual *self interest* (emphasis mine) channeled by competitive Supply and Demand incentives (Johnson 1991: 53–54).

This excerpt (and similar ones can be selected from almost any text or monograph), with its emphasis on self-interest, obscures the fact that the market operates in a pervasive social context and the ordering principle is not self-interest but is, instead, reciprocity.

There is an entire community, nation, or world out there stating its egoistic Demands or wants, which are indexed by the price mechanism. A supplier or businessperson looks at this egoistic demand or want indicator of price and decides how much or what empathetic services or products she/he will produce or perform for provisioning or responding to this demand.

The businessperson then fulfills the empathetic, nurturing, or provisioning side of the economic equation, fulfilling the egoistic demands of the individuals grouped into the concept of market. She/he then receives payment in reciprocal acknowledgment to his/her own egoistic demands or needs—and the reciprocity is complete.

The ubiquitous equivalent reciprocal of *thank you* and *you're welcome* is always there. The mechanism is reciprocal because if the community, nation, or world were not out there, the businessperson would simply not provide.

True, given the scale of inclusiveness, the market as described is impersonal and rarefied. Therefore, subjective feelings of Ego and Empathy may be weak to almost nonexistent. Nevertheless, the reciprocal algorithms of behavior are clearly the driving source of the market mechanism—not self-interest alone as claimed by the prevailing market theory and set out as gospel by economic, rational choice, and public choice texts.

Market or exchange theory, as it exists today is inaccurate, distorted, and has the unfortunate side effect of promoting self-interested egoism, Social Darwinistic propensities, and cynicism throughout the society. It does so by failing to understand and grasp the empathetic nature of the provisioning required to fulfill the equation.

Legitimacy: The Reciprocal Relation of Political Unit and Citizen

In political science one of the most important issues is that of legitimacy—the question of how people are bound into a political community—a local, national, or even worldwide identity.

Patriotism and loyalty illustrate that Empathy, with its roots in affection, accompanies identification with the political unit, community, nation, or perhaps world, as kin, as benefactor, as provider of safety and services.

In keeping with the algorithms of reciprocity, when the political unit provides, the citizens reciprocate Empathy, attachment, identity, loyalty. It would be easy to obscure these essential issues of politics within a self-interested, rational choice model.

FROM CONFLICT TO RECIPROCITY:
THE IMPLICATIONS FOR NEW INSTITUTIONS

The reciprocal algorithms of behavior prescribed by our evolved brain structure show us how to get from conflict to reciprocity by the balancing of our self-interested and empathetic programming.

These algorithms of reciprocity have been shown to be the guiding dynamic of social organization and exchange. What then do they require of us in building new institutions and behaviors to accommodate self-consciously, in a more enlightened manner appropriate to the new millennium, their inevitable dynamic?

Orienting Political Science

First, I would point out the implications for orienting the discipline of political science.

Although it has stirred controversy and cleavages, there is no question that the rational choice model of economics and exchange theory, under the rubric of public choice, has become the dominant model in political science (Bates 1997, Johnson 1997, Lusick, 1997).

After several decades of effort, however, the judgment on the ultimate contribution of the public choice is quite diverse and qualified and there has developed an active discussion for a more pluralistic approach to political science research (cf. Schram & Caterino 2006; Buchanan 2003; Flyvbjerg 2001; McQuaig 2001, Green & Shapiro 1996).

By adopting the alternative model presented here, political science connects with evolutionary neuroscience, as well as avoiding the negatives, the moral discomfort and criticism that have plagued the overly self-interested economic and exchange theory models.

It also gains a heuristic that can better account for such important political phenomena as loyalty, commitment, and the shifting involvements of private interest and public action (e.g., Hirschman 1982).

Finally, the model shows the moral basis of exchange and choice which is increasingly important to our society, and avoids the implicit and troubling academic endorsement and propagation of a one-sided self-interested egoism in public affairs.

And hopefully, with the dethroning of unmitigated self-interest by the appropriate acknowledgment of the balancing role of Empathy, the last vestiges of Social Darwinism will begin to fade from our social, economic, and political thought.

Even Kenneth Arrow, Nobel prize recipient and the acknowledged creator of social choice theory, has commented in an oral history interview:

People just do not maximize on a selfish basis every minute. In fact, the system would not work if they did. A consequence of that hypothesis would be the end of organized society as we know it (Arrow in Feiwel 1987: 233).

This position is increasingly recognized in the new institutional economic literature although no effective model to account for it has yet been devised. For other examples, see also Raymond Plant's article on the moral limits of markets (1992) and Lars Udehn (1996: esp., pp. 60–114).

And economist Thrainn Eggertsson of the University of Iceland refreshingly and candidly puts it in terms that match those used here when he writes:

A society where everybody behaves solely in an *egotistical and cold-blooded* (emphasis mine) fashion is not viable (1990: 75).

It is further interesting that Eggertsson, intuitively, as most of us do since we all share similar brain structures, associates egotistical with cold bloodedness—our protoreptilian or premammalian heritage. Our mammalian heritage gives us warm bloodedness, nurturing, the capacity for cooperation, trust—and the warmth and comfort of friendship.

Now that we can more clearly see the natural state of humankind, proceeding from our evolved brain structure, we can proceed to more self-consciously and intentionally construct our institutions and conduct our behaviors within these institutions to exploit these insights.

Concerning our domestic institutions and behavior, the reciprocal algorithms of behavior driven by behavioral tension, are the foundation of all social organization. They prescribe that such institutions in their structure and methods of operation should facilitate the give and take, the reciprocity, among the citizenry. Such reciprocity allows the expression of the tension between self- and other-interest as it tends toward balance. It is noteworthy that the findings from brain structure, gene theory, and ethology reported in this book support the emphasis on Empathy, cooperation, and altruism by scholars in economics, social and political science (e.g., Mansbridge 1990; Etzioni 1988; Frank 1988; Hirschman 1982; Margolis 1982).

The facilitation of such reciprocal expression should begin early, especially in our socially critical educational institutions, and it should permeate the socializing curricula throughout the education process.

This means such institutions must respect and facilitate both dynamic aspects of our makeup. They must preserve and facilitate the freedom to express our Ego, our self-interest, our individuality, in the form of self-expression, productivity, and creativity.

And they must also facilitate and cultivate our expressions of Empathy, relatedness, and social responsibility.

The proper balance of the two means that individual self-interested creativity and productivity is performed empathetically in the process of social exchange as a gift or contribution to society.

Creativity and productivity in fact make no sense except as a gift or contribution to be shared with others—with society. Said another way individual creativity and productivity invariably have a social context.

The Biological Source of
Liberty vs. Equality Tension

This tug-and-pull between Ego and Empathy, self-preservation and affection, is the biological source of the tensions between our values of liberty vs. equality that so pervade our modern thinking.

As we saw in the contrasting positions of Dugger and Hayek (Ch. 20: 192). The innate dynamic, that we all share and strive to articulate, divides well-intentioned scholars into opposing camps depending on which derived value, liberty or equality, they feel most strongly about, and their assessment of the means by which we can best achieve the most socially desirable balance between the two.

Although liberty and equality need not theoretically be in conflict, this is an issue with deep divisions in current thinking. Total liberty would seem inevitably, even on an ideal level playing field, to involve some inequality, because of innate individual differences in intelligence, skills, talents, energy, and/ or developmental factors of health, age.

Total equality would likewise, seem inevitably to involve some suppression of liberty, because it would, inhibit or redistribute the advantages gained through the same innate and developmental factors.

THE NEURAL DYNAMIC:
SHAPING OUR POLITICAL CHOICES

The dynamic, shaping forces of our neural architecture expressed as the reciprocal algorithms and the related equation set the fundamental political options open to us.

First, is the *egoistic* option by which we pursue self-interest relentlessly, with all our physical and psychological energies. To the extent that we pursue this option, according to our reciprocal algorithms, the ultimate product would be a physical as well as a psychological world filled with the tension and conflict of our contending behavioral forces, internally within each of us and externally as inequities in society. Only force would prevail to control the conflict.

This world would require an imposed authoritarianism in the nature of Hobbes' *leviathan* to which we surrender power in the face of coercion—whether in fascism or some other form of totalitarian statism.

Second, is the path of *self-sacrifice* along which we surrender our selves to the primacy of others in the form of a subordinated collectivism. The ultimate result would be an absorption of self, a loss of identity, in the identity of others. This, too, according to the reciprocal algorithms of our behavior, produces a physical and psychological world of tension and conflict in which some dominate and some submit. This, too, would be a path toward a collective form of oppression.

The alternative option is the pursuit of *Dynamic Balance* of self with others. Physically and psychologically, this path leads to a partnership in unity. Here, tension and conflict may be limited and managed, if not fully resolved, in a free and full interplay of Ego and Empathy, self-preservation and affection, acceptance of self and others—a unity in diversity inclusive of all humankind.

We do not yet have a full and proper definition or concept of such a system, but it would surely include the essentials of free choice (freedom) and fundamental equality.

Our brain was structured for such choices. And the possible range of socio-political choices are set by our evolved brain structure. These again can be expressed by the CSN Model of our neural architecture.

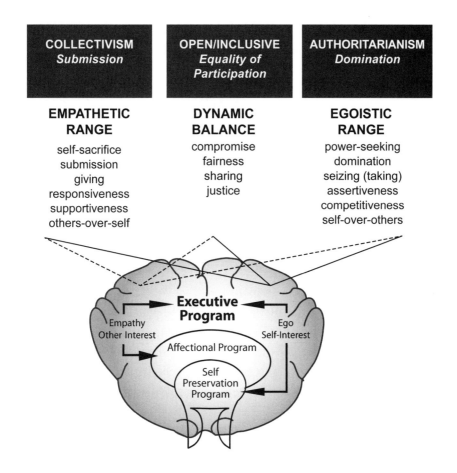

Figure 21.1. Socio-political Options Set by the Reciprocal Algorithms of Our Neural Architecture.

Falteringly, the innate dynamic seems to be moving us generally in the direction of the center option. Academia sometimes leads, sometimes obscures this process.

For example, concerning the world situation, the late Kurt Steiner, emeritus professor of political science at Stanford University, in discussing his study on the Tokyo war crimes trial, pointed out that the overwhelmingly predominant paradigm in international relations theory today is the so-called realist theory.

This theory has a Hobbesian concept of conflict and power at its core. As a result of this paradigm the study of international law has all but disappeared from the political science curriculum in America.

This myopic focus on power alone obscures the considerable progress made since World War I in limiting sovereignty in cases of human rights and crimes against peace and in the growing significance of international organizations.

At the turn of the 21st century, we had a former head of state, Slobodan Milosevich, brought before the international court at The Hague. The movement has become so strong that the United States, in its role as principal international peacekeeper, has insisted upon exemption of its military personnel from the court's jurisdiction. The leaders of other rogue states also face the possibility or threat of being brought before the court of international justice.

In more recent years, a reaction to the realist approach has set in. A main thrust comes from feminist thought that emphasizes a more empathetic, idealistic, and transformational approach to counter the raw power egoism of the realists (e.g., see Ackerly, et al. 2006). The continued expansion of these academically neglected phenomena in international relations, despite the prevalent "realist" paradigm, indicates that the tug-and-pull of Empathy vis-à-vis Ego (power) is alive and well and that Empathy and cooperation invariably are invoked as counters to excesses of power.

THE NECESSITY FOR A FRAMEWORK OF POWER AND AUTHORITY

In our political thinking, however, we must remember, that polar swings between Ego (power) and Empathy (cooperation) are misleading. The extremes produce socio-behavioral tension and leave us vulnerable.

The tug-and-pull dynamic of our neural architecture dictates the necessity for Dynamic Balance in socio-political as well as market operations. An ordered society, to include international society, must, therefore, have a framework of power and authority. Given our dual motive neural architecture, anarchy has never worked historically and is not an option for the future.

That is why the *type* of power structure (Figure 21.1) is so important. The *type* of power structure *formalizes* the structural behavioral tension (inequalities) of the system. Within that structure the tug-and-pull of the reciprocal architecture goes on within and among individuals, groups, and organizations.

The power structure either suppresses, distorts, or allows the relatively free venting or expression of this tension.

As we absorb the horror and the threat to human life of a total reliance on power, we are perhaps, stumblingly, but relentlessly, moving in the direction of choosing a more balanced, reciprocal path between Ego and Empathy, not only in our domestic society, but also in our international social and political relations.

The equation of our social brain provides us with a mathematically expressed index whereby we can estimate our progress toward a dynamically balanced political system. Such a system can be best expressed as an increasingly open, inclusive, participative, and freely functioning system.

As the ratio between dominance and submission increases to the extremes, we approach one of the fascist or collectivist alternatives fraught with socio-behavioral tension. As we move progressively toward Dynamic Balance or approximate homeostatic equilibrium we become increasingly open and inclusive.

$$BT = \frac{\text{Domination}}{\text{Submission}} \text{ or } \frac{\text{Submission}}{\text{Domination}} = \pm 1$$

Our institutions of open, inclusive participation and economic upward mobility, although until now lacking a satisfactory scientific foundation, implicitly recognize the instability of imbalance between Ego and Empathy, dominance and submission.

At a minimum, they allow institutional vents for the behavioral tension, promoting social stability amidst social change. At best they lead us toward a minimizing of social and political inequality in a transformational direction for domestic as well as global socio-economic political organization.

THE HISTORICAL VIEWPOINT

The entire story of human society, economics, and politics can be seen as the expression of the tug-and-pull of the alternatives presented us by our brain structure. At this point in history it seems to have a circular or returning quality about it—shall we say a *dé jà vu*?

Scholars mostly agree that our species began in small egalitarian foraging bands some probable 100,000 years ago. We continued to live in such generally equal conditions until sometime about 10–12,000 years ago (e.g., see Knauft 1991, 1994).

Human political life begins with the nuclear family. But what we usually think of as the political aspect becomes more clearly expressed in the increasingly larger social units of bands, tribes, chiefdoms, and ultimately nations.

In the larger social units the empathetic scale of inclusiveness thinned out, and with the increasing division of labor, small, normally self-correcting differences become amplified into significant wealth and power inequalities. The naturally, self-corrective tendency of our neural architecture became blocked or stymied by multiple contingencies and at multiple levels.

The dynamic, and the associated tension, do not go away, however. They remain locked in states of varying tension by customs, ideology, institutions, and coercive power.

In the Western world we emerged through the theocratic absolutism of Egypt and Mesopotamia to the early return to relative egalitarianism in Greece. Then we passed from republican

Rome through the imposing hierarchical, yet all-inclusive power of Imperial Rome.

With the fall of Rome we entered the somewhat chaotic Middle Ages dominated by the contesting powers of theocratic church, feudalism, and, eventually, emerging new states.

Entering the Renaissance we saw the self-conscious rebirth of egalitarian ideals from the Greek world. Society opened, institutions loosened, power relaxed sufficiently to permit the self-corrective tendency of social architecture to emerge into open discussion. In America, especially, these ideals expressive of our dynamically balanced neural architecture burst forth in fullest political expression.

Driven from their homelands by the social tensions of hierarchy and inequality, the early European settlers spread out into a sparsely populated continental expanse with no all-pervasive pre-existing customs, institutions, or ideologies to block the natural expression of human brain structure.

In some cases, the bands and tribes of the Native Americans provided reinforcing examples of egalitarian lifestyles. The last century especially has marked the dramatic struggle between the dynamically balanced participatory ideals and the extremes of authoritarianism and collectivism.

The extremes simply don't work in an open human society. They suppress one or both of the primary dynamics of our social brain. In doing so, they create the behavioral and social tensions that lead to their own ultimate demise.

As a young person, I pondered in awe the seemingly vast scale of human civilization. A 5000-plus years of recorded human history! It seemed an eternity. Now, as I approach my eighties, I marvel at the exceedingly brief span.

How young we still are! Hardly, my own age multiplied by itself! That is, my own age squared—to the second power. The length of our recorded history is captured by a most elementary of mathematical operations—eighty times my own approaching age of eighty.

And our brain has not changed much in the past 100,000 years. For over 90 percent of this time we lived—driven by our evolved neural architecture—as essential egalitarians.

Now, after a brief 5000-year interlude, we face planet-wide globalization, with our new technologies bringing virtual face-to-face communication and powers of mutual destruction. We now replicate on a large scale the conditions of our overwhelmingly predominant history.

In the virtual face-to-face interactions, as in the earlier nuclear family and kinship bands, the interactive dynamic of our brains drives us toward resolution of our relative differences in essential equality or Dynamic Balance.

AND TO THE FUTURE

As we move into the future, the same choices face us as before. This time, however, we confront them in the self-conscious maturity of our species. As now customary, thinkers emerge to express the variable options provided by our neural architecture.

On one side, as I review much of the so-called leftist literature, I see increasingly detailed prescriptions offered to achieve the essential equality we desire. Such detailed prescriptions—well-intended though they may be—would require bureaucratic invasion of privacy and freedom on a massive scale.

The dynamic of our neural architecture will never tolerate the ultimate collectivist authoritarianism such invasiveness would eventually lead to. The cumulative behavioral tension would provoke repression, responded to by growing resistance—and, eventually, probable social upheaval.

On the other hand, the radical "hands off" idealizations of free market and political libertarians would lead us ultimately to a society of increasing inequality as the self-corrective tendency of our social architecture is blocked and frustrated by the exercise of cumulative differentials of wealth and power.

The trick, of course, is in the Dynamic Balance—the ever illusive, never quite satisfactory state of shifting homeostatic equilibrium.

In the frustratingly indeterminate, groping process by which we self-correct, pragmatics not ideology must be the rule. Pragmatically and situationally, we may place shifting and variable limits on the market and on the politico-legal system as well—to correct the inevitable instances of failure in both. We must also prevent one from overwhelming or swallowing up the other, lest the corrective balance be lost.

There will be no final answers in a process that, by its very nature, takes us back and forth between conflict and reciprocity as it gropes for a Dynamic Balance of our inner motivations as well as their expression in our socio-political institutions.

22

THE NEURAL DYNAMIC IN CHINESE POLITICAL AND MARKET THOUGHT: CAN EAST MEET WEST?

Gerald A. Cory, Jr.
Yau-Gene Chan
Jin (Helen) Luo

The previous two chapters examined the relation between the political system and the market system as viewed from the reciprocal algorithms of our neural architecture. The primary focus was on the perspective of the Western world.

In any quest for a model suitable for globalization, however, we must find a commonality or accommodation with other major cultures. None is more important than that of China.

This jointly authored chapter, accordingly, explores the common basis between the Western and Chinese viewpoints with the participation of two scholars familiar with the latter tradition.

And it considers a crucial question confronting globaliztion.

Can East meet West?

The answer to this question is especially important to the issue of compatibility in market and political thinking so fundamental to global unity.

THE HISTORICAL AND CULTURAL EXPRESSION OF EGO AND EMPATHY

Historically, the dual motives of Ego and Empathy have expressed themselves pervasively in Western thought and practice (Cory 2000, 2010). The beginning question, then, becomes: Do the dual motives of Ego and Empathy express themselves as pervasively in Eastern thought and practice as represented by China?

Although we can touch only briefly on this broad subject in this single chapter, the answer is unequivocally, yes. The neural dynamic has been expressed in Chinese thought and practice for several millennia.

Confucius

The neural dynamic can be seen at work in the writing of Confucius (551–479 BCE). Confucius claimed that the just order for society sprang from the character and virtue of the prince and his subjects.

The ideal ruler, expressing Empathy for subjects, was just in behavior. The ideal subjects, receiving this affirmation by the ruler of their Ego demands for security and just treatment, reciprocated loyalty and obedience in return. The result was a harmonious society.

Confucius introduced the ideas of *li,* meaning rules of conduct, and *ren*, meaning agape or benevolent love. These two, proper conduct and benevolence, working together in accord with the neural dynamic, produced justice and social harmony in practice.

Mencius

Mencius (c. 372–c. 298 BCE), a later follower of Confucius, believed that one could govern the entire world easily based upon the principle that is common to all mankind—that one cannot bear to see others suffer. Mencius held the feeling of distress at the suffering of others to be the first sign of humanity. This, of course, amounts to the emergence of Empathy.

He further said that every child in his mother's arms knew about love for his parents. Such love, extended first as love and respect to elders, ends with one having love and respect for everyone (Mencius, 1970 [298 BCE]; cf. Shun, 1997: 145–146). This reflects not only the interactive dynamic of Ego and Empathy but an intuition or appreciation of the scale of inclusiveness.

Mencius, then, saw the origin of justice in society as stemming from love and respect for others. This is, in effect, the balance of self and others, Ego and Empathy. Mencius seems to have intuited the dynamic of the neural architecture rather well.

THE NEURAL DYNAMIC IN WARLORD CHINA: AN OVERVIEW

Let us now take a look at the neural dynamic in historical practice. We begin in a period when the homeostatic balance breaks down allowing us to do comparison and contrast most definitively.

The Nature of Standard Warlord Rule

In the 1920s through the 1930s, China's governmental rule was dominated by regional military rulers, or Warlords. Warlords themselves, in this period, were generally concerned only with maintaining or increasing their power and increasing their personal wealth at the expense of the Chinese citizens.

The most tragic characteristic of warlordism was the oppression, injury, and hardship that it inflicted on the Chinese people. During the warlord era there was little constructive governmental action, even in critical emergencies. When famine or plague struck, provincial warlord governments often failed to provide effective relief; their disorder and greed also rendered it difficult or impossible for foreign relief organizations to aid the suffering people (Sheridan 1966: 23–24).

In analyzing the nature of Warlord rulership in China as described by Sheridan, the neural dynamic of Ego and Empathy allows us to see that such unfair oppression between a ruler and his citizens would create an enormous amount of behavioral tension.

In other words, such poor—Empathy-lacking—measures taken by the greedy and purely self-interested Warlords at that period would necessarily create an imbalance and a state of conflict between the ruling regime and its people. This was, of course, also in violation of Confucian standards.

Socio-behavioral Tension
Between Warlord and People

In keeping with the homeostatic nature of the neural dynamic, such extended oppression, injury, and hardship inflicted against the Chinese people would build enormous behavioral tension between the rulers and their subjects.

Predictably, according to the CSN Model, there would accumulate a great deal of energy in the populace to self-correct this imbalance. Given the realistic opportunity for the people to reject this Ego-centered rulership, they would overthrow such governance in favor of a more empathetic one.

Extreme Socio-behavioral Tension
Fostered Extreme Social Transformation

Had imbalances of Warlord rule been less extreme, a more moderate form of correction would likely have taken place. For example, if the conditions in the society were less harsh, exploitative, and oppressive, if the people had received provisions for their basic needs, the Chinese people would perhaps have favored a more peaceful, longer-term social transformation.

However, because the oppressive rule of the Warlords, on a national scale, was so extreme, the people of China would collectively choose a revolutionary system—such as communism —that was ideologically promoted and structurally conceived to be empathetic towards the population.

Whether or not communism delivered, in fact, the kind of empathetic governance the Chinese people were fighting to realize is a topic outside the scope of this chapter. However, the impetus of the people to create drastic change during this time can be attributed to the imbalanced Ego-centric rulership, pervasive in China by most Warlords.

Such massive stored behavioral tension by the population inevitably led to the drastic and wave-like violent overthrow of such governance on a national level.

It has been estimated that loss of life in determining the system of government in China in this period surpassed 48 million (Rummel 1991).

DYNAMIC BALANCE IN WARLORD-DOMINATED GUANGDONG: THE CASE OF CHEN JITANG (1928–1936)

Chinese culture stretches out longer than any other existing culture in the history of humankind. For such a culture to exist and thrive, it must fundamentally and structurally contain the cultural elements and teaching of a social protocol or moral behavior. Such a protocol must be interwoven into its people to create a fair, balanced social behavior that sustains itself successfully over such a long time.

But if upwards of 48 million lives were lost due to the imbalances created by the negative legacy of Warlord control, where was represented this 5000 year traditional Chinese culture built on *li, ren,* and the interactive dynamic of Ego and Empathy seen in the teachings of Confucius and Mencius?

The answer may lie in the regime of Chen Jitang in the Guangdong Province of Southern China.

Chen Jitang, Warlord of Guangdong, was unquestionably the most powerful ruler in Southern China and surrounding areas. Chen's air force was the most technologically advanced, best trained, and bigger than the rest of Nationalist China combined. In the Sino-Japanese war, it was Chen's air force that defended the nation against the invading Imperialist Japanese.

Unlike his Ego-centric ruling contemporaries, Chen's rule was characterized by service or Empathy toward the people. Chen promoted economic growth, foreign technology exchange and investment, large-scale social infrastructure, establishment of new industry to support the economy.

He also placed strong emphasis on public education that extended from K-12 to the relocation and massive expansion of Southern China's present elite universities. He also instituted a centralization of social welfare services accompanied by the systematic purging of governmental corruption, and enforcement of laws ensuring the safety of the general public.

There exists a wealth of documentation establishing the fact that during Chen's rule public service was effective, fruitful, and far-reaching in its vision. In fact, his determination to promote social relief work was a large factor surrounding Chen's ability to assume provincial command.

In the words of a recent scholar:

As the leader of a semi-independent regime that stood to rival the Nationalist government's claim to legitimate leadership…, Chen needed to show the people of Guangdong that his government had much to offer (Lin 2004).

In the 1930s, under Chen's aggressive development, Guangzhou became the city of high-tech advancement that the whole nation would point to as a model for the modernization of China. This period in modern Chinese history has been coined the "Golden age of Guangdong."

Foreign reporters noted that there were no beggars on the streets of Guangzhou. Early or late in the evenings, all the big restaurants were brimming with business. Chen's rule is remembered fondly and widely by the citizens recalling that time in history (Guangzhou Flower City Publishing, Jan 1, 2005).

In contrast to his contemporaries then, Chen Jitang found harmony and balance in the ratio of dominant control (Ego) to the goal of public service (Empathy). He did so by directing the predominance of military, political, and industrial power to the creation of infrastructure, service, general safety, education, and economic opportunity for the Southern lands.

Chen and the Conscious Application of Confucian Teaching

When asked the secret to his successful rule of Guangdong, Chen cited Confucian teaching to live the principles of: Loyalty; Respect for Elders; practice of Charity and Love; to maintain Integrity and Live Peacefully (capitalized words translate the characters in the Chinese vernacular).

He believed that his province became great because they were able to successfully train the population to live out those principles and help others in the communities throughout Southern China.

It is interesting to note that although his rule was characterized by tangible, industrial development, construction, growth, and political accomplishments, Chen stressed and gave credit to all "empathetic" qualities in his rule and in the effective training of his citizens to realize those qualities.

Not only does Chen's rule affirm the Ego/Empathy neural dynamic, but the derived Confucian ideal of the just and benevolent ruler.

RECENT CHINESE THOUGHT ON MANAGEMENT

Recent Chinese thought on management practice is reflected in the work of Su Dongshui.

The Tri-oriented or Three-dimensional Approach to Economics and Business Management

Su's tri-oriented, or three-dimensional approach to management—people-centered, principle-based, empathy-powered—is the source of many publications and is well renowned to scholars of Chinese management.

The tri-oriented concept with its essential emphasis on Empathy and social responsibility stands clearly in contrast to the classical Western emphasis on Ego and self-interest. Both cultures overemphasize one side of the behavioral spectrum.

Taken separately, then, both the Eastern and Western emphases, at the extremes, are only half right.

If the emphasis is too much toward Empathy or social responsibility, it shuts off the creativity that comes from self-interest and individual initiative.

If emphasis is too much toward self-interest or individualism it shuts off social responsibility and leads to greed and selfishness.

The Dual Motive Approach: Fusing the Eastern and Western Approaches

The interplay of Ego and Empathy expressed in the CSN Model, allows the fusion or integration of the traditional Eastern (Chinese) concept of the market and management as emphasizing Empathy, virtue, social responsibility with the Western (Anglo-American) approach emphasizing self-interest and individual initiative.

The merger of these two approaches provides the foundation for an economic and management philosophy that combines the best of Eastern philosophical thinking and Western scientific research. The merger, further, offers a modern international model of market, management, and political thinking suitable for globalization.

It is in the Dynamic Balance of these two traditions, in accordance with the archetypal neural circuitries common to us all, that we find the optimal match between the social and individual that leads to creativity, productivity, and social contribution.

CONCLUSION

In summary, the Ego/Empathy neural dynamic is clearly expressed in Chinese thought.

The CSN Model of that dual motive dynamic permits analysis of politico-economic development as expressed in the warlord period of China. It can also be considered to bridge longstanding Western and Eastern emphases in thinking about social exchange and management.

Lastly, the dual motive dynamic provides the conceptual basis for a global exchange system based on a Dynamic Balance of individual initiative and social responsibility that combines the best of Eastern and Western thinking.

23

GLOBAL POLITICS
AND THE DUAL MOTIVE DYNAMIC

In previous chapters, I have explored the dual motive dynamic of our neural architecture in shaping our overall social, market, and politico-legal exchange systems.

In the last chapter, I examined, with the aid of two other scholars, the same shaping effect in Chinese thought and culture. We offered the view that the CSN Model of Ego and Empathy interplay, had the capacity to integrate the Eastern philosophical system and the Western more scientifically based system, overcoming their deficiencies, to create a truly global model for economic, business enterprise, and political thinking.

This chapter will explore the application of the pervasive dynamic of our neural architecture to global economics and politics.

THE GLOBAL EXCHANGE SYSTEM

Balanced reciprocity is the optimal homestatic outcome of the dual motive dynamic captured in the CSN Model of our neural architecture. And the hopeful possibility of reciprocity undergirds the worldwide exchange system.

From the beginning, reciprocity has loomed large in American economic thought. Over the history of United States trade relations, however, the term *reciprocity* has been used very ambiguously. Since it had a positive popular ring to it, it was frequently used inappropriately as a catchword to defend, not true reciprocity, but partisan and parochial preferences.

Nevertheless, despite opportunistic usage, reciprocity has been an important part of the trade vocabulary of the United States since the signing of its first commercial agreement. That first treaty with France, signed in 1778, provided for reciprocal trade concessions between the two nations. Between that early date and the entry of the US into World War II in 1941, reciprocity in trade had been the watchword.

Following World War II, a worldwide commercial exchange system was established. The General Agreement on Trade and Tariffs (GATT) was setup as a reciprocal, multilateral trading system. The road to peace and harmony among nations was seen to follow along the trade routes of commercial exchange.

The GATT was replaced by the World Trade Organization (WTO) in 1995. Reciprocity and multilateralism continued to be the foundational principles. The WTO, in fact, claims among its top benefits to humankind the promotion of world peace.

The WTO objectives are to serve the benefit of all and allow the exploitation of none. Such principles reveal clearly an extended expression of our neural dynamic, the tug-and-pull of Ego and Empathy, respect for self and others.

Worldwide exchange, like social exchange at all levels, is propelled by human brains interacting with like human brains sharing a common reciprocal architecture.

DIFFUSE RECIPROCAL VS. SPECIFIED RECIPROCAL

In earlier chapters (8 through 10), I traced the evolution of social exchange as driven by the neural dynamic. In the family and small groups of our primitive ancestry the reciprocal obligated response to a sharing or giving act was diffuse. That is, it created generalized bonds underpinned by affectional and Ego circuitry that held us together for mutual protection, nurture, and survival.

As we evolved larger social exchange units, what has been called the gift economy emerged. In gift exchanges the reciprocal lost some of its diffused character and became anticipated. An even exchange maintained equal status in social relationships, unequal exchanges led to inequalities of status or hierarchy.

In accord with Dual Motive Theory, hierarchy, like other forms of inequality is, of course, structured behavioral tension. The social bonding effect of obligation, nevertheless, remained. It became expressed more fully and formally in such social phenomena as patron-client and other dominant/submissive social relations based upon mutual but unequal obligation.

I think it is noteworthy that thinkers in recent feminist international relations theory, without reference to brain science or Dual Motive Theory, define inequality and equality in terms of the presence or absence of hierarchy, rather than purely economically or as sameness (see Ackerly & True 2006: 246).

The Transactional Market:
Limiting the Scale of Inclusiveness

As the transactional market emerged from sharing and gift-giving, we came to exchange or trade with strangers. Social bonding was neither necessary nor desired. The reciprocal became specified or quantified. The transaction left little or no residual social bonding or obligation, thereby limiting the scale of inclusiveness characteristic of the family and larger kinship groups. Impersonal market exchange, however, still operated by the same reciprocal algorithms of our neural architecture.

Reciprocity as Neural: A Solid Foundation
For a Previously Begged Assumption of IR Theory

The sourcing of reciprocity in the dynamic of neural architecture provides a solid foundation for understanding its appeal in exchange relations among nations. Reciprocity is driven by and a necessary response to behavioral tension. When reciprocity fails in trade, there is always behavioral tension. When reciprocity works—that is, when it moves toward Dynamic Balance or equilibrium—it tends to produce harmony or peace among nations, as hoped for by the WTO.

Previously, in the literature on reciprocity and international trade, the motivational source of reciprocity has been begged. That is: Its motivational source has been assumed, intuited, or taken for granted. But it has not been explained. Discussion has centered not on reciprocity's source, but on how it should be defined.

RECIPROCITY IN INTERNATIONAL RELATIONS (IR) THEORY

Robert Keohane, a leading IR theorist, has given considerable thought to the question of reciprocity in international relations. In *After Hegemony* (1984, revised 2005) Keohane counterpoises egoism and empathy as conflicting motives in international relations (see also, Keohane 1990). He makes no connection with neuroscience and makes no effort to source either egoism or empathy in human nature. Nevertheless, the writing of the book is clearly motivated by the neural dynamic, the tug-and-pull of Ego and Empathy.

In a subsequent work (1989), Keohane broke the general concept of reciprocity down into two forms: specific reciprocity and diffuse reciprocity.

Without attempting to source reciprocity, he described the two types in terms that we can equate with the transition from the exchange practices of family and gift economies to the exchange practices of market economies.

Keohane identified specific reciprocity with prisoners' dilemma or tit-for-tat exercises in game theory. Such games allow two players, who might seek maximum gain by defecting in a single game, to develop cooperation for maximum total payoffs over a series of continuing games. Reciprocals are clearly specified for each individual transaction and are cumulative over the series.

The prisoners' dilemma represents a highly simplified, idealized exchange situation. It is divorced from reality, and rarely if ever, found in real life situations. It, nevertheless, by some considerable stretching of one's imagination, can be seen to approximate roughly a series of market transactions between two individuals.

Keohane finds it hard to apply specific reciprocity so defined to actual bilateral international trade situations. He finds it even more difficult to apply it to multilateral trade relations. This situation led him to suggest diffuse reciprocity as the more appropriate principle for international trade. Diffuse reciprocity requires a general commitment to a set of rules and practices, rather than a case-by-case response to a series of transactions.

Such a conclusion is tantamount to suggesting reversion to a form of premarket reciprocity—that of the family or the gift economy—as the foundation for global trade.

Keohane, in effect, found specific reciprocity, grounded in game theory, inadequate as a standard in international trading relations. As a consequence, he went to an intuited but unrelated concept of diffuse reciprocity to fill the need. Without knowledge of the neural algorithms and their shaping role in the evolution of exchange, it is impossible, however, to see the relation between the two concepts. Keohane, thus, has difficulty accounting for why this should be or for what is actually going on.

A second major conceptual problem with reciprocity in the social sciences rests in the artificial dichotomy between egoistic and empathetic (altruistic) behavior. Such a dichotomy obscures the evolved linkage between the two—the fact that behavior is an Ego/Empathy spectrum, not a polar set of extremities. The reciprocal outcome shows respect for the interests of self and others. Such is the essence of the Ego/Empathy dynamic.

Reciprocity can never be *just* self-interested as claimed by some. Nevertheless, it is always *inclusive* of self-interest.

Peter Blau, a prominent sociologist who wrote on power and exchange (1964), refused to associate reciprocity with norms. He did so on the ground that such association would make reciprocity inconsistent with self-interest.

Keohane expressed agreement with Blau. He asserted that a concept of reciprocity, to be valuable, must be consistent with self-interested practice. Keohane, then, attempted to resolve the dilemma of Blau's statement by adding to the confusion.

He changed the definition of norms, which included a moral component, to include standards of behavior to which even egoists could sometimes conform.

This concession, in effect, grants that egoists could sometimes express Empathy. Such tortuous devices show how distorted arguments can become in the absence of a grasp of the underlying neural dynamic.

In contrast to Keohane, Christine Sylvester (2002), in her work on international relations from a feminist perspective, seems to intuit the contradictions inherent to the view of reciprocity as purely self-interested or egoistic.

But back to diffuse reciprocity which has subsequently become well established in IR theory (e.g., see Bolewski 2007, especially pp. 45–49).

MULTILATERALISM: A REVERSION
TO THE FAMILY OR GIFT ECONOMY?

According to Keohane, the transition from specific reciprocity to diffuse reciprocity depends on sequential rather than simultaneous or one-shot exchange. He sees diffuse reciprocity as desirable for an effective global system.

Diffuse reciprocity means that subscribing nations seek not balanced trade reciprocity on a nation-by-nation basis, but balanced reciprocity in the overall system of global exchange. Such a position allows for the principle of comparative advantage to work effectively. Comparative advantage requires that each nation do what it does best in contributing to the global trading system.

From the broad perspective of economic history, it is interesting, if not ironical, to watch what is going on here. Diffuse reciprocity characterized premarket or premodern societies. This was pointed out by Harvard sociologist Talcott Parsons several decades ago in a set of so-called pattern variables that he thought up to contrast such societies.

Anthropologists have long known that diffuse reciprocity pervaded premarket or so-called primitive societies. Such diffuseness is also characteristic of family exchange, probably from the beginning of time. It still pervades family giving and sharing to this day.

Now, as we proceed to globalization of exchange, we see the clear call for a return to an earlier principle of social exchange. A reverse movement from the modern market principle of specificity to premarket diffuseness of reciprocal obligation.

And the call has been heeded—even if without conscious intent.

If you visit the website of the WTO at the turn of the present century, you will see the institutionalization of diffuse reciprocity implicit in its objectives and its proclaimed benefits for international society.

The ten benefits provide for:

(1) promoting peace among nations,

(2) resolving disputes,

(3) rules for proper exchange behavior,

(4) reducing cost of living,

(5) making more choices available to worldwide consumers,

(6) raising incomes in poorer countries,

(7) promoting growth and jobs,

(8) improving efficiency,

(9) reducing lobbying of governments by special interests, and

(10) promoting good government in general.

In principle, if not always in practice, the WTO exemplifies the promotion of diffuse reciprocity as integral to the global exchange system.

Not just the WTO, but the World Bank has also recognized the essential importance of reciprocity. Business scholars Robert Wood and Gary Hamel report on that institution's efforts to confront the persistent problem of global poverty through innovative market procedures (Wood & Hamel 2002).

THE WORLDWIDE HUMAN FAMILY: EXTENDING THE SCALE OF INCLUSIVENESS

These days, we hear a lot about the global village and other one-world concepts proceeding from the information age. Technology has made face-to-face real-time relations a virtual if not tangible reality. We can look down on our planet from space and see its isolation, its fragility, and its unity. And we are confronted with a shared fate in the exhaustion of resources, excessive carbon emissions, and the threat of global warming.

At such times we turn naturally to such thoughts as the worldwide human family. We appreciate, subliminally if not in full consciousness, the importance of overcoming and extending the scale of inclusiveness. In doing so, the concept of stranger vanishes before our very eyes. We extend the neural dynamic, which evolved originally in small family units, to now include all people and nations.

Such thoughts are surely ideal, but they are neither hokey nor softheaded. They rest solidly on what we are—they rest upon the very affectional and self-preserving core dynamic that prescribes our humanity.

In the present global situation, any international organization, claiming to represent all nations, must reflect this common core of our humanity in both its principles and conduct. That is, if it is to be acceptable and successful in the long-term.

From Categorical Imperative to Reciprocity

Immanuel Kant (1724–1804), the great German philosopher of the 18th century, with no knowledge of brain science, saw such acceptable common principles based upon a categorical imperative that all thinking humans would inevitably come up against through careful retrospection.

In the absence of brain science, the categorical imperative was the bedrock of just and equitable behavior. More modern scholars fall back, instead, on the poorly grasped concept of reciprocity.

In 1978, social historian Barrington Moore, Jr. in his *Injustice: The Social Basis of Obedience and Revolt* wrote as follows:

Without the concept of reciprocity—or better, mutual obligation…it becomes impossible to interpret human society as the consequence of anything other than perpetual force and fraud…such an interpretation would be a manifest exaggeration (1978: 506).

Moore went on to say that only a pure form of reciprocity could serve as a universal code for the organization of society if all authority were removed (1978: 510).

Much has been written on the subject of reciprocity, and the writing continues to this day. I do not intend to review the literature or acknowledge every worthy contributor and contribution.

The centrality of the concept of reciprocity in trade among nations has been fully established. No international organization, no international statesperson, can avoid its foundational implications.

Neural Architecture and Balanced Reciprocity: The Physiological Foundations of Natural Law

If the global economic system as well as the global political system truly evolves toward greater freedom on principles of mutual benefit, the homeostatically balanced reciprocity based in our neural physiology will emerge ever more clearly. Such balanced reciprocity is the only principle, minimally acceptable by all, upon which a long-term global system vested in freedom can hope to exist.

It is the only system fully consonant with the common core of humanity.

It is as close to natural law as we can get.

It is the balanced expression of our human nature—our evolved neural structure.

The equation of our social brain is a mathematical tool for estimating how close we get to, or how far we depart from, matching the demands of the common core of our humanity. It is, further, a guide in physiological or natural science, for transformational thinking in international relations theory.

The equation of our social brain also provides a broader, more accurate and comprehensive foundation for the naturalistic model in IR theory which has long encouraged emulation of the natural sciences.

At the same time, however, it should not be used to disavow the importance of the competing model of a human sciences approach which draws upon historicism and hermeneutics in social inquiry (see the discussions in King, et al. 1994; Flyvbjerg 2001; Caterino & Schram 2006).

Given the complexities of history, culture, and social context, we need all the help we can get in the identification, understanding, and coping with the many silent as well as not so silent barriers that frustrate the global transformation that most wholesomely expresses the common core of our humanity.

When we achieve the assent of all nations, the principles adopted will invariably reflect the dynamic of our neural architecture—the balance of self- and other-interest, Ego and Empathy, freedom and equality, which express the essence of reciprocity in its fullest, most balanced sense.

CONCLUSION
AND
EPILOGUE

24

EMERGENCE OF A NEW PARADIGM:
THE CSN MODEL AND
DUAL MOTIVE THEORY

In this concluding chapter I return to the comparison of the Maslow hierarchy with the CSN Model—the graphic of Dual Motive Theory, begun in Chapter 2.

The Maslow hierarchy was the first and most influential attempt to construct a complete model of the human biological needs. In essence it was a model of human nature. Other models followed in the succeeding nearly seven decades since its articulation. Many follow-on models were either partial models or were variants that sprung from the foundational Maslow concept.

Although I early sensed its inadequacies when confronted with the emergent thinking in physiology and evolutionary neuroscience, it, nevertheless, had a great influence on my thinking. The Maslow hierarchy was, rightly or wrongly, co-opted by, and came to represent and give psychological support to the mainstream of thinking in economics and business of the period. Therein lies its historical significance.

In conclusion, this chapter compares the Maslow hierarchy with the CSN Model developed from physiology and evolutionary neuroscience and calls for a shift in thinking appropriate to accomodate new scientific findings as well as new challenges in global thinking about economics, society, and politics.

I will begin my analysis with a partial review of the discussion in Chapter 2.

THE MASLOW HIERARCHY

Maslow had arranged his hierarchy from bottom to top in the form of a pyramid, staircase, or stepladder. He put the physiological needs such as hunger and thirst at the base. On top of these basic needs he stacked the safety needs, then the belonging or social needs; and next esteem or ego needs in ascending order. At the very top of the pyramid or stepladder he put what he called the need for self-actualization.

Maslow theorized that these needs were emergent: That is, as we satisfied our basic needs of hunger and thirst, our safety needs would then emerge. Accordingly as we satisfied our newly emerged safety needs, the next level, the belonging or social needs, would come into play. Next came esteem needs, and finally, as these were satisfied, the self-actualizing need at the top of the hierarchy emerged. In self-actualizing we were projected to become all that we could be.

Maslow's hierarchy has appeared in every basic text on psychology and behavior for the past four decades. It also appears in most texts on organizational behavior and business management. Its influence has been widespread as a behavioral scheme of ready and easy reference. It has also been popularized in casual and popular writing about motivation.

SHORTCOMINGS OF THE MASLOW MODEL

The Maslow hierarchy has, however, serious shortcomings that limit its usefulness for thinking about our evolved brain structure.

For one thing, it lacks an evolutionary perspective. The hierarchy of needs is presented as a given, disconnected from the evolutionary process which produced it.

Secondly, Maslow put the concept together in the days before the full emergence of evolutionary neuroscience. It, therefore, makes no connection with neural architecture. The needs are asserted from informed intuition more than solid science or reliable empirical research.

Thirdly, the concept of hierarchy is not fully developed. Maslow did not adequately spell out the interaction of the levels of hierarchy nor did he satisfactorily account for those cases that violate the proposed normal priority of needs.

The hierarchy has also been criticized for being culture bound. That is, it fit neatly with particularly the U.S. concept of material achievement and success as a steady stair step progression of higher development (Yankelovich 1981). It thereby tends to ignore or diminish the great accomplishments in thought, morality, and service to humanity of many of the great figures of human history (Maddi 1989).

Additionally, Maslow's hierarchy, with its almost exclusive focus on the individual, affords little insight into the dynamics of social interaction. In other words it is not an interactive model. In fact, it turned us away from social interaction.

Maslow's focus on a staircase-like hierarchy of inner needs, therefore, tended to turn us inwardly away from the social environment. Co-opted and blended with the prevailing view of self-interest as the sole primary human motive in American business and economics, Maslow's theory of self-actualization, with its lofty connotations of self-fulfillment and creative expression became reduced, especially in the decades of the 70s and 80s, to a license for indulgent self-interest. It has retained this identification in the years since.

In blaming Maslow's concept for the excesses of that self-indulgent time, well-known pollster Daniel Yankelovich, writing in 1981, dubbed it the Maslow escalator. This isolated, indulgent version of self-interest, as expressed in our social and business experience, earned the labels of "narcissistic" and "me first."

One of the great popular appeals of the Maslow hierarchy is that it could be interpreted to fit so well with the prevailing emphasis on self-interest in our everyday as well as academic thinking on economics, business, and politics.

CONFLICT, NOT EMERGENCE

But inward focus and simplistic hierarchy were not the only problems with Maslow's hierarchy. It allowed us to be drawn excessively toward our inner selves and away from society because it missed a point central to human behavior—that *conflict*, not *emergence*, is behavior's most definitive characteristic.

Maslow placed the social or relatedness needs (Empathy) lower on the escalator than esteem and self-actualization needs (Ego). His theory contains the clear suggestion that we pass through these social needs or rise above them in the trek up the hierarchical ladder. This was a fundamental error, resulting in a considerable distortion of our view of human social nature.

The two sets of needs, social and self-interested, although hierarchical to some extent, are wired together in the same brain to produce the tug-and-pull, conflictual dynamic of interpersonal or social behavior.

We are not autonomous, but at best semiautonomous creatures, completely immersed in a pervasive social context, which is, at this point in our evolution, both demanded and made possible by our evolved brain structure.

Maslow's hierarchy does not fit well with the emergent, newly prevailing concept of the social brain.

FOR ME? FOR YOU? OR FOR US?
IT'S ALWAYS THE SAME!

The dynamic of our neural architecture shows that the tug-and-pull of Ego and Empathy drives interpersonal behavior not only at the levels of Maslow's social and esteem needs, but at all levels. The basic questions of interaction are the same anywhere in the hierarchy.

These questions are:

Do I do it or take it for myself (Ego)?

Do I do it for or give it to others (Empathy)?

Or do I do it for both myself and others? (Dynamic Balance).

It is enlightening to try out these questions at each level of Maslow's staircase.

Take the physiological needs first. I can see myself lost in the desert with a friend. I have one remaining canteen of water. It's half full, and I don't know if or when we'll find more. My interpersonal choices are three: Do I keep it all for myself (Ego)? Do I give it all to my friend (Empathy)? Or do we share it (Dynamic Balance)? I would face the same choices if my companion were a spouse, child, friend, or enemy.

These three questions would likewise apply to the next level of needs, those of safety. Suppose we are threatened by a wild beast? Or a natural disaster? An intruder? A terrorist? Do I protect myself'? Others? Self and others? The conflict is more or less evident depending on the urgency of what is happening, but it is always present.

At the next level the social needs are directly related to affection and Empathy, while above them, the esteem needs are related to Ego. But as we have seen, Ego and Empathy and their inexorable conflict pervade all three levels of Maslow's hierarchy.

In evolutionary terms, the conflict did not exist prior to the appearance of affectional circuitry in the mammalian brain; but ever since it appeared, it has influenced all needs and all behaviors.

The Ego-Empathy conflict even pervades Maslow's highest need level—self- actualization.

Behaviorally speaking, the need for self-actualization has to do with Ego rather than Empathy, but again the choices are the same as at all the other need levels. Do I put my own priorities, feelings, and objectives first? Or do I first consider the priorities, feelings, and objectives of my parents, spouse, children, friends, company, church, nation, or world-wide humanity itself'? Or do I struggle to achieve a balance?

The self reference perspective of Maslow's hierarchy fit well with the self-reference perspective of economics. And it had the same distorting effects that I have noted in earlier chapters.

There is, however, a general hierarchical quality to human behavior as Maslow proposed. The tri-level brain structure is itself hierarchical. The basic self-preservational circuitry is more ancient and lies essentially in the brain stem below the more recent mammalian and neocortical modifications and structures.

And sometimes the basic circuitry does override the newer. At such times ancient, often socially undesirable behaviors burst forth, disrupting our civilized social interaction.

On the other hand there are also clearly times when the affectional circuitry overrides the earlier self-preservational circuits in favor of pro-social, caring behavior.

THE EVOLUTION OF BEHAVIORAL CHOICE

The tug-and-pull of these circuitries, when connected to the frontal executive leads to the capacity for behavioral choice.

Normally the wiring between the levels and their input to the frontal cortex allows the subcortical circuits of self-preservation and affection to function at a roughly equal level in the tug-and-pull of Ego and Empathy.

Experience, Education, and Socialization: A Nondeterministic Process

This is not a deterministic process, however. Through experience, education, socialization, discipline, and practice, we may strengthen the control circuitry of the frontal cortex to manage more effectively the dynamic tug-and-pull between the conflicting circuits.

Extending the Scale of Inclusiveness

And equally, if not more importantly, through education, socialization, discipline, and practice, we can neuronally tune the emotional, caring, and bonding capacities of the fundamental circuitries to progressively extend the scale of inclusiveness from family, to humankind, to all life—even to the universe.

This capacity to manage—to choose—to extend, emerged with the development of general purpose neural network architecture which was connected with, but not dedicated to, the service of earlier life-preserving and affectional circuitry. This general purpose six-layered frontal circuitry, located in the neocortex, allowed us to partially escape and transcend the blind instinctual tyranny of the earlier circuits.

Of Choice, Growth, and Free Will

We became, thus, creatures of choice and of growth. That is, we can be said scientifically to have an element of free will, and the capacity for social, even moral growth.

The exercise of this free will—the making of choices—may, however, involve varying degrees of emotional and motivational intensity as the significance of the choices to the fundamental self-preservation and affectional circuitry varies.

SO WHAT, THEN, IS ACTUALIZATION?

If Maslow's hierarchy is in error, what, then, does the CSN Model of our neural architecture offer to replace the previously highly valued and popular concept of self-actualization? How do we express the highest and best of our behavioral potential?

Here's how:

We blend Ego and Empathy in Dynamic Balance or unity. At the highest levels of emotional abstraction—in philosophical terms—we synthesize the two powerful motives in unconditional acceptance and love for self and others, extending the synthetic scale of inclusiveness even to the universe. (I deal with this aspect more fully in my book *Consilience and Spirituality: The Scientific Foundations for the Choice to Believe or Not to Believe.*)

At the practical level we affirm ourselves, our Ego, with an empathic contribution or gift of our very best to society.

Rarely, such unifying experiences occur spontaneously— beyond our control. Circumstances may unexpectedly release the fully synthesized expression of the dual circuitry. Maslow called such moments *peak experiences*.

Such synthesized, or dynamically balanced experience is expressed by the social dynamic as it approaches equilibrium.

Likewise, the behavioral conflict, tension, and ultimate stress of our daily lives may be indexed by the social equation as the ratio diverges to the extremities of Ego and Empathy circuitry.

Since the present book focuses on the neural dynamic in economics, society, and politics, what might I suggest, in conclusion, as a practical application to those critical areas?

Nothing less than a significant shift from the last two centuries of socio-economic thinking.

A NEW PARADIGM FOR THINKING
ABOUT GLOBAL ECONOMICS AND POLITICS

Before getting on with the detailed discussion of the proposed shift, it may be helpful to deal with the fundamental question:

What, after all, Is a Paradigm Shift?

A paradigm shift is a shift in scientific perspective. The most famous paradigm shift in history was the shift from the Ptolemaic geocentric theory of the solar system to the Copernican heliocentric system. Other shifts may be attributed to the discoveries of Newtonian mechanics and quantum theory.

What Does a Paradigm Shift Do?

A paradigm shift may be considered to do at least four essential things:

1. It makes necessary accommodation with new scientific findings.

2. It allows us to see old things in a new, more accurate way.

3 It allows us to see things we could not see before.

4. It allows us to explain things we could not explain before.

CURRENT PARADIGM:
AN ETHNOCENTRIC ANGLO-AMERICAN VIEWPOINT

The current paradigm is an ethnocentric view of economics and free enterprise reflecting essentially an Anglo-American viewpoint.

It dates roughly from 1776, the publication of Adam Smith's *Wealth of Nations,* and it emphasizes self-interest as the sole primary motive driving economics and free enterprise, ascribing that position erroneously to Smith.

It has remained largely unchallenged despite misgivings of many scholars about the adequacy of rational self-interest as the sole primary motive. The lack of a credible scientifically sound alternative has limited serious empirical challenge to its claim of scientific accuracy.

EMERGING NEW PARADIGM
OF DUAL MOTIVE THEORY

The emerging new paradigm of Dual Motive Theory has been traced extensively throughout this book. It is based upon the interaction of the archetypal neural circuitries of Ego and Empathy, as graphically expressed by the CSN Model, and mathematically represented by the homeostatic equation of the social brain.

In the following paragraphs I will, first, compare the traditional paradigm with the emergent one. Secondly, I will show the relevance of the emergent paradigm by contrasting the advantages it brings with the disadvantages of the traditional paradigm.

Paradigm Shift Made Possible by
New Findings in Neural Architecture

Current Paradigm	Suggested New Paradigm
Ethnocentric View of Economics & Free Enterprise Theory 1776–2000	Global View of Economics & Free Enterprise Theory 2001→

Current	Suggested
1. Based on sole self-interest motive	1. Based on dynamic tug-and-pull of Ego (self-interest) & Empathy (other-interest)
2. Psychological model of Maslow pyramid	2. Conflict Systems Neurobehavioral (CSN) Model
3. Demand & Supply based on sole primary motive of self-interest (Empathy hidden/implicit)	3. Demand & Supply based on interaction of dual motives of Ego and Empathy
4. No equation linking economics with human nature	4. $BT = \dfrac{Ego}{Emp} = \dfrac{Dem}{Sup} = EP = \pm 1$

Relevance of New Shift for Global Business/Society

Traditional Paradigm	New Paradigm
Disadvantages	**Advantages**
1. Inaccurate scientifically	1. Scientifically accurate
2. Inherent selfishness Can breed and justify greed	2. Golden Rule Justifies responsible behavior; Respect for self and others
3. Supports & justifies inequality	3. Supports & justifies equality
4. Bad press for global free enterprise as selfish, materialistic system	4. Supports moral basis of free enterprise system as caring, responsible system
5. Builds behavioral tension	5. Mitigates behavioral tension

6. Encourages conflict	6. Encourages conflict resolution

7. Basis for national centeredness
    Seeking national self-interest
	7. Basis for global centeredness
	    Global respect for self & others

8. Domination, exploitation in trade & business	8. Reciprocity in trade & business
9. Ethnocentric	9. Global or universal

In conclusion, based on the above comparisons, I feel that Dual Motive Theory meets the requirements necessary to a paradigm shift.

Firstly, it makes necessary accommodation with the relevant new scientific findings.

Secondly, it allows us to see our economics, society, and politics in a more accurate way.

Thirdly, it allows us to see the underlying driving dynamic that we could not clearly see before.

Fourthly, it allows us to explain the organic behavior of economics, society, and politics which has previously eluded us for lack of a proper model of human nature.

Altogether, Dual Motive Theory provides a more accurate, positive, and hopeful model to guide the achievement of a global free enterprise and open, inclusive, and participatory political system.

EPILOGUE:
LET'S STOP TEACHING GREED

As I was completing this book, the economic crisis of 2008–2009 had burst upon us in full fury—with the devastating, but much wider effect, than a Hurricane Katrina. As we sought for answers amid unprecedented bailouts and stimulus packages, there have been calls for a new paradigm.

This epilogue is condensed from a paper that I presented at the combined meeting of the International Association for Research in Economic Psychology (IAREP) and the Society for the Advancement of Behavioral Economics (SABE) held at Saint Mary's University, Halifax, Nova Scotia, July 7–10, 2009.

The two associations include a wide range of international scholars in the emergent and significant new field of behavioral economics—a field that because of its multidisciplinary range holds the hope of developing new thinking and approaches.

The paper I presented, like those from of other participating scholars, responded to a call for papers addressing the causes and solutions of the largest economic crisis since the Crash of 1929.

In that paper, I offered Dual Motive Theory, the topic of the present book, as a candidate for the called-for paradigm. Dual Motive Theory, as extensively explored throughout this book is based on evolved brain physiology, links economics with the more fundamental science of physiology and prescribes the market—and indeed all social exchange as an expression of the organic, homeostatic interaction of archetypal Ego (self-interest) and Empathy (other-interest) neural circuitries from our ancestral vertebrate and mammalian heritages.

The reasons supporting this offer, that substantially summarize the arguments presented in this book, are as follows:

1. Dual Motive Theory links economics and business theory, consiliently, with a more fundamental science.

2. It demonstrates correctly that the market expresses the interaction of neural circuitries driving self- and other-interest (we are mammals), rather than a sole primary motive of self-interest (attributable to our ancestral reptiles and earlier ancestral vertebrates) that has so dramatically demonstrated its negative side effects in human social exchange activities in the form of flagrant greed.

3. It demonstrates the organic (not Newtonian) basis of the market as expressed in Demand and Supply (two primary motives, not one), General Equilibrium Theory, and the venerable Invisible Hand.

4. It provides a homeostatic equation from physiology that expresses also the interaction of Demand and Supply.

5. It provides a consilient, holistic theory that helps to overcome the isolated "silo" effect that by general agreement contributed significantly to the financial crash and that also inhibits scholarship in our similarly isolated departmented ("silo"-ed) university system.

6. It permits the unification of Eastern (Chinese) and Western approaches to the market. Each overemphasizes one motive or circuitry over the other. The Eastern, based on Confucian and other traditions over-emphasizes social or collective responsibility (Empathy), inhibiting the creativity of self-interest or individual initiative. The Western over-emphasizes self-interest and inhibits social responsibility.

7. Dual Motive Theory, thus, provides a proper paradigm for global free enterprise emphasizing a Dynamic Balance of the two motives, thereby capturing the advantages of creative self-interest and social responsibility as well as emphasizing the reciprocity and mutual respect essential to such a system.

THE CURRENT ECONOMIC CRISIS

The current economic crisis has made dramatically and undeniably clear that the classic assumption of economics and free enterprise theory—that a market driven by a sole primary motive of self-interest will be self-regulating and stable—is simply untrue.

Even such a libertarian stalwart as Alan Greenspan has finally been forced to acknowledge the flawed nature of the assumption (testimony before Congress, October 2008).

And even a former member of the J. P. Morgan team that developed the derivative concept that lead to such flagrant greed and catastrophe has called for a new paradigm (Tett 2009: 251).

In my judgment, emergent Dual Motive Theory, which links economics to hard neuroscience, provides the best candidate for the soughtafter new paradigm.

THE PROBLEM OF GREED
AND THE FAUSTIAN BARGAIN OF ECONOMICS

In recent articles on the current economic crisis, *pundits still do not get it.*

Although they openly and emphatically acknowledge that flagrant greed was a fundamental contributor to the crisis, they continue to suggest that *Greed is Good (To A Point)*—as the title of Fareed Zakaria's recent article in *Newsweek* (June 22, 2009) goes. See also the rather trite article by George Will, *Greed's Saving Graces* (Washington Post, May 17, 2009).

The above follow along with the Faustian bargain that economics has made with the term "greed" over the past several decades under the false belief that it was necessary to free enterprise or capitalism. Even if tongue-in-cheek, the acknowledgment by professors of economics and business to classrooms of budding business executives that "*a little greed is good*" needs to be stopped.

Such statements or implications may be considered equivalent to:

Leaving the barn door a little open—(the horse will still get out),

or worse,

Racism is good (to a point),

Religious discrimination is good (to a point),

Hatred is good (to a point).

According to a standard dictionary, the core definition of greed is

a selfish and excessive desire for more of something (as money) than is needed.

Usually it implies a negative or harmful social impact by taking from or depriving others in the short- or long-term (e.g., sustainability). Since the emphasis is on the "selfish" and "excessive" it is traditionally considered a personal and social negative or pernicious quality by the wider human society.

That certainly has proved to be the case in our often fraudulent and misleading business practices (e.g., misleading customers on loans and financial information, risking shareholder investments for short-term personal gain, cheating in general etc., etc., etc.).

Greed, by definition, is *not* good. It is harmful to social interests because of its "excessiveness," and we should not teach it in any form.

GREED SHOULD NOT BE CONFUSED
WITH SELF-INTEREST OR PERSONAL INITIATIVE

On the other hand, greed should not be confused with healthy self-interest, Ego, or personal initiative. This confusion has been a great terminological mistake/distortion often cynically promoted by those who want to justify their antisocial, anti-business behavior —often, perhaps, "tongue-in-cheek" among the good ole' boys.

Self-interest, Ego, and individual initiative are healthy and necessary, but only when balanced with an empathetic, other-interested socially responsible behavioral component. We are mammals who are wired for essentially balanced social exchange behavior.

Dual Motive Theory, as I conceive and present it, is a spectrum of homeostatic counterbalancing physiological forces in which Ego- and Empathy-producing neural circuits are always present and active in social exchange in a tug-and-pull dynamic in some proportional mix except at the extremes of nonsurvivable behavior (Greed as well as self-sacrifice essentially belong at the nonsurvivable extremes).

I think we would do well to avoid such terms as "good greed," "a little greed," and other variants when we probably mean healthy self-interest with a substantial proportion of socially responsive Empathy.

In fairness to Zakaria whom I quoted above, at the close of his ill-titled article he wrote:

But at heart, there needs to be a deeper fix within all of us, a simple gut check. If it doesn't feel right, we shouldn't be doing it...

A simple gut check? A rather overly simple, but perhaps intuitive prescription. And perhaps, in commonsense parlance, that may be, in part, what Empathy is about—it is the source of ethical conscience. And greed has no place in it or in a market that serves us all. In other words, we really do, unless we are sociopaths, know better.

A CONSILIENT, HOLISTIC THEORY NEEDED

If we are to attempt a new paradigm, we must avoid the narrow perspective of a single discipline that has been forced upon us by the departmented university system of which we are the products and inhabitants. A departmented university system equates to the isolated "silos" that Tett and others found so problematic in the financial world.

To overcome the departmented or silo effect, Tett, a social anthropologist PhD and *Financial Times* journalist, concludes we need a holistic approach to the market and related political issues that face us. This is especially the case in the pressing issues of sustainability and climate change.

The highest form of holistic theory would be a consilient theory—one that unifies not only the social sciences but also unifies or links them with the natural sciences.

Dual Motive Theory, as I and others (e.g., Chan 2007, 2008; Duffy 2007, 2008; Levine 2006; Li 2009; Luo 2008; Lynne 2006; Patlolla 2008; Wilson 2006) have developed in numerous publications is suggested as a candidate for such a theory. It is a consilient meta-theory inclusive of physiology, neuroscience, anthropology, economics, sociology, and political science.

THE SCALE OF INCLUSIVENESS
AND THE RESPONSIBILITY OF PROFESSORS

Since we evolved for several million years in small, essentially kinship groups, our social exchange architecture works most effectively in family and similar small groups that exist in close proximity. Empathy is strongest in such groups. It tends to weaken or thin out as the groups become larger and impersonal—thus creating a scale of inclusiveness.

Education and socialization are needed to extend the basic social circuitries to include the larger societies we now live in, reaching even to globalization. The scale of inclusiveness, thus, places a great responsibility upon teachers of economics and business. In a global economy, we need to teach empathetic mutual respect and reciprocity—not a little greed or a little racism.

Our neural circuits of Ego and Empathy are the basic resources of human nature that we build upon to create such a viable and productive global society.

THE UNIFICATION OF EASTERN AND WESTERN THINKING

At the International Federation of Scholarly Associations of Management (IFSAM) conference held in Shanghai, China, 2008, I presented a jointly authored paper (with Chan & Luo) demonstrating that Dual Motive Theory permits the fusion or integration of the traditional Eastern (Chinese) concept of the market and management as emphasizing Empathy, virtue, social responsibility with the Western (Anglo-American) approach emphasizing self-interest and individual initiative. Both emphases, at the extremes, are only half right.

If the emphasis is too much toward Empathy or social or collective responsibility, it shuts off creativity that comes from individual initiative. If emphasis is too much toward self-interest or individualism it shuts off social responsibility and leads to greed and selfishness. It is in the Dynamic Balance of these two archetypal neural circuitries that we find the optimal match between the social and individual that leads to creativity, productivity, and social contribution.

The in-conference paper was so well-received that it became repeated by invitation as the closing plenary session.

Perhaps the time for change has come.

BIBLIOGRAPHY

Ackerly, B., Stern, M., & True, J. (2006). *Feminist methodologies for international relations.* Cambridge University Press.

Ackerly, B. & True, J. (2006). Studying the struggles and wishes of the age. In B. Ackerly, et al. (Eds.), *Feminist methodologies for international relations* (pp.241–260). Cambridge University Press.

Alexander, R. (1987). *The biology of moral systems.* New York: Aldine de Gruyter.

Appadurai, A. (Ed.). (1986). *The social life of things.* Cambridge University Press.

Arrow, K. (1987). In G. Feiwel (Ed.), *Arrow and the ascent of modern economic theory.* London: Macmillan.

Arrow, K. (1963). *Social choice and individual values* (2nd ed.). Yale University Press.

Arrow, K. & Debreu, G. (1954). Existence of an equilibrium for a competitive economy. *Econometrica, 22,* 265–290.

Arrow, K. & Hahn, F. (1971). *General competitive analysis* San Francisco: Holden-Day.

Axelrod, R. (1984). *The evolution of cooperation.* New York: Basic Books.

Axelrod, R. & Hamilton, W. (1981). The evolution of cooperation. *Science, 211,* 1390–1396.

Baal, J. van. (1975). *Reciprocity and the position of women.* Amsterdam: Van Gorcum.

Barfield, T. (Ed.). (1997). *The dictionary of anthropology.* Malden, MA: Blackwell.

Bates, R. (1997). Area studies and the discipline: A useful controversy? *PS: Politics and Political Science, 30*(2), 166–169.

Batson, C. (1991). *The altruism question: Toward a social-psychological answer.* Hillsdale, NJ: Lawrence Erlbaum.

Beauregard, M. & O'Leary, D. (2007). *The spiritual brain.* San Francisco: HarperOne.

Becker, G. (1987). Economic analysis and human behavior. In L. Green & J. Kagel (Eds.), *Advances in behavioral economics* (Vol. 1, pp. 3–17). New York: Ablex Publishing.

Becker, L. (1986). *Reciprocity.* London: Routledge & Kegan Paul.

Bendor, J. & Swistak, P. (1997). The evolutionary stability of cooperation. In *American Political Science Review, 91*(2), 290–303.

Bentham, J. (1907)[1789]. *An introduction to the principles of morals and legislation.* (Reprinted from 1823 ed. by Oxford, UK: Clarendon Press.)

Berridge, K. (2003). Comparing the emotional brains of humans and other animals. In R. Davidson, et al. (Eds.) *Handbook of affective sciences* (pp. 25–51). Oxford University Press.

Bianchi, M. (1993). How to learn sociality: True and false Solutions to Mandeville's problem. *History of Political Economy*, *25*(2), 209–240.

Birtchnell, J. (1999). *Relating in psychotherapy*. Westport, CT: Praeger.

Birtchnell, J. (1993). *How humans relate*. Westport, CT: Praeger.

Blair, R. (2003). Facial expressions, their communicatory functions and neurocognitive substrates. *Philosophical Transactions of the Royal Society B: Biological Sciences.*, *358*, 561–572.

Blau, P. (1964). *Exchange and power in social life*. New York: Wiley.

Boehm, C. (1999). *Hierarchy in the forest: The evolution of egalitarian behavior*. Cambridge, MA: Harvard University Press.

Bohannon, P. (1963). *Social anthropology*. New York: Holt.

Bolewski, W. (2007). *Diplomacy and international law in globalized relations*. New York: Springer.

Bowles, S. & Gintis, H. (1998). *Recasting egalitarianism*. New York: Verso.

Breggin, P. (2008). *Brain-disabling treatments in psychiatry.* New York: Springer.

Brownell, H. & Martino, G. (1998). Deficits in inference and social cognition: The effects of right hemisphere brain damage on discourse. In M. Beeman and C. Chiarello (Eds.), Right hemisphere language comprehension: Perspectives from cognitive neuroscience. Mahwah, NJ: Lawrence Erlbaum.

Buchanan, J. (2003). *Public choice: The origins and development of a research program.* Fairfax, VA: George Mason University, Center for Public Choice.

Buchanan, J. (1991). *The economics and the ethics of constitutional order.* University of Michigan Press.

Buchanan, J. & Tullock, G. (1962). *The calculus of consent: Logical foundations of constitutional democracy.* University of Michigan Press.

Buss, D. (1999). *Evolutionary psychology: The new science of the mind.* Boston: Allyn & Bacon.

Cacioppo, J., Berntson, G., et al., (Eds.). (2002). *Foundations in social neuroscience*. MIT Press.

Carter, C., Ahnert, L. et al. (Eds.). (2006). *Attachment and bonding: A new synthesis*. MIT Press.

Carter, C., Lederhendler, I., & Kirkpatrick, B. (Eds.). (1997). The integrative neurobiology of affiliation. *Annals of the New York Academy of Sciences, 807*, 213–238.

Cannon, W. (1932). *The wisdom of the body*. New York: W.W. Norton.

Cannon, W. (1929). *Bodily changes in pain, hunger, fear, and rage*. New York: D. Appleton.

Chan, Y.-G., Cory, G., & Luo, J. (2008, July). The tri-orientedapproach and Dual Motive Theory. In D.-S. Su (Chair), *Fusion and development of East and West management*. Paper presented at the Annual Conference of International Federation of Scholarly Associations of Management (IFSAM), Shanghai, China.

Chan, Y.-G. (2008, September). *Dual Motive Theory in China: A case study analyzing the warlord rule of Chen Jitang, Canton (1928–1936)*. Paper presented at The International Association for Reserach in Economic Psychology (IAREP) and The Society for Advancement of Behavioral Economics (SABE) World Meeting, Luiss University, Rome.

Chan, Y.-G. (2007, May). *Governing power as evaluated by Dual Motive Theory: A case study of China*. Paper presented at the Society of Behavioral Economics (SABE) 25th Conference of Economists, New York University.

Chan Y.-G., Cory, G., & Rajaram, K. (2007, January). *Neuroeconomics and Dual Motive Theory: Can East meet West? Bridging Eastern and Western economics*. Paper presented at WEAI Pacific Rim Conference, Guanghua School of Management, Peking University, Beijing, China.

Chang, C. (1975). *Tao: A new way of thinking*. New York: Harper & Row.

Cheal, D. (1988). *The gift economy*. New York: Routledge.

Coleman, J. (1990). *Foundations of social theory*. Harvard University Press.

Cook, K., O'Brien, J., & Kollock, P. (1990). Exchange theory: A blueprint for structure and progress. In G. Ritzer (Ed.), *Frontiers of social theory: The new synthesis* (pp. 158–181). Columbia University Press.

Cook, K. (Ed.). (1987). *Social exchange theory*. London: Sage.

Corning, P. (1983). *The synergism hypothesis*. New York: McGraw-Hill.

Cory, G. (2009, July). *Let's stop teaching greed: Dual Motive Theory as a new paradigm for global economics*. Paper presented at the International Association for Research in Economic Psychology (IAREP) and the Society for the Advancement of Behavioral Economics (SABE) joint conference, Saint Mary's University, Halifax, Nova Scotia.

Cory, G. (2006a). Physiology and behavioral economics: The new findings from evolutionary neuroscience. In M. Altman (Ed.), *Handbook of contemporary behavioral economics: Foundations and developments*. Armonk, NY: M.E. Sharpe.

Cory, G. (2006b). A behavioral model of the dual motive approach to behavioral economics and social exchange. *The Journal of Socio-Economics, 35*(4): 592–612.

Cory, G. (2004). *The consilient brain:The bioneurological basis of economics, society, and politics*. New York: Kluwer Academic/ Plenum.

Cory, G. (2003). MacLean's evolutionary neuroscience and the CSN Model: Some clinical and social policy implications. In A. Somit and S. Peterson (Eds.)., *Human nature and public policy* (pp.161–180). New York: Palgrave MacMillan.

Cory, G. (2002a). Reappraising MacLean's triune brain concept. In G. Cory & R. Gardner (Eds.)., *The evolutionary neuroethology of Paul MacLean: Convergences and frontiers* (pp. 9–27). Westport, CT: Greenwood/Praeger.

Cory, G. (2002b). Algorithms of neural architecture, Hamilton's Rule, and the Invisible Hand of economics. In G. Cory & R. Gardner (Eds.)., *The evolutionary neuroethology of Paul MacLean: Convergences and frontiers*. Westport, CT: Greenwood/Praeger.

Cory, G. (2000a). From MacLean's triune brain concept to the Conflict Systems Neurobehavioral Model: The subjective basis of moral and spiritual consciousness. *Zygon: Journal of Religion & Science, 35*(2), 385–414.

Cory, G. (2000b). *Toward consilience: The bioneurological basis of thought, behavior, language, and experience*. New York: Kluwer Academic/Plenum.

Cory, G. (1999). *The reciprocal modular brain in economics and politics: Shaping the rational and moral basis of organization, exchange, and choice*. New York: Plenum.

Cory, G. (1992). *Rescuing capitalist free enterprise for the twenty-first century*. San Jose, CA: Center for Behavioral Ecology.

Cory, G. (1974). *The biopsychological basis of political socialization and political culture*. Doctoral dissertation, Stanford University.

Cory, G., Chan, Y.-G., & Luo, J. (2008, July). The tri-oriented approach and Dual Motive Theory. In D.-S. Su (Chair), *Fusion and development of East and West management*. Paper presented at the Annual Conference of International Federation of Scholarly Associations of Management (IFSAM), Shanghai, China.

Cory, G. & Duffy, M. (2007, May). Dual Motive Theory and development: A look at Sen's development as freedom through brain physiology. Paper presented at the *Annual Meeting of the Society for the Advancement of Behavioral Economics (SABE)*, New York University.

Cory, G., Chan, Y.-G., & Rajaram, K. (2007, January). *Neuroeconomics and Dual Motive Theory: Can East meet West? Bridging Eastern and Western economics.* Paper presented at WEAI Pacific Rim Conference, Guanghua School of Management, Peking University, Beijing, China.

Cory, G. & Wilson, D. (2007). *The Evolutionary Epidemiology of Mania and Depression.* New York: Mellen Press.

Cory, G. & Gardner, R., (Eds.). (2002). *The evolutionary neuro-ethology of Paul MacLean: Convergences and frontiers.* Westwood, CT: Greenwood/Praeger.

Cournot, Augustin. (1929)[1838]. *Researches into the mathematical principles of the theory of wealth* (N. Bacon, Trans.). New York: Macmillan.

Damasio, A. (1999). *The feeling of what happens.* New York: Harcourt.

Damasio, A. (1994). *Descartes' error: Emotion, reason, and the human brain.* New York: Grosset/Putnam.

Darwin, C. (1964) [1859]. *On the origin of species by means of natural selection* (facsimile ed. published in 1964 with an introduction by E. Mayr). Harvard University Press.

Davidson, R., Scherer, K., & Goldsmith., H. (Eds.). (2003). *Handbook of affective sciences.* Oxford University Press.

Davies, J. (1991). Maslow and theory of political development: Getting to fundmentals. *Political Psychology, 12*(3), 389–420.

Davies, J. (1963). *Human nature in politics.* New York: Wiley.

Davis, N. (2000). *The gift in sixteenth century France.* University of Wisconsin Press.

Dawkins, R. (1976). *The selfish gene.* Oxford University Press.

Decety, J. & Ickes, W. (2009). *The social neuroscience of empathy.* MIT University Press.

Descartes, R. (1952). Rules for the direction of the mind. In R. Hutchins & M. Adler, et al. (Eds.)., *Great books of the western world* (Vol. 4), Chicago, IL: Encyclopedia Britannica.

Devinsky, O. & Luciano, D. (1993). The contributions of cingulate cortex to human behavior. In B. Vogt, M. Gabriel, & M. Boston (Eds.)., *Neurobiology of Cingulate Cortex and Limbic Thalamus: A Comprehensive Handbook.* Boston: Birkhauser.

de Waal, F. (1996). *Good natured: The origins of right and wrong in humans and other animals.* Harvard University Press.

de Waal, F. (2002). Evolutionary psychology: The wheat and the chaff. *Current Directions in Psychological Science, 11*(6), 187–191.

Donaldson, Z. & Young, L. (2008, November 7). Oxytocin, vasopressin, and the neurogenetics of sociality. *Science, 322*(5903), 900–904.

Donnerstein, E. & Hatfield, E. (1982). Aggression and Inequity. In J. Greenberg & R. Cohen (Eds.), *Equity and justice in social behavior* (pp. 309–329). New York: Academic Press.

Douglas, M. (1990). No free gifts. In M. Mauss, *The gift* [Foreword] (W. Halls., Trans.). New York: W.W. Norton.

Duffy, M. & Li, L. (2009, July). A neural network application of Dual Motive Theory to manage customer relationships. Paper presented at the International Association for Research in Economic Psychology (IAREP) and the Society for the Advancement of Behavioral Economics (SABE) joint conference, Saint Mary's University, Halifax, Nova Scotia.

Duffy, M. & Cory, G. (2007, May). Dual Motive Theory and development: A look at Sen's development as freedom through brain physiology. Paper presented at the annual meeting of the Society for the Advancement of Behavioral Economics (SABE), New York University.

Dugger, W. (1996). Four modes of inequality. In W. Edgar (Ed.), *Inequality: Radical institutionalist views on race, gender, class, and nation* (pp. 21–38). Westport, CT: Greenwood.

Dyson, F. (1999). *Origins of Life*. Cambridge University Press.

Ebenstein, A. (2001). *Frederich Hayek: A biography*. New York: St. Martins.

Eckel, C. & Grossman, P. (1997). Equity and fairness in economic decisions: Evidence from bargaining experiments. In G. Antonides & W. F. van Raaij (Eds.), *Advances in economic psychology* (pp.281–301). New York: Wiley.

Edelman, G. & Tononi, G. (2000). *A universe of consciousness*. New York: Basic Books.

Edelman, G.(1992). *Bright Air, Brilliant Fire*. New York: Basic Books.

Eggertson, T. (1990). *Economic behavior and institutions*. Cambridge University Press.

Eisenberg, N. (1994). Empathy. In V. S. Ramachandran (Ed.), *Encylopedia of Human Behavior* (pp. 247–253). New York: Academic Press.

Erdal, D. & Whiten, A. (1996). Egalitarianism and Machiavellian intelligence in human evolution. In P. Mellars & K. Gibson (Eds.), *Modelling the early human mind* (pp.139–150). The McDonald Institute, Cambridge University Press.

Etzioni, A. (1988). *The moral dimension: Toward a new economics*. New York: MacMillan.

Etzioni, A. (1986). The case for a multiple-utility conception. *Economics and Philosophy*, *2*: 159–183.

Fehr, E. & Gachter, S. (2000). Fairness and retaliation: The economics of reciprocity. *Journal of Economic Perspectives, 14*(3),159–181.

Feiwel, G. (Ed.). (1987). *Arrow and the ascent of modern economic theory*. New York: Macmillan.

Fennell, L. (2002). Unpacking the gift. In M. Osteen, *The question of the gift* (pp. 85–101). London: Routledge.

Flyvbjerg, B. (2001). *Making social science matter: Why social inquiry fails and how it can succeed again.* Cambridge University Press.

Frank, R., Gilovich, T., & Regan, D. (1993). Does studying economics inhibit cooperation? In *Journal of Economic Perspectives*, *7*(2), 159–171.

Frank, R. (1988). *Passions within reason: The strategic role of the emotions*. New York: W.W. Norton.

Freud, S. (1961)[1920]. *Beyond the pleasure principle* (J. Strachey, Trans.). New York: W.W. Norton.

Freud, S. (1915–1917). *Introductory Lectures*. Psychoanalytic Training Institute.

Fukuyama, F. (1992). *The end of history and the last man*. New York: Free Press.

Fulton, J. (1951). *Frontal lobotomy and affective behavior*. New York: W.W. Norton.

Gardner, R. (1982). Mechanisms in major depressive disorder: An evolutionary model. *Archives of General Psychiatry, 39*, 1436–1441.

Gehring, W. (1998). *Master control genes in development and evolution*. Yale University Press.

Gérard-Varet, L.-A., Kolm, S.-C., & Mercier Ythier, J. (Eds.). (2000). *The economics of reciprocity, giving, and altruism.* New York: St. Martin's Press.

Gintis, H. (2000). Strong reciprocity and human sociality. *Journal of Theoretical Biology, 206*, 169–179.

Gloor, P. (1997). *The temporal lobe and the limbic system*. Oxford University Press.

Godelier, M. (1999). *The enigma of the gift*. University of Chicago Press.

Goldin-Meadow, S. & So, W.-C., et al. (2008). The natural order of events: How speakers of different languages represent events nonverbally. *Proceedings of the National Academy of Sciences, USA, 105*(27), 9163–9168.

Gopnik, A. (2007, April 26). Cells that read minds? What the myth of mirror neurons gets wrong about the brain. *Slate's special issue on the brain*. Retrieved May 12, 2008, from http://www.slate.com/id/2165001

Gouldner, A. (1960). The norm of reciprocity: A preliminary statement. *American Sociological Review, 25*,161–178.

Gray, J. (1987). *Fear and stress* (2nd ed.). Cambridge University Press.

Green, D. & Shapiro, I. (1996). *Pathologies of rational choice theory.* Yale University Press.

Gregory, C. (1982). *Gifts and commodities*. New York: Academic Press.

Guerrero, L., Andersen, P., & Afifi, W. (2007). *Close encounters: Communication in relationships* (2nd ed.). London: Sage.

Hameroff, S. & Penrose, R. (1996). Orchestrated reduction of quantum coherence in brain microtubules: A model for consciousness. In S. Hameroff, A. Kaszniak, & A. Scott (Eds.), *Toward a science of conciousness: The first Tuscon discussions and debates* (pp. 507–539). MIT University Press.

Hamilton, W. (1964). The genetical evolution of social behavior (Pts. 1 & 2). *Journal of Theoretical Biology, 7*, 1–52.

Harel, D. (1987). *Algorithms: The spirit of computing.* Reading, MA: Addison-Wesley.

Harrington, A. (Ed.). (1992). *So human a brain*. Boston: Birkhauser.

Hatfield, E. & Traupmann, J. (1981). Intimate relationships: A perspective from equity theory. In S. Duck & R. Gilmour (Eds.), *Personal relationships: Studying personal relationships* (pp. 165–178). New York: Academic Press..

Hayek. F. (1991). *Economic freedom*. London: Basil Blackwell.

Hayek. F. (1988). *The fatal conceit*. University of Chicago Press.

Hayek. F. (1973, 1976, 1979). *Law, legislation, and liberty (Vols*. 1–3). University of Chicago Press.

Hayek. F. (1944). *The road to serfdom*. University of Chicago Press.

Heller, W., Nitschke, J., & Miller, G. (1998). Lateralization in emotion and emotional disorders. *Current Directions in Psychological Science, 7*(1), 26–32.

Henry, J. & Wang, S. (1998). Effects of early stress on adult affiliative behavior. *Psychoneuro-endocrinology, 23*(8), 863–875.

Herbert, J. & Schulkin, J. (2002). Neurochemical coding of adaptive responses in the limbic system. In D. Pfaff, et al. (Eds.), *Hormones, brain and behavior* (pp. 659–697). New York: Academic Press.

Hicks, J. (1939). *Value and capital*. Oxford University Press.

Hirschman, A. (1982). *Shifting involvements: Private interest and public action*. Princeton University Press.

Hobbes, T. (1971)[1651]. *Leviathan*. New York: Pelican Classics, Penguin Books.

Hobhouse, L. (1906)[1951]. *Morals in evolution: A study in comparative ethics*. London: Chapman & Hall.

Hoffman, M. (2000). *Empathy and moral development*. Cambridge University Press.

Hoffman, M. (1981). Is altruism part of human nature?. *Journal of Personality and Social Psychology*, *40*, 121–137.

Homans, G. (1961). *Social behavior: Its elementary forms*. New York: Harcourt Brace & World.

Homans, G. (1950). *The human group*. New York: Harcourt Brace Jovanovich.

Housepian, E. (1998, Fall). Bilateral frontal resection for psychoses revisited. *P & S Medical Review, 5*,(2). Retrieved July 6, 2000, from http://www. cumc.columbia.edu/news/review/archives/medrev_v5n2_0005.html

Hunt, R. (2002). Economic transfers and exchanges: Concepts for describing allocations. In J. Ensminger (Ed.) *Theory in Economic Anthropology* (pp. 105–118). Walnut Creek, CA: AltaMira Press.

Humphrey, N. (1976). The function of the intellect. In P. Bateson & R. Hinde (Eds.), *Growing points in ethology* (pp. 303–317). Cambridge University Press.

Iidaka, T. & Terashima, S., et al. (2003). Dissociable neural responses in the hippocampus to the retrieval of facial identity and emotion: An event-related fMRI study. *Hippocampus, 13*, 429–436.

Jones, E. (2007). *The Thalamus* (2nd ed.). Cambridge University Press.

Ingrao, B. & Israel, G. (1990). *The Invisible Hand: Economic equilibrium in the history of science* (I. McGilvray, Trans.). MIT University Press.

Isaac, G. (1978). The food-sharing behavior of protohuman hominids. *Scientific American, 238*, 90–108.

Jevons, W. (1888). *The Theory of Political Economy*. London: Macmillan.

Jevons, W. (1905). *Essays of economics*. London: Macmillan.

Johnson, C. (1997). Perception vs. observation, or the contributions of rational choice theory and area studies to contemporary political science. *PS:Politics and Political Science, 30*(2),170–174.

Johnson, D. (1991). *Public Choice: An introduction to the new political economy*. Mountain View, CA: Mayfield.

Johnson, G. (1986). *Research methodology for economists*. London: Macmillan.

Kahneman, D., Diener, E., & Schwarz, N. (Eds.). (1999). *Well-being: The foundations of hedonic psychology*. New York: Russell Sage.

Kandel, E., Schwartz, J., & Jessell, T. (2000). *Essentials of neural science and behavior*. Norwalk, CT: Appleton & Lange.

Kant, I. (1964)[1797]. *The doctrine of virtue: Part II of metaphysics of ethics* (M. Gregor, Trans.). University of Pennsylvania Press.

Keohane, R. (1990). Empathy and international Regimes. In J. Mansbridge (Ed.), *Beyond Self-Interest* (pp. 227–236). University of Chicago Press.

Keohane, R. (1989). *International institutions and state power*. Boulder, CO: Westview Press.

Keohane, R. (2005). *After Hegemony*. Princeton University Press.

Keohane, R. (1984). *After Hegemony*. Princeton University Press.

Knauft, B. (1991). Violence and sociality in human evolution. *Current Anthropology, 32*, 391–428.

Knauft, B. (1994). Culture and cooperation in human evolution. In L. Sponsel & T. Gregor (Eds.), *The anthropology of peace and nonviolence* (pp. 37–67). Boulder, CO: Lynne Rienner.

Knutson, J. (1972). *The human basis of the polity*. Chicago: Aldine-Atherton.

Koch, C. (1999). *Biophysics of computation: information processing in single neurons*. Oxford University Press.

Kolb, B. (1995). *Brain plasticity and behavior*. Mahwah, NJ: Erlbaum. Kolb, B., Gibb, R., & Robinson, T. (2003, February 1). Brain plasticity and behavior. *Current Directions in Psychological Science, 12*(1), 1–4.

Kohlberg, L. (1984). *The psychology of moral development* (Vol. 2). San Francisco: Harper & Row.

Lambert, K., & Gerlai, R. (Eds.). (2003). A tribute to Paul MacLean: The neurobiological relevance of social behavior. *Physiology and Behavior, 79*(3), 341–342.

Landsburg, S. (1992). *Price theory and applications*. Chicago: Dryden Press.

Lasley, E. (2009). A road paved by reason. In D. Gordon (Ed.), *Cerebrum 2009*. Washington, DC: Dana Press.

Leven, S. (1994). Semiotics, meaning, and discursive neural networks. In D. Levine (Ed.), *Neural networks for knowledge representation and inference* (pp. 65–82). Mahwah, NJ: Erlbaum.

Levi-Strauss, C. (1949)[1969]. *The elementary structures of kinship*. London: Eyre & Spottiwoode.

Levine, D. (2006, August). Neural modeling of the Dual Motive Theory of economics. *Journal of Socio-Economics, 35*(4), 613–625.

Levine, D. & Yani, N. (2002). Toward a neural network theory of the triune brain. In G. Cory & R. Gardner (Eds.), *The evolutionary neuroethology of Paul MacLean: Convergences and frontiers.* New York: Praeger.

Levine, D. (1991). *Introduction to neural and cognitive modeling.* Mahwah, NJ: Erlbaum.

Lin, A. (2004). Warlord, social welfare and philanthropy: The case of Guangzhou under Chen Jitang. *Modern China, 30,* 151–198.

Lieberman, P. (2000). *Human language and our reptilian brain.* Harvard University Press.

Luo, J. Chan, Y.-G., & Cory, G. (2008, July). The tri-oriented approach and Dual Motive Theory. In D.-S. Su (Chair), *Fusion and development of East and West management.* Paper presented at the Annual Conference of International Federation of Scholarly Associations of Management (IFSAM), Shanghai, China.

Lynne, G. (2006, August). Toward a dual motive economic theory. *Journal of Socio-Economics, 35*(4), 634–651.

MacLean, P. (1990). *The triune brain in evolution: Role in paleocerebral functions.* New York: Plenum.

Maddi, S. (1989). *Personality Theories* (5th ed.). Chicago: Dorsey Press.

Malinowski, B. (1926). *Crime and custom in savage society.* London: Routledge & Kegan Paul.

Malinowski, B. (1922). *Argonauts of the Western Pacific.* London: Routledge & Kegan Paul.

Mandeville de, B. [1714]. *The Fable of the Bees.*

Mansbridge, J. (Ed.). (1990). *Beyond self-interest.* University of Chicago Press.

Margolis, H. (1982). *Selfishness, altruism, and rationality: A theory of social choice.* Cambridge University Press.

Margulis, L. & Sagan, D. (1997). *Slanted truths: Essays on Gaia, symbiosis, and evolution.* New York: Copernicus Books.

Margulis, L. & Schwartz, K. (1988). *Five kingdoms* (2nd ed.). New York: W.H. Freeman.

Margulis, L., Schwartz, K., & Dolan, M. (1994). *The illustrated five kingdoms.* New York: HarperCollins.

Margulis, L. (1998). *Symbiotic planet: A new look at evolution.* New York: Basic Books.

Marx, K. (1906). *Capital.* New York: Modern Library.

Maslow, A. (1970). *Motivation and personality* (2nd ed.). New York: Harper & Row.

Maslow, A. (1968). *Toward a psychology of being* (2nd ed.). New York: Van Nostrand Reinhold.

Maslow, A. (1943). A theory of human motivation. *Psychological Review, 50,* 370–396.

Mauss, M. (1990). *The Gift* (W. Halls, Trans.). New York: W.W. Norton.

Mauss, M. (1954). *The Gift*. (I. Cunnison, Trans.). New York: W.W. Norton.

McQuaig, L. (2001). *All you can eat: Greed, lust and the new capitalism*. Toronto: Penguin Books.

Mencius. (c. 298 B.C.E.). *The mind of Mencius* (D. Lau, Trans., 1970). London: Penguin.

Moore, B. (1978). *Injustice: The social basis of obedience and revolt*. Armonk, NY: M.E. Sharpe.

Morgane P., Galler, J., & Mokler, D. (2005). A review of systems and networks of the limbic forebrain/limbic midbrain. *Progress in Neurobiology, 75*, 143–160.

Morishima, M. (1992). General equilibrium theory in the twenty-first century. In J. D. Hey (Ed.), *The future of economics*, Oxford: Blackwell.

Nelson, R. (2000). *An introduction to behavioral endocrinology* (2nd ed.). Sunderland, MA: Sinauer.

Nash, J. (1953). The two person cooperative games. *Econometrica, 21*, 405–421.

Nash, J. (1951). Non-cooperative games. *Annals of Mathematics, 54(2)*, 286–295.

Nash, J. (1950). The bargaining problem. *Econometrica, 21*, 155–162.

Neumann, J. von & Morgenstern, O. (1947). *Theory of games and economic behavior* (2nd ed.). Princeton University Press.

Newmarch, W. (1861, December). The progress of economic science during the last thirty years: An opening address [before Section F]. *Journal of the Statistical Society, 24*(4), 451–467.

Newman, J. & Harris, J. (2009). The scientific contributions of Paul D. MacLean (1913–2007). *Journal of Mental and Nervous Disease, 197*(1), 3–5.

O'Callaghan, M. & Carroll, D. (1982). *Psychosurgery: A scientific analysis*. Lancaster, MI: MTP Press.

Osteen, M. (Ed.). (2002). Gift or commodity. In *The question of the gift: Essays across disciplines* (pp. 229–247). London: Routledge.

Panksepp, Jaak (2004). *Textbook of biological psychiatry*. New York: Wiley.

Panksepp, Jaak (2002). The MacLean legacy and some modern trends in emotion research [Foreword]. In G. Cory & R. Gardner (Eds.), *The Evolutionary Neuroethology of Paul MacLean: Convergences and Frontiers* (pp. ix-xxvii). Westport, CT: Praeger.

Panksepp, Jaak (1998). *Affective neuroscience*. Oxford University Press.

Panksepp, Jaak & Panksepp, Jules. B. (2000). The seven sins of evolutionary psychology. *Evolution and Cognition, 6*, 108–131.

Parsons, T. (1960). Pattern variables revisited. *American Sociological Review, 25*, 467–488.

Parsons, T. (1951). *The social system*. London: Routledge & Keegan Paul.

Patlolla, B. (2008, September). The neuro-physiological foundations of Dual Motive Theory: A review of the brain model set forth in Wilson and Cory's *The Evolutionary Epidemiology of Mania and Depression*. Paper presented at The International Association for Reserach in Economic Psychology (IAREP) and The Society for Advancement of Behavioral Economics (SABE) World Meeting, Luiss University, Rome.

Penrose, R. (1994). *Shadows of the mind*. London: Oxford University Press.

Penrose, R. (1991). *The emperor's new mind*. New York: Penguin.

Piaget, J. (1977). *The development of thought* (A. Rosin, Trans.). New York: Viking.

Piaget, J. (1968)[1947]. *Psychology of intelligence*. Totowa: NJ: Littlefield Adams.

Piaget, J. (1965)[1932]. *The moral judgement of the child*. New York: Free Press.

Pinker, S. (1997). *How the mind works*. New York: W.W. Norton.

Plant, R. (1992). Enterprise in its place: the moral limits of market. In P. Heelas & P. Morris (Eds.), *The Values of the Enterprise Culture: The Moral Debate* (pp. 85–99). London: Routledge.

Plato. (c. 380 B.C.E.). *The Republic* (G. Grube, Trans.,1982). Indianapolis, IN: Hackett.

Polanyi, K. (1957)[1944]. *The great transformation*. Boston: Beacon Press.

Pollard, K. (2009). What makes us human?. *Scientific American, 300*(5), 44–49.

Porter, T. M. (1986). *The rise of statistical thinking, 1820–1900*. Princeton University Press.

Pressman, J. (1998). *Last resort: Psychosurgery and the limits of medicine*. Cambridge University Press.

Price, J. (1967). Hypothesis: The dominance hierarchy and the evolution of mental illness. *Lancet, 2*, 243–246.

Rajaram, K., Cory, G., & Chan Y.-G. (2007, January *Neuroeconomics and Dual Motive Theory: Can East meet West? Bridging Eastern and Western economics*. Paper presented at WEAI Pacific Rim Conference, Guanghua School of Management, Peking University, Beijing, China.

Robbins, L. (1952). *An essay on the nature and significance of economic science* (2nd ed.). New York: MacMillan.

Rummel, R. (1991). *China's bloody century*. New Brunswick, NJ: Transaction.

Saarela, M. & Hlushchuk, Y., et al. (2007). The compassionate brain: Humans detect intensity of pain from another's face. *Cerebral Cortex, 17(1)*, 230–237.

Sahlins, M. (1976). *Culture and practical Reason.* University of Chicago Press.

Sahlins, M. (1963). On the sociology of primitive exchange. In M. Banton (Ed.), *The Relevance of Models for Social Anthropology.* (pp. 139–236). London: Tavistock.

Samuelson, P. (1947). *Foundations of economic analysis.* Harvard University Press.

Say, J.-B. (1855). *A treatise on political economy* (C. Princep., Trans.) Philadelphia, PA: Lippincott.

Schram, S. & Caterino, B. (Eds.). (2006). *Making political science matter: Debating knowledge, research, and method.* New York University Press.

Schumpeter, J. (1954). *History of economic analysis.* Oxford University Press.

Schulkin, J. (2002). Hormonal modulation of central motivational states. In D. Paff (Ed.), *Hormones, Brain, and Behavior* (Vol. 1, pp. 633–657). New York: Academic Press.

Sheridan, J. (1966). *Chinese warlord: The case of Feng-Yuhsiang.* Stanford University Press.

Sherman, S. & Guillery, R. (2001). *Exploring the thalamus.* New York: Academic Press..

Sen, A. (1997). *On economic inequality* [exp. ed.]. Oxford: Clarendon Press.

Sen, A. (1979). Rational fools: A critique of the behavioral foundations of economic theory. In F. Hahn & M. Hollis (Eds.), *Philosophy and Economic Theory.* Oxford University Press.

Seymour-Smith, C. (1986). *Dictionary of anthropology.* Boston: G. K. Hall.

Shun, K. (1997). *Mencius and early Chinese thought.* Stanford University Press.

Simmel, G. (1950). *The Sociology of Georg Simmel* (K. Wolff, Trans.). New York: Free Press.

Singer, T. (2006). The neuronal basis and ontogeny of empathy and mind reading. *Neuroscience and Biobehavioral Reviews, 30*, 855–863.

Smith, Adam. 1977(1740–90). The correspondence of Adam Smith. In E. Mossner & T. Ross (Eds.), *The Glasgow Edition of the Works and Correspondence of Adam Smith* (Vol. 6). General editing by D. Raphael and A.Skinner. Oxford: Clarendon Press.

Smith, Adam. (1911)[1789]. *The theory of moral sentiments* (New ed.). London: G. Bell.

Smith, Adam. (1937)[1776]. *The Wealth of Nations* (E. Cannan, Ed.). New York: Modern Library.

Smith, J. M. (2002). Equations of life: The mathematics of evolution. In G. Farmelo (Ed.), *It must be beautiful: Great equations of modern science.* London: Granta Books.

Smith, J. M. (1982). The evolution of social behavior: A classification of models. In King's College Sociobiology Group (Eds.), *Current problems in sociobiology* (pp. 28–44). Cambridge University Press.

Smith, M. (1991). Comments on Davies's *Maslow and theory of political development. Political Psychology,12*(3), 421–423.

Stapp, H. (1972). The Copenhagen interpretation. *American Journal of Physics, 40*(8), 1098–1116.

Steiner, K. Personal communication.

Stuss, D. & Knight, R. (2002). *Principles of frontal lobe function.* Oxford University Press.

Su, D.-S. (2006, December) Tri-oriented Managerial Ideology. Paper presented at *The 10ᵗʰ World Management Forum.* Shanghai, China.

Sylvester, C. (2002). *Feminist international relations: An unfinished journey.* Cambridge University Press.

Tankersley, D., Stowe, C., & Huettel, S. (2007). Altruism is associated with an increased neural response to agency. *Nature Neuroscience, 10*(2), 150–151.

Tett, G. (2009). *Fool's gold: How the bold dream of a small tribe at J. P. Morgan was corrupted by Wall Street greed and unleashed a catastrophe.* New York: Free Press.

Thurnwald, R. (1932). *Economics in primitive communities.* Oxford University Press.

Tickell, C. (1993). The human species: A suicidal success. *Geographical Journal.* Vol. 159. 219–226.

Titmuss, R. (1972). *The gift relationship: From human blood to social policy.* New York: Pantheon Books.

Trivers, R. (1981). Sociobiology and politics. In E. White (Ed.) *Sociobiology and Human Politics* (pp. 1–44). Lexington: Heath.

Trivers, R. (1971). The evolution of reciprocal altruism. *The Quarterly Review of Biology, 46*, 35–57.

Tucker, D., & Luu, P., et al. (1995). Social and emotional self-regulation. In *Annals of the New York Academy of Sciences, 769*, 213–239.

Udehn. L. (1996). *The limits of public choice.* London: Routledge.

Van Baal, J. (1975). *Reciprocity and the position of women.* Amsterdam: Van Gorcum.

Valenstein, E. (1986). *Great and desperate cures: The rise and decline of psychosurgery and other medical treatments for mental disorders.* New York: Basic Books.

Vaughan, G. (1997). *For-giving: A feminist criticism of exchange.* Austin, TX: Plain View Press.

Walras, Léon. (1954). *Elements of Pure Economics* [4ᵗʰ ed.] (W. Jaffe, Trans.). Homewood, IL: Richard D. Irwin.

Walster, E., Walster, G., & Bersheid, E. (1978). *Equity: Theory and research.* Needham Heights, MA: Allyn and Bacon.

Will, G. (2009, May 17). Greed's saving graces. *The Washington Post.*

Wilson, D. (2006). The evolutionary neuroscience of human reciprocal sociality: A basic outline for economists. *Journal of Socio-Economics, 35*(4), 626–633.

Wilson, D. (1992). Evolutionary epidemiology. *Acta Biotheoretica, 40,* 87–90.

Wilson, D. & Cory, G. (2008). *The evolutionary epidemiology of mania and depression.* New York: Mellen Press.

Wilson, E. (1993). Analyzing the superorganism: The legacy of Whitman and Wheeler. In R. Barlow, et al. (Eds.), *The biological century.* Harvard University Press.

Witter, M. & Groenewegen, H. (1992). Organizational principles of hippocampal connections. In M. Trimble, et al. (Eds.), *The temporal Lobes and the limbic system.* Petersfield, UK: Wrightson Biomedical Publishing.

Wood, R. & Hamel, G. (2002). The World Bank's innovation market, *Harvard Business Review, 80*(11), 104–113.

Yankelovich, D. (1981). *New rules: Searching for self-fulfillment in a world turned upside down.* New York: Random House.

Zakaria, F. (2009, June 22). Greed is good (to a point). *Newsweek, 153*(25), 41–45.

Zigler, E. & Child, I. (1973). *Socialization and personality development.* Reading, MA: Addison-Wesley.

NAME INDEX

SUBJECT INDEX